# THE PSYCHOLOGY OF BUDDHIST TANTRA

# The Psychology of
## Buddhist Tantra

Rob Preece
*Foreword by Stephen Batchelor*

SNOW LION PUBLICATIONS
ITHACA, NEW YORK • BOULDER, COLORADO

Snow Lion Publications
P.O. Box 6483
Ithaca, NY 14851 USA
(607) 273-8519
www.snowlionpub.com
e.mail: info@snowlionpub.com

An earlier version of this book was published in the UK
under the title *The Alchemical Buddha*.

Typest and design by Gopa & Ted2, Inc.

ISBN-13: 978-1-55939-263-1
ISBN-10: 1-55939-263-0

*Library of Congress Cataloging-in-Publication Data*
Preece, Rob.
  The psychology of Buddhist tantra / Rob Preece ; foreword by
Stephen Batchelor.
      p. cm.
  Includes bibliographical references.
  ISBN-13: 978-1-55939-263-1 (alk. paper)
  ISBN-10: 1-55939-263-0 (alk. paper)
  1. Tantric Buddhism—Psychology. I. Title.

BQ8918.6.P74 2006
294.3'925019—dc22

                                                         2006025889


Printed in Canada

*This book is dedicated to Lama Thubten Yeshe,*
*whose inspiration made it possible,*
*to Thubten Zopa Rinpoche,*
*whose example is impeccable,*
*and to*
*Gen Jampa Wangdu,*
*whose kindness is unforgettable.*

*I would like to offer my gratitude to all those who have supported me*
*in the process of writing this book, in particular to my wife, Anna.*
*I would also like to dedicate this book to those who have*
*shared their experiences and struggles of integrating*
*Buddhism into their lives.*

# *Contents*

# Illustrations

"Tantra" is a word that is increasingly familiar to readers of books on Hinduism and Buddhism, but the complex body of practices and ideas to which the term refers still remains a source of considerable confusion. Tantra evokes a sense of the dark, esoteric underbelly of Eastern religion. It is associated with death and sex, mysterious rituals undertaken at night by initiates, terrifying gods and goddesses, as well as breathtakingly beautiful mandalas and deeply moving chants intoned by brocade-draped Tibetan monks to the syncopated rhythms of bells and drums.

*The Psychology of Buddhist Tantra* succeeds in clarifying the nature of tantric practice without reducing the tradition to a set of merely rational beliefs, exercises, and techniques. Rob Preece does not seek to explain away the undeniably evocative and darkly potent language and imagery of Tantra, but to recognize them as transformative symbols of the rich complexity of our own inner lives. In contrast to the approaches of conventional religion, Tantra does not attempt to soothe the turmoil of existence with consoling promises of heaven and salvation. The tantric practitioner chooses to confront the bewildering and chaotic forces of fear, aggression, desire, and pride, and to work with them in such a way that they are channeled into creative expression, loving relationships, and wisely engaged forms of life.

In order to make the processes of Tantra psychologically intelligible for a contemporary reader, Rob Preece makes judicious use of the work of Carl Jung. For in the writings and therapeutic methods of Jung, we find an approach that enables us to forge a compelling link between a Western tradition that hearkens back to the alchemical traditions of our own past, and the comparably "alchemical" strategies of Tibetan Buddhist tantric practices. In keeping with the pragmatic and therapeutic aims of both Jungian psychotherapy and Buddhist meditation, *The Psychology of Buddhist Tantra* never loses sight of the central importance of applying these ideas to the concrete realities of day-to-day life.

For those from other Buddhist traditions, this book will serve to shed light not only on some of the inner workings of Tibetan Buddhism, but also the transformative process that underpins all forms of Buddhist practice. While the term "Tantra" might be alien and even suspect to Theravada or Zen Buddhists, any practice that leads from confusion to insight, from self-centered anxiety to compassion, from arrogance to humility, is necessarily engaged in a process of transformation. By illuminating the richly symbolic language of Tantra through the intermediate language of psychology, *The Psychology of Buddhist Tantra* points to the transformative nature of Buddhist practice as such.

Stephen Batchelor
Sharpham College

❖ ❖ ─────────────────────────────────────────────

W HEN WE ENTER the world of Tantra, we may need to loosen some of our preconceptions about the nature of reality. We begin to inhabit a twilight world where the distinctions between the material and the symbolic are less defined. We discover that *psyche* and *soma*, the unconscious and matter, are in an intimate interrelationship. The tantric view of reality does not make such solid differentiation between them; they are simply two reflections of the same ultimate nature. In the West, we habitually make a clear distinction between spirit and matter, whereas, in the East, these two are not separated.

Tantra, or Vajrayana, has emerged from a culture where nature is still animated. Spirits still inhabit rocks and rivers; demons and goblins live in wild places, and interfere with the lives and health of those who disturb them. People make offerings to the local guardians and protectors to maintain the fertility of their crops and the security of their households, and sickness is seen as the interference of spirits. As Westerners engaging in Tantra, we may find it convenient to overlook this animism as superstition or primitive medieval belief. We would, for example, go to a doctor when we were sick, rather than consider pacifying an interfering spirit.

Tantra has thus become sanitized, and is largely practiced in the West as a series of sophisticated practices performed in the contained environment of the local temple. This may make Tantra more accessible to Western taste, as many aspects of the tantric worldview are alien to our cultural background, but it is not how tantric adepts, particularly in India, would have pursued their practice. They were often found in wild hostile places, such as cremation grounds, mountain caves and forests; environments where the elemental energies they were awakening and relating to were alive and potent.

We cannot assume that Tantra will find an easy resonance in the Western psyche when our cultural psychological background is so different, even if we feel an attraction. So we require a bridge between the complex practices of Tantra and our Western disposition for psychological understanding. The work of Jung has much to offer in this respect, throwing light on some of the more obscure aspects of these esoteric practices.

I first encountered the work of C. G. Jung while I was at university, but the importance of the link between Tantra and the work of Jung was made in 1976, when my teacher, Lama Thubten Yeshe, was visiting the UK, and introduced many of his students to the Jungian sandplay analyst Dora Kalff. This link was further deepened during retreat in India from 1980 onwards, when I was fortunate enough to have with me several volumes of Jung's *Collected Works*, including *Psychology and Religion*.[1] This somewhat unusual opportunity gave me the chance to explore tantric practice while drawing connections to Jung's ideas. The parallels between the two seemed remarkable, and gave me a clear feeling for the alchemical nature of the tantric path. Jung's understanding seemed to open up psychological meaning within tantric practice helping to bridge two worlds. In exploring Tantra from a more psychological perspective, it also seemed possible that Tantra itself could broaden or deepen our understanding of Western archetypal psychology.

When I eventually returned to the West in 1985, underwent training as a psychotherapist, and began to teach workshops on comparative Jungian and Buddhist psychology, the implications of a psychological basis for the practice of Tantra became more and more relevant. It became apparent to me that the practice of Tantra needs a fertile ground in which to grow. It relies less on intellectual and philosophical knowledge than on an innate trust in the intuitive and creative faculties of the mind. The language of Tantra is not the abstract intellectual concepts of philosophy, but the language of symbol and myth, which follow a different rationale. The poetic metaphorical reality of Tantra takes the power of symbol to perhaps its most refined potential. Jung once said that in the East they reject fantasy not because it is irrelevant and childish as we often consider in the West, but because its essence has long ago been transformed into a religion.

Mythical truth and historical truth become subtly interwoven in Tantra in a way that tries to express the inner meaning and symbolic nature of our experiences. The extraordinary events described in the biographies of tantric adepts like Padmasambhava, Milarepa, and Gesar show how Tantra inhabits a twilight zone where our familiar, material, outer world and the inner world of the psyche begin to merge. The outer world becomes suffused with inner reality.

Tantra focuses our attention on the underlying vitality and energy of our aliveness. It brings us into contact with the subtle influences that shape and motivate the dynamics of life, thus inevitably has been linked with sexuality. Consequently many people have seen this as the central practice of Tantra. Unfortunately, the popularization of "tantric sex" has led to much misunderstanding. When placed in the wider context of this profound path, the energy of our sexuality may well be an aspect of the creative process of Tantra, but it bears little relationship to the exotic sexual possibilities some Westerners like to imagine. Our sexuality is only one expression of the subtle forces that flow through our lives, bringing vitality and creativity. In Tantra, this vitality is seen as the root of transformation in order to awaken our full potential.

The tantric path brings us back into relationship with the source of the vitality of our lives, and then offers a vehicle for its creative manifestation. This source is intrinsically connected to our physical body, but is visualized in the aspect of a deity. There are many deities, but tantric practitioners need not practice them all. Rather, they attune to the deity or deities that are constitutionally the most transformative for them. A deity is not like an external god; it arises as a manifestation of the mind's primordial clear nature. Our true relationship to the deity comes, therefore, from within, and is felt as a deep inner resonance, or as an energetic quality that pervades the body. Once this is awakened, practicing just one deity allows us to experience the underlying source of them all.

The Tibetan word for Tantra is *gyu,* a term which is often translated as "continuity," but which can also be understood to mean "the process of transformation." Tantra is the unfolding of a creative process, which occurs moment by moment in the act of manifestation and transformation. In this sense, we continually experience the process of creative transformation in every aspect of our lives. When the process unfolds naturally, as an expression of our true nature, we experience a flow of vitality in all we do. But when this process becomes stuck or blocked, we experience varying degrees of dis-ease and suffering. As Jung pointed out, the gods that inhabit the underworld of the psyche "have become our diseases."[2]

Each of us has the innate potential to awaken fully, and to give individual expression to our true nature in our lives. This potential is the seed of our Buddha nature, which, once awakened and allowed to manifest, can creatively enrich our lives. The transformative nature of tantric practice is like the yogurt culture that turns milk into yogurt. Activating the deity within the psyche of a practitioner gradually awakens and brings to manifestation the full potential within.

Tantra has more in common with the creative arts than with philosophy or science. Its visionary nature is intimately linked with a process that brings deep inner wisdom into expression, similar to that which we see in great works of art. The essential principle of Tantra can live through an individual in different ways, and the tantric adept is often a mixture of healer, shaman, artist and medieval alchemist.

In this book I have tried to bring out some of the elements of an alchemical process, as explored by Jung, which have a direct bearing on our understanding of the transformation process of Tantra. The structure I have used reflects something of this approach. In Part I, I have introduced some of the necessary preliminary conditions for entering into the process of Tantra as a kind of alchemical apprenticeship. Here I will look at the need for a sound psychological ground and also the significance of a relationship to some form of guide or mentor who holds the process.

In Part II, I introduce some of the significant elements involved in actually embarking upon the process of Tantra as we place ourselves within the alchemical vessel. Here I explore the nature of that vessel, and those aspects of ourselves that are the essential ingredients of transformation.

Part III then looks in more depth at the actual processes that are practiced within this vessel. We look at the psychological nature of deity practice as a means of transformation, drawing particularly on Jung's insights.

Finally, Part IV explores the completion of the alchemical process and its implications for us as we apply our experiences out in the world. Here I try to show how the essential principle of Tantra is to encourage the expression of our true nature through the creative process. Once we are attuned to it, this creative principle can then be present in every aspect of our lives.

Detailed descriptions of tantric practices can be found in many recent translations of and commentaries on Tibetan tantric texts, and will not be explained here. (See, for example, Stephan Beyer's *The Cult of Tara*; Gavin Kilty's translation of the *Ornament of Stainless Light*; and Lama Yeshe's *Tantric Path of Purification*.) We will rather explore the underlying psychological processes intrinsic to tantric practice, and look at some of the difficulties Westerners might encounter when meeting this Eastern tradition. Much of the work here has come from my own struggles and insights while attempting to bring tantric practice into my life.

I have also drawn on my experience as a psychotherapist and meditation teacher over the past twenty years, and I focus on a process that is relevant to both men and women. However, I have made no attempt here to address specific issues relating to women's relationships to Tibetan Buddhism, or to Tantra in particular.

It has become increasingly apparent that some of the problems that arise in integrating the practice of Tantra are a reflection of our own psychological and cultural dispositions, while others arise from the fact that Tantra has been colored for so long by a particularly influential Tibetan culture. Much is owed to the Tibetans for preserving this tradition. To become genuinely integrated into the Western psyche, however, Tantra needs to be freed from some of its Tibetan influence. What I have attempted to do here is to remain true to the essential principles at the heart of tantric practice and to bring to light its psychological significance as a process of creative transformation.

# PART I
## *The Ground*

*Figure 1. Shakyamuni Buddha*

I N THE INDIAN VILLAGE of Bodhgaya stands a large pipal tree; it is
called the Bodhi Tree. Beneath an ancestor of this tree, the prince
Siddhartha once sat in meditation. His mind was utterly absorbed in a
state of unobstructed clarity of emptiness, like a clear sky. The Buddhas abiding in a realm called Akanishta (Highest Pure Land) recognized that this meditation alone would not lead to the totally unified
state of a Buddha. Through their innate wisdom they spontaneously
manifested within the sphere of emptiness a celestial vision of totality. Siddhartha arose from his absorption and was initiated into this
mandala of perfected form. In his meditation he was finally able to
attain a state of unification, and to manifest the qualities of a fully
evolved buddha.

This is how tantric texts describe the final process of enlightenment
for the Buddha Shakyamuni. There are, however, many different views
of the Buddha's final incarnation as Siddhartha up to the point of his
awakening as the Buddha Shakyamuni, the originator of the present
teaching of the Dharma. Each view arises partly from different levels
of understanding within the Theravada, Mahayana, and Tantra traditions, and each has come to describe this process in accordance with
their particular path.

The origins of Tantra are particularly difficult to define because historical truth and symbolic reality have become interwoven. Tantra as an
esoteric tradition originated primarily through vision and revelation
rather than the spoken or written word, which makes conventional validation difficult. No passage in Buddhist literature records an instance

in which the Buddha sat with a group of disciples and taught a specific tantra. Transmission is rather expressed in terms such as this: "The Buddha manifested in the aspect of Vajrapani seated on the summit of Mount Meru and initiated the tantra." This teaching would have been experienced on a psychic or visionary level to those open and ready to receive it.

As a consequence, the origins of Tantra are obscure and mystical. Some people feel they are not teachings of the Buddha. Others think they emerged from Hindu Tantra, but these views are refuted by great tantric adepts such as Lama Tsongkhapa. To understand the significance of Tantra, a different perspective is therefore necessary. Tantra and its symbolic expression of Buddha nature are fundamentally processes of creative revelation.

Most tantras, the generic term for deity practices, originated as visions or revelations of highly developed meditators. In the teachings of each tantra there is almost always a description of how a practitioner, man or woman, experienced a vision of a particular aspect of a deity and then began to teach its essential practice. Many such lineages originated from a group of tantric practitioners known as the eighty-four *mahasiddhas* of India, who lived in the period soon after the Buddha's passing. While some tantric lineages originated at the time of the Buddha, many others have emerged more recently. Today these lineages are to be found primarily within the Tibetan tradition, which has preserved their practice intact for hundreds of years.

Tantra, also meaning "continuity," or "thread," can be understood in another way than the process of transformation mentioned previously. Great emphasis is placed on the sense of continuity that comes from a lineage of the unbroken transmission of a deity practice that has been kept without degeneration. This has also maintained its power. While a tantra may be taught from a text, the real transmission occurs when an experienced practitioner helps to inspire the same deity quality in another. This traditionally occurs when the lineage of experience of a deity is passed on through some form of initiation. In Tibet, as a result, semi-political hierarchies arose with lamas in positions of great power as so-called lineage holders. Many Westerners find this confusing when they encounter the Tibetan tradition. Regrettably, the politics of some Tibetan teachers can complicate the validity of a tantric lineage.

Over the centuries the practice of Tantra has been shaped and structured into formalized systems, passed on from teacher to disciple. Maintaining the various styles of practice free from innovation to preserve the integrity of the system has been seen as essential. This has kept the purity of the traditions intact over many generations as living lineages. While it is important to preserve the precision of the system and its formalized practices, this is not, however, the essence of Tantra. The essential ingredient of any tantric practice must be the inner vision and inspiration that is gained through a deep inner awakening.

Many people still believe that the system of practice must be strictly maintained to preserve the purity of the tradition. But this needs to be balanced against the danger of losing the essence of its meaning by rigid adherence to form, particularly when that form has been styled by a specific culture. It is difficult to see the degree to which the Tibetan culture and approach to spirituality has flavored tantric practice. This inevitably calls into question the necessity of strictly maintaining the Tibetan style when the tantric tradition is practiced by Westerners.

Tantra is a creative process and must be allowed to be creative and expressive. Many of the mahasiddhas of India who originated these practices were great craftsmen, poets, and musicians. Others were roughnecks, drinkers, and vagabonds who were more comfortable frequenting the whorehouse than the monastery. Tantric practitioners have a history of breaking the rules of orthodoxy and have often been condemned as decadent and sometimes heretical, even while their approach may have acted as a necessary balance to orthodox practice.

Those who have a disposition to be controlling and live within constrained boundaries of thinking may find the strict adherence to a set form of tantric practice very tempting. It should be borne in mind, however, that Tantra is not designed to make our lives safe by providing a neat system. Nor is the system the ultimate meaning of tantric practice. When we awaken the aspect of ourselves that is our creative vitality it may not be comfortable. It will, however, require a creative vehicle for expression, and Tantra can provide such a channel. The dynamic process of transformation lies at the heart of all creative aspects of our lives, even though sometimes we may fear its potency and block its expression. Tantra offers one of the richest, most potent, and most inspiring ways of creative transformation to enable us to embody fully our true nature.

For the practice of Tantra to continue as a living experience within the lives of Westerners there are a number of important questions that need to be considered. First, to what extent is maintaining a tradition more important than developing a style of practice that suits Westerners? I am not an advocate of diluting the tradition in an attempt to make Tantra accessible to Westerners. With our very different cultural history and psychological development, however, an authentic creative expression of Tantra may not evolve fully for some time in the West. Second, our need for creative innovation and individual expression is alien to the culture that has been holding Tantra for the past thousand years.

Can the practice of Tantra be developed to the same depth in a new way that includes a more creative dimension, but without losing its essence? I do not claim to have an answer, but if we look at the origins of Tantra, there is little doubt that creative transformation is central. Perhaps the future of Tantra lies in genuinely developing a deeper understanding of this process rather than simply holding to formal practices because they are traditional. Somewhere between tradition and creative renewal lies a middle path that each of us must tread for ourselves. There is no clear map, only the need to be authentic and true to our inner nature as it unfolds.

E NTERING THE PATH of Tantra in a traditional way is considered a significant step on the journey. Those who take this step need to have a foundation of understanding of basic Buddhist principles to sustain the process that will unfold. This foundation gives practitioners a sense of whether they are ready to engage in the tantric path. According to Tsongkhapa, these foundations are traditionally known as the "three principal aspects of the path," and are the heart of the Sutra teachings of Mahayana Buddhism. Simply, these three are: renunciation; *bodhichitta,* the aspiration to attain full awakening or buddhahood for the benefit of all sentient beings; and the realization of emptiness, or *shunyata.*

The first of these, renunciation, is traditionally considered to be an attitude that abandons attachment to *samsara,* the cycle of existence, and the seductions of worldly life. Although the familiar translation of the Tibetan word *ngejung* is "renunciation," a more accurate one would be "definite emergence," or, as my teacher, Lama Thubten Yeshe, described it, "a determination to wake up." The psychological implications of this go beyond renunciation. They imply a willingness to wake up and emerge from the unconscious habits and patterns within which we usually take refuge. We use many activities of our worldly life—television, work, relationships, or food—as an escape into unconsciousness. Even spiritual practices such as meditation can be used to avoid feelings, responsibilities, relationships, and even living fully in our bodies. We can drift into a detached, disconnected, but peaceful state that avoids reality and the deeper aspects of ourselves.

Definite emergence is the willingness to abandon the habitual disposition of avoiding facing ourselves. It challenges the habit of letting ourselves sink into unconscious, anesthetized states of denial.

The intention of Mahayana Buddhist practice is not avoiding or escaping from our human condition, but the transformation of our relationship to it. Meditation is not a soft, quiet, easy way to generate a peaceful dissociation from the trials of life. If this is our wish, then Tantra is not the path to follow. When practiced properly, Tantra will confront us with our emotional problems so we have the opportunity to grow through them. Therefore our first prerequisite is a willingness to face the challenge, and no longer seek refuge in habits that keep us unconscious. Definite emergence is not abandoning life, as renunciation might imply, but living it fully and consciously. Rather than running away from difficult times when we are challenged, we wake up to the situation and face what there is to learn.

Spiritual practice often brings to the surface aspects of ourselves that are extremely painful. We have a deep reservoir of emotional wounds and patterns that may be hard to accept in ourselves, and which we have consequently often ignored or denied. This forms a powerful "Shadow," to use Jung's term. As we begin to develop some aspects of tantric practice, these repressed emotions will be resurrected from the underworld of our psyche. This enables the energy bound up in them to then be addressed and potentially transformed. This can sometimes be an uncomfortable process, and it is important to accept and value ourselves even though we feel dreadful, or are frightened of or disgusted with what we see. When we practice Tantra, the dark aspects of our Shadow will almost certainly be evoked, and it requires great courage, honesty, and humility to face and transform them.

Definite emergence, therefore, is the willingness to wake up and face ourselves as we embark on the tantric path. In this willingness to face unconscious habits we also need compassion towards ourselves as we pass through periods of struggle and discomfort in our practice. Through a genuine love, self-acceptance, and sense of humor about ourselves we can potentially uncover even the darkest inner monsters.

Healthy self-value and self-worth gives us a solid basis from which to explore the tantric path.

While traditional teachings speak of insights and realizations experienced on the spiritual path, it is seldom made clear that these often come through pain and turmoil. Tantra aims at transforming our most basic emotional nature, and to hold this process we must cultivate compassion for ourselves. This compassion is the recognition that we are human, that we have our qualities and failings, and that we need to value ourselves with them. Compassion towards others begins when we are able to love ourselves through our pain, and in doing so empathize with the pain of others.

Renunciation as definite emergence combined with a healthy sense of self-worth is the basis for the second foundation, *bodhichitta*, the aspiration to attain full awakening or buddhahood for the benefit of all sentient beings.

Our motivation for practicing Tantra may at first be mixed. We may engage in it for our own healing and transformation, or to be of benefit to others. In the practice of Tantra as an aspect of Mahayana Buddhism, the bodhisattva's intention to work for the welfare of others is a vital basis of practice. It is the quality of motivation that safeguards tantric practice from becoming potentially harmful to others.

If we consider that the happiness we experience in our lives arises through the efforts, support, and kindness of others, it can seem indulgent to remain preoccupied only with our own welfare. We live in mutual interdependence. On the basis of our own experience of suffering, our empathy and capacity to have compassion for the suffering of others grows. As a natural outcome of this compassion, we can recognize the need to respond to the suffering of others in a meaningful way. This is not sentimentality or compulsive caring, but the desire to be of real lasting benefit to others to repay their kindness. Bodhichitta, the awakening mind, grows as we bring together two psychological insights. One is the growing desire to serve the welfare of others; the second is a vision of our own innate potential buddhahood.

Bodhichitta is a profound openness that seeks to respond to others without judgment or discrimination. It is a big heart that has the capacity to accept and value all living beings, holding them dear and precious. This is not a passive principle that wishes only that all beings may be happy. Rather, it is an active dynamic quality of intention, sometimes known as the "great will," that will engage in a demanding journey to awaken for the welfare of others. Bodhichitta is the willingness to surrender to a higher purpose and let go of our limited neurotic ego needs. This is the bodhisattva's intention, formally acknowledged through the bodhisattva vows, which are central to Mahayana Buddhism. These vows exemplify a willingness to serve the welfare of others and protect them from the shadowy side of our nature, which seeks to gratify personal needs and thereby harm others.

Tantra contains the power to heal and transform, but this must be held in a context of great sensitivity, compassion, and awareness. Those who are still blind to their own shadowy and unconscious needs may use the power of Tantra misguidedly. Tantric practitioners must therefore get to know their own Shadows, and clarify their intentions in awakening the potential powers of the psyche.

Although "Shadow" is not a tantric term, it is a useful way of viewing much of what is unconscious and needing to be faced in our path. Jung's idea of the Shadow primarily referred to aspects of ourselves that we have repressed and denied, our blind spots. The Shadow can contain both the negative destructive emotions and habits we deny or repress, as well as positive helpful qualities we have been unable to express. Thus, the Shadow is the side of ourselves that is of particular importance in the process of tantric transformation. It contains the forces that are the manure of transformation. It will also hold the ego's wounds that must be addressed in our path.

Our tendency to get caught in harmful egotistical needs and habits, whether conscious or unconscious, is rooted in ignorance, the fundamental cause of suffering. Ignorance in Buddhism is seen in two ways. One is the failure to understand the laws of karma, or cause and effect. The other is our misunderstanding of the nature of reality. This refers to a particular misconception of the nature of both the ego and phenomena; that is, the belief that they have inherent self-existence. Unless this misconception is rectified, the tantric path is extremely misleading. This brings us to the third prerequisite foundation for Tantra: understanding emptiness, or *shunyata*.

The distinction between the two levels of truth—relative and absolute—is fundamental to Buddhist understanding. Relative truth is the way in which phenomena appear to exist; ultimate truth is the way in which phenomena actually exist. Thus, our confusion is that the way things appear is not how they actually exist. We cling to the idea that objects are independent, permanent, solid, and reliable because they give the illusion of being so, and yet the way they actually exist is interdependent, transient, unstable, and empty of inherent characteristics. This confusion leads to endless suffering.

The tantric path is based on the view that all relative appearances arise in dependence upon the consciousness that cognizes them; in other words, the world each of us inhabits is the creation of our own mind. We can understand this on the level that our attitudes, beliefs, and values color our world and create the problems we experience. To resolve the difficulties that arise in our lives, we need to change our inner attitudes rather than blaming the world outside.

On a more subtle level, we mistakenly believe that our world has intrinsic substance independent of consciousness. When we hold this view of reality, the world and its events and objects become separate and solid, and we lose sight of their interdependent, insubstantial, transitory nature. This misconception makes us turn relative phenomena into absolute or ultimate entities. Our relative beliefs, for example, become absolutes that then give rise to endless conflict.

Our mind then acts as a powerful projector of reality, and yet we fail to recognize it. We solidify our projected reality and endlessly create a world of confusion, struggle, and limitation. Perhaps the most common experience of this occurs when we exaggerate and fantasize the qualities of something. It leads to disappointment and frustration when the object is unattainable, and disillusionment when its actual nature shows through the veneer of our fantasy. The degree to which we suffer is generally the degree to which we are clinging to a distorted view of reality.

The reality we experience is an illusion, just like the film on a cinema screen. When we go to the cinema, the projected play of images has a significant effect on how we feel, as if what we see were real. We respond as if the images had lives of their own rather than being fabricated illusions. Understanding emptiness on a subtle level is recognizing that the material world is like an illusion, a mirage, and that the mind that apprehends it is no more than a mirror. The mirror takes on the color of whatever appears. The mind's nature is clear and empty. Objective phenomena, and the mind that cognizes them, both arise moment by moment as a fleeting play of emptiness. This subtle view does not imply that the relative world does not exist. It has a perfectly valid relative existence, but we need a deeper understanding of how it ultimately exists.

This is particularly relevant to our understanding of what we mean by the ego. Buddhist practice aims to clarify our sense of self-identity through an understanding of the distinction between its relative and ultimate nature. While the ego's relative existence is necessarily an aspect of our normal life, when we explore this more deeply we begin to recognize that there is no self to be grasped at as true, or ultimately real. Rather than becoming caught in a tight, emotionally contracted sense of self, it becomes possible to let go of this grasping, and to remain open.

When we practice Tantra, the solidity of ego-identity must be softened to enable us to have a special relationship with the two levels of truth. The aim of practicing Tantra is to develop an awareness that lives on the threshold between relative appearance and ultimate nature. When we let go of believing relative appearances to be ultimately true we can begin to live on this threshold, realizing that all phenomena, including our ego identity, are mere appearances, fleeting and illusory. That their nature is emptiness does not, however, negate the validity of their relative existence.

Alongside these three principal foundations for the practice of

Tantra, I would like to add one further ingredient: a trust in our innate potential for transformation and in the process itself. Trust and faith grow with experience and there are many aspects of the tantric path that at first can only be taken on through faith. The development of a deity practice and all that this entails does not bring instant results. Yet faith and confidence in the effectiveness of Tantra can be greatly enhanced through a clear understanding of how Tantra works. This is not always easy to gain through the explanation of teachers, so it becomes important to test the validity and relevance of the practice ourselves. With the gradual awakening of an inner taste of Tantra, faith grows. Some people are easily inspired by these exotic Eastern practices, but to genuinely experience their potential takes time and work. Great patience is needed, as Tantra requires repeated practice with results that grow slowly with time.

Faith combined with a genuine testing of the process leads to trust based on experience, and the confidence to go deeper and further on the journey. To engage in a path that requires deep commitment requires great trust to surrender to its transformative power. When we commit to this path our trust will enable us to open to the challenges and changes the process demands. Faith enables us to step into the unknown and let go of the ego's fears that limit us.

Thus the three primary foundations of the path of Vajrayana are the willingness to wake up and face ourselves; the capacity to let go of self-will and surrender to a higher purpose based on a deeply rooted love and compassion; and an understanding of the nature of reality. If we are then willing to trust in the process of transformation that our journey will take us through, the ground of the path is prepared. Creating a fertile ground is said to be vital for the experiences of Tantra to arise naturally. When obstacles occur, they usually do so because this ground is not yet prepared.

*Figure 2. Manjushri*

◆ ◆

IN ORDER TO INTEGRATE the processes involved in practicing Tantra it is important to have a sound and stable identity. When water is poured into a clay pot that is cracked or has not been fired properly, the pot will not be able to contain the liquid. The water may eventually weaken and destroy the pot. In a similar way, the practice of Tantra requires a vessel that will remain stable and be able to contain the process. A grounded, healthy identity will remain stable as the process of transformation unfolds. This may sound obvious, but some of those who become involved in exotic spiritual practices do so from an unstable psychological basis, and are therefore unsuited to the practice of Tantra.

Unless they have considerable experience of Western students, Eastern teachers are often unaware of how much emotional wounding we suffer. They usually assume we have well-established, strong egos, and speak of abandoning or surrendering the ego and its related self-oriented egotism as the root of misery in our lives. However, this teaching requires the student to have a healthy ego and sense of self-worth that has become a solid center of identity. When the occasional Westerner becomes psychologically unstable through practicing Tantra, Eastern teachers often don't know how to deal with it.

Perhaps the most common misconception among Westerners is that Buddhism aims to negate the ego. This is a misunderstanding of emptiness and egolessness, which is more subtle than simply meaning we have no ego. This misunderstanding generally arises from a failure to recognize the difference between relative and ultimate truth. The object of emptiness is not to negate the existence of the ego on a relative level, but to cut through ego-grasping (Tib. *dagdzin*), which holds the ego to be a solid self-existent entity, an ultimate truth. When we erroneously negate the relative self, we are in danger of becoming nihilistic. If we are to function normally in a relative world, we need a stable sense of ego identity, a focus of awareness that cognizes, filters and understands the events of the day, both inner and outer. This enables even a highly evolved individual to say "I am eating," "I am sitting," and so on. This "I" is a valid relative truth. Without it we can have severe psychological problems, and even go into psychosis where our normal sense of self is flooded by material coming from the unconscious.

The ego has two dimensions, which for most of us are not differentiated. One is healthy; the other is emotionally wounded. Problems arise when the ego is damaged through traumatic experiences particularly in childhood. Ego-identity gradually becomes overwhelmed by layer upon layer of emotionally held beliefs about the sense of "I" or "me." These are often painful wounds that we cling to and believe to be real and solid. We become fearful for our safety, and feel we are bad, worthless, unlovable and so on. We cling to this core traumatized sense of "I" as absolute and permanent, and experience a powerful emotional feeling of "I" as bad, worthless, and so on. This is the emotional tone of ego-grasping which we instinctively cling to as though it were real and absolute. It is not therefore the ego that must be eliminated, but the ego-grasping that clings to these emotional wounds as absolutes.

Another way in which the ego becomes damaged has less to do with being wounded, and more to do with how it is formed. This often occurs in early infancy when a normal sense of identity fails to develop. In the normal mother-infant relationship, a process unfolds that enables the infant over time to become aware of itself as a separate entity. Slowly this consolidates a sense of "I" and "other" that gradually stabilizes, giving a clear feeling of identity. Individuals who fail to develop this because of a dysfunction in some aspect of the early maternal relationship often feel they are losing their sense of self and disappearing. They may have terrifying feelings of annihilation, as though they were on the edge of a black hole. These feelings can arise both when alone and in relationship to others.

A spiritual practice that negates the ego is not the answer when the ego has failed to form in this way, as egolessness and emptiness are not useful concepts when there is no solid sense of self in the first place. There are people who enter a spiritual practice such as Tantra in the belief that it will help solve this problem, but psychotherapy would be more useful for them first, to prepare the ground for later spiritual practice.

The practice of Tantra therefore requires a well-formed, stable sense of self, which for most people means few problems will arise. This stable identity provides the necessary foundation to practice, and gives an appropriate vessel to contain the experiences of the tantric process. Milarepa, a renowned figure in Tibetan Buddhism, once said, "It is easy to meditate upon the sky, but not so easy to meditate upon the clouds." He was implying that to understand the spacious nature of emptiness is not difficult; the difficulty is in understanding how conventional forms such as the ego exist.

In the sixties, Zen was perhaps the most familiar Buddhist tradition in the West. Zen emphasizes viewing reality from the perspective of ultimate truth as a negation of false conceptions about reality. In this view there is no ego, no path, no person. It is the path of no practice, no goal. However, it is easy to misunderstand Zen, and to think that because there is no ego, there is no personal responsibility, either, no matter what may happen. Sadly, this misinterpretation of one of the essential aspects of Buddhist thought can lead to much confusion. We need to establish the ego before we negate it, or we negate the wrong thing.

The Dalai Lama once said that a bodhisattva—one who aspires to rescue all beings from the ocean of suffering through becoming a Buddha—must have a huge ego. He was, of course, joking, but his point was that even to contemplate becoming a bodhisattva requires a strong sense of personal identity. What the bodhisattva does not do is to cling to that identity as an ultimate truth. The ego-grasping that leads to inflated omnipotence is entirely absent. This is the principle behind the bodhisattva, although in practice the human predisposition to cling to a sense of "I" may still be subtly present.

Understanding the need for a stable yet relatively true identity is extremely important in the practice of Tantra. Like many esoteric practices, Tantra requires the establishment of a solid basis sufficient to stabilize and ground experiences. Without it there is the danger that as the forces of the psyche are released and transformed there is no vessel to contain them. Rather than being able to integrate them, these liberated forces will make us increasingly disoriented and unable to maintain a normal, functional life, like a lightning rod with no ground wire connected to the earth. In extreme cases, powerful experiences can disrupt the normal sense of identity, bringing about disorientation close to psychosis.

Several years ago, in Italy, I was part of a group of Western students participating in a program of teachings and initiations given by a high Tibetan lama. There was an almost tangible energy of excitement in the atmosphere, and several young Englishmen seemed particularly enthralled and captivated by the power of what was happening. I began to notice however that they had intense mood swings. While they had great inspiration and enthusiasm for the Dharma teachings, they seemed to have great difficulty relating to more worldly demands, particularly with respect to how they were going to live and work. They took part in the empowerment into some particularly powerful tantric practices, and appeared to become highly charged by the energy generated. However, the high they felt seemed disconnected from reality.

Some weeks later, back in England, I received a phone call from a relative of one of these young Englishmen asking if I knew of anywhere that would help him, as he had gone into a psychosis. This did not surprise me, and I was aware that few mental hospitals would grasp the peculiarity of his experience. This sad tale demonstrates how important it is to have a clear sense of identity, a stable ego, before starting to practice Tantra. It also confirms my belief that some people would benefit from a psychotherapeutic experience before becoming involved so intensively in Tantra.

However, anyone with a normal, healthy sense of self, and who is well grounded in life, can enter the practice of Tantra with little concern. Danger only arises when someone has the tendency to be ungrounded, caught in idealistic, fanciful notions of spirituality, or whose self-identity is severely emotionally wounded. Some people may also be drawn by the exotic nature of Tantra and naively wish to play with it, which could prove hazardous.

When entered skillfully, Tantra is a vast resource with many profound approaches to transformation, and practicing this path can be a deeply integrating experience. The dangers mentioned can be avoided so long as a balanced lifestyle is maintained and a healthy practical basis to life is kept so that the transformation process has a grounded form in which to manifest. I have heard my own teacher, Lama Thubten Yeshe, say many times, "You be practical," when we tend to get caught in idealistic fantasy. Another highly venerated old lama, Song Rinpoche, was clear in his pragmatism. During an initiation of many Westerners into a Highest Tantra deity, he stated that first we needed to get our livelihood together, then build the foundations. He would then gladly "open the door to Vajrayana."

*Figure 3. Chenrezig*

The Role of the Teacher  4

✦✦ ───────────────────────────────

Having CREATED a fertile ground, the seeds of the tantric
process can now be sown. At this point it is usually necessary to
enter into a relationship with someone who can act as mentor, like
the relationship between an apprentice and a master. The relationship
to a guru, or spiritual guide, is emphasized more in the tantric tradition than in any other school of Buddhism. As Tibetan Buddhism
becomes increasingly familiar and widespread in the West, many
Tibetan lamas have visited and gathered around them groups of disciples. Many Western students are keen to find the kind of relationship
and potential guidance a spiritual teacher offers. Some people have
found this relationship easy to develop, others not so, but increasingly
it is apparent we have much to learn about how to relate to a spiritual
teacher, and about the value and the pitfalls that such a relationship
presents.

To gain an awareness of our own inner wisdom we may need the
guidance of a teacher. Our limited insight into our own nature is part
of the human condition, and leads us into confusion and suffering
time and again. From a Buddhist viewpoint, our fundamental ignorance of the nature of reality leads us to circle endlessly in the cycle
of death and rebirth. While we lack the insight to free ourselves from
this cycle of existence, the teacher can offer us a way to break free of
our ignorance and suffering. The Mahayana and Vajrayana traditions
consider the guru to be the root of the path, the source of realizations
and the one who liberates us from the bondage of ignorance. The
tantric teachings of *guru yoga* say that the guru should be considered

synonymous with the Buddha, and emphasize that without the guru the student cannot proceed.

Because the role of the guru is given such emphasis, it is important to examine it closely, and in recent years awareness has grown of the hazards involved in the guru-disciple relationship. When students meet a teacher who touches them deeply, the experience can be overwhelming. They might become aware of their potential in a way they have never recognized previously. Disciples still captivated by the inspiration of their teacher often speak as if they have fallen in love, full of wonder and admiration. The teacher has opened their eyes, and they see him or her as fundamental to that experience. What empowers this experience is partly the quality of the teacher, who acts as a catalyst to awaken an inner quality that was unconscious.

Each of us has an innate inner wisdom that is for the most part unconscious. Access to this inner knowledge-wisdom may at first elude us, and be primarily experienced projected onto an outer teacher in whom we place our trust. This inner wisdom is our inner archetypal guru, which is constellated by projection upon an outer teacher. Jung first introduced to the West an understanding of the archetype of the wise man or wise woman as a personification of the Self in the aspect of a teacher or guide. When we have no inner relationship to this quality, there is no inner resource in which to trust. At such times the outer guru can be a vital guide, an oasis in the desert, but a guide who should be approached cautiously. The outer teacher becomes the guru because we imbue them with this archetypal quality. Their task is to gradually bring the disciple to experience this quality internally through a continual process of empowerment.

The teacher-disciple relationship in Tantra is similar to an apprentice in relation to a master craftsman. The master-craftsman provides a stable context in which an apprentice passes through a process of transformation. Adepts in Western alchemy had apprentices they instructed in the practices of crafting alchemy. The significance of this relationship is not to be underestimated, as it creates an environment for the development of a disciplined and contained experience of powerful inner forces. In this contained and clearly defined space, instructions into the esoteric aspects of practice can be safely transmitted and then practiced under guidance. The tantric teacher considered in this way is a vital resource to pass on an oral tradition of the finer details of a deity practice. He or she will instruct the apprentice in the visualizations and rituals of the generation stage, and the yogic practices of the completion stage.

From my own experience, detailed knowledge and understanding of the performance of ritual practices is almost impossible to gather without the guidance of a teacher. An oral tradition ensures a degree of protection that prevents those ill-prepared being able to develop the practice. This may sound exclusive or restrictive, but it has preserved intact an authentic lineage of some of the most significant tantric traditions over hundreds of years. The guru's role is to transmit a lineage of experience, which cannot be received merely through reading texts, as we might hope in the West.

The outer guru acts as a vehicle for initiating and empowering certain experiences. He or she serves as a model or example to inspire the apprentice into believing in the possible effects of the practice by embodying certain qualities. The teacher can only function within certain parameters, however, and while in the tantric teachings the guru's place is paramount, there are limitations. Contrary to the hopes of some disciples, the guru is not omnipotent. It is said that if the Buddha could have enlightened his disciples, his compassion would have led him to do so, but he was not able to change and eliminate the karma of individuals. He could guide them to their own liberation through his insight, but ultimately disciples must practice the guru's instructions.

In the tantric tradition the guru is understood on three levels known as "outer," "inner," and "secret." Understanding these three is crucial to deepening the experience of the guru-disciple relationship. The outer guru is therefore partly the expression of an archetypal need for someone to embody the inner guru through projection, or what in psychotherapy is called "transference." This is similar to the need for someone to embody the father or mother so that we transfer this inner need onto an outer figure. While we are unable to consciously experience the qualities of our Buddha nature fully, they are constellated through projection. A teacher with integrity will be aware that ultimately the quality he or she has been imbued with must be given back to the disciple. Such teachers awaken the disciple's inner potential through a process of empowerment that is free and unconditional.

For a tantric practitioner to grow, the projected outer guru must be gradually brought back into the psyche so as to stabilize the inner experience. This is often cultivated within a practice of guru yoga, where the visualized guru is brought repeatedly into the heart so as to remind the disciple of this inner quality. The awakening of the inner guru gradually enables disciples to stand in their own power and become adepts. The outer teacher is significant as the person who temporarily holds the vessel within which the disciple is being transformed. As the relationship grows, a good teacher gradually allows disciples to express their own inner experiences, enabling them to manifest in the world. When this process of empowerment is positive and supportive, it allows disciples to express their full potential. This manifests in greater individuality and autonomy, and a growing sense of inner authority that increases the capacity to trust the inner intuition of their own spiritual needs.

The relationship moves forward when a disciple draws back some of the projection and begins to experience the inner aspect of the guru for him or herself. This frees both teacher and disciple, as they are no longer bound by so much idealization. The teacher is freer to relate to the disciple in the most beneficial way, and the disciple's behavior becomes more natural and less caught in stilted deference. This can make the relationship more challenging, as the romantic phase has ended, but it is more real. The deferential behavior of many students towards their teachers creates a tension and falsity in the relationship that can inhibit genuine contact.

My own relationship to some of my teachers went through a phase during which I held them in such awe that I created an unnecessary distance between us because of my awkwardness. My manner was contrived, self-conscious, and pious, with lots of bowing and softly uttered politeness, and this deference made real communication almost impossible. As I allowed the guru to be more human, I allowed myself to be so, too. I developed a more natural friendship that respected and valued their special gifts, but included their human fallibilities. This must have been as great a relief to them as it was to me.

Cultivating the inner guru in the tantric tradition concentrates particularly upon the development of a deity practice. This in turn gradually enables deeper access to the wisdom of the secret guru, which is the innate clarity of our true nature. The inner guru may be seen as the relative guru, and the secret guru as the ultimate guru. As the experience of these two grows, the sense of inner authority, inner resourcefulness, and trust also grows. As Lama Thubten Yeshe emphasized many times in his teachings, both privately and publicly, "You must learn to trust your inner knowledge wisdom." This became vital for disciples who were soon to experience his death at the age of forty-nine due to a heart disorder.

Thus the teacher's role works in different ways. One is to act as a catalyst to empower the disciple into the experience of the inner guru, often in the aspect of a deity. This process may take time, and so the teacher must also provide a container in which the disciple can grow. Once this has reached a certain point, the disciple begins to turn the emphasis of the relationship inward. Only then will the disciple begin to take responsibility and truly trust his or her innate inner wisdom. The deity acts as a bridge to access inner wisdom, and the guru's role is to initiate this relationship so that the deity can gradually be awakened in the disciple.

Song Rimpoche said that the tantric guru opens the door to an entirely new world of experience by introducing the disciple to the mandala of the deity he or she will practice. Having received this initiation, the disciple is usually expected to maintain certain commitments to the guru called *samayas*. Often these commitments are seen as the most sacrosanct aspect of the tantric path, as they are intended to protect and preserve the essential quality of the relationship to the deity through the vehicle of the guru. Formally these commitments are the tantric vows, but informally this refers to the practitioner's deep-rooted devotion to the deity, and to their innate clear nature.

Eventually, the inner awakening initiated by the guru stabilizes and leads to a level of awareness that is present at all times as an inner resource of insight and inspiration. The disciple has gradually become a vehicle for the deity to manifest in the world, and to take responsibility for any effects this may have. The outer guru has enabled greater autonomy in the disciple through stabilizing the inner guru in the aspect of the deity, and making possible a profound insight into the secret guru as the ultimate truth of emptiness, or *dharmakaya*.

If there is any disruption of the essential trust in the guru-disciple relationship, the consequences can be painful, and occasionally extremely psychologically disturbing. The hazards in the guru-disciple relationship are unfortunately as present in the Tibetan Buddhist world as they are in many other spiritual traditions. Many Westerners have become deeply involved in a relationship with a teacher, but a lack of understanding has often led to confusion. This confusion became particularly apparent recently as a result of the inappropriate behavior of certain renowned teachers. This arose partly from teachers denying their deficiencies and having unclear boundaries, but also from the naiveté of the students. The fundamental question is whether we assume the guru to be enlightened and therefore not manifesting any personal flaws. Regrettably, there are unscrupulous teachers who do have personal needs and problems, which we overlook or deny to our cost.

There is considerable ongoing debate regarding the traditional view of the guru-disciple relationship, which asserts that seeing the guru as Buddha, impeccable and without failings, is vital to ripen the disciple's potential to attain the fruits of the path. This is reinforced by the admonition that to see faults in one's guru will result in karmic downfalls and future suffering for the disciple. Any faults in the teacher should be seen as the disciple's aberrations projected outside. The tantric teachings insist this pure view should be held at all times to protect the disciple from accruing negative karma.

However, underlying this is also the need to preserve the integrity, authority, and status of the teacher. This leads to a great deal of confusion when students begin to see evident flaws in teachers, and it would be folly to explain them away as the students' impure perception. Consequently it has become necessary to cultivate a less dogmatic, more pragmatic view. A teacher may not be a perfect carrier of the projection, but this does not contradict the tantric view that essentially the guru, an inner phenomenon projected outside, is Buddha.

If we literalize this principle of the teacher as the embodiment of perfection, we are in danger of blinding ourselves to the reality that most teachers are human, and therefore not perfect. An individual can have deep insights into the nature of reality and still have human failings, a shadow that has not been fully eradicated. According to teachings on the Ten Grounds or Stages of the Bodhisattva, until the final ground is reached, there are still subtle obscurations to full enlightenment that can manifest in flawed behavior. Believing without question that the outer guru is Buddha also traps the teacher in an unrealistic, unconscious position. This can feed into the shadowy side of the guru's nature, inflating his or her own sense of omnipotence and power. The Dalai Lama has commented that too much deference harms the teacher, because we never challenge him or her.

When disciples become devoted to teachers, considerable power and authority is entrusted to them. While a teacher's role is to support and empower disciples to discover their own potential, sometimes this does not happen. Some teachers become caught in the powerful position they have been endowed with and are unaware of their own desire for power and authority. They may begin to enjoy their power too much and take advantage of it for their own needs. This keeps their disciples disempowered, and ultimately does not allow growth and individual responsibility to emerge. Teachers may be unconsciously afraid to empower their disciples and allow them to gain a sense of their own authority and autonomy. They may try to hold on to their disciples, when to genuinely empower them could lead to their leaving to engage in their own journey.

Devoted disciples may also be caught in unconscious habits that are not addressed and become destructive. Sometimes reluctance to take personal responsibility is like the struggle to separate from a perfect parent who solves our life problems. It is not uncommon for disciples to project many of their childhood needs for the perfect parent onto the teacher. This can lead to unconscious collusion from both sides, making a perpetually infantilizing and dependent relationship. If there is a sexual dimension in the relationship, this can be very hazardous. Disciples may project sexual fantasies, and the teacher may take advantage of them to satisfy his or her own needs. Regrettably, this does occasionally occur when teachers are unable to keep their boundaries clearly. When this happens it is also evident that disciples involved have often suffered sexual abuse of some form in childhood.

A romantic view of Eastern teachers creates a mystification around their qualities and abilities that can have serious consequences. All too frequently, those who enter the role of devotee have no objectivity around the relationship. Romantic, idealized falling in love with a teacher can be a wonderfully opening and inspiring experience, but can also be fraught with confusion and the potential for abuse. Absence of the guru role in our own culture tends to make us naive about the shadowy side of a guru-disciple relationship, and disillusionment may play a significant part in waking us up to the illusion we can create around a teacher. Disappointment, however, helps us separate psychologically from a teacher so we can take more responsibility for our own journey, even while we maintain the relationship.

While we may need a relationship to someone who can awaken us to our inner nature, the dangers of placing ourselves too willingly in the power of a teacher must be recognized. In meeting someone who becomes a teacher or guru, the student places an inner power and wisdom into that person's hands. This leaves the disciple vulnerable, as he or she trusts the teacher's integrity to use that power and wisdom skillfully. The Dalai Lama has clearly expressed in recent years that Westerners who engage in such a relationship should take time and check a teacher carefully before making a commitment. When the projected idealization of a spiritual teacher is made conscious, we are able to clearly see the qualities and failings of a teacher. We are also able to develop greater autonomy in our spiritual journey, and suffer less from the inconsistencies that arise from idealized projection onto a fallible teacher.

A practitioner will need to relate to an outer teacher for periods along the path to facilitate deeper insight and understanding of the practices he or she is developing. If this relationship is engaged in skillfully and with awareness of the hazards from both sides, it can be immensely rewarding. When the teacher gradually enables a genuine empowerment of disciples, they gain the maturity to develop their own inner integrity and authority.

Each of us must ultimately be true to our own inner potential in order to discover the appropriate path that awakens us. The role of the teacher in this process can be a very special one that develops over many years. Devotion towards a teacher does not have to imply blindness to the teacher's human fallibilities. As this relationship matures there can be greater freedom, mutual respect, and love arising from each valuing the other without illusion. The human dimension to the relationship will then become as important as the sublime one. Allowing the teacher to be human allows disciples to have understanding and compassion for their own fallibility as well.

*Figure 4. Green Tara*

J UNG WROTE that the psyche's inner disposition is always to attempt
to move towards the healthiest state in any given situation. He considered this to be an important function of the Self as the archetype
of wholeness. The Self has a fundamental homoeostatic intention that
will enable the individual to adjust and integrate life experiences in a
way that always attempts to remain unified and whole. We may be
unconscious of this capacity of the Self to maintain wholeness, but
once awakened it becomes central to every aspect of life, giving it
meaning and value.

However, our habitual failure to listen to this inner call towards
wholeness leads to endless suffering, confusion, and sickness. Our
experience of emotional or physical problems could from one perspective be seen as reflections of the imbalance of the body/psyche
whole. They could equally be seen as symptoms emerging as the psyche adjusts to life's traumas. Symptoms of dis-ease are the psyche's
way back towards wholeness. Symptoms become a source of chronic
suffering only when they are stuck and cannot move through.

If we refuse to listen to the body's expression of dis-ease through
symptoms, the voices of those symptoms will become louder until we
take notice and change. Similarly, when we are out of relationship to
the source of our potential wholeness, we consequently suffer psychological ill health. When we fail to respond to the psyche's archetypal intent, "the gods become our diseases," to use Jung's phrase. Once
this happens we experience a sense of alienation, meaninglessness, and
lack of purpose, because we are out of relationship to the Self.

Just as Jung saw that the process of individuation was to open to and trust in the Self's pull towards wholeness, so too must we begin to open to the potential of our Buddha nature. Our innate Buddha potential is said to be like a priceless jewel buried beneath our homes, while we live our lives in ignorance of it. As a result, we flounder, lost in endless confusion. We tend to spend our lives in a constant search for security, and freedom from anxiety and fear, yet the materialistic methods we employ continue to leave us out of relationship with this innate wisdom. The intention of Tantra is to gradually awaken the seeds of our innate wisdom as a source of health, power, love, and peace that can then live through every aspect of our lives. We can engage in life more fully and confidently because we are in relationship to our true nature personified in the deity.

To practice Tantra successfully we must also begin to respond to our innate disposition to unfold towards wholeness. Even though the notion of no-Self (Skt. *anatma*) is a central tenet of Buddhism, the Buddhist tantric path conceives that our potential for wholeness is personified in the symbolic form of a deity. Perhaps the most significant experience of the tantric path, therefore, is the introduction to a deity that will embody our innate enlightened potential, the seed of our eventual wholeness. In this introduction the outer guru plays an important role as one who can provide a context within which a transmission occurs into an experience of the deity's nature. The guru initiates a relationship to powerful archetypal forces that transform the disciple as they awaken. These seeds of transformation and healing are present within each of us, but need to be awakened, usually through a process of initiation. Because we all have different dispositions, however, the deity practices that suit each individual will vary. It then requires skill and understanding to recognize the deity forms that will best suit a particular person. This is one of the most important roles of the tantric teacher.

The deity in Tantra can be understood as a gateway or bridge between two aspects of reality. Buddhism has no concept of a creator God, as do theistic religions. The deity is not to be viewed as a god in the sense of an entity that has an autonomous existence beyond human consciousness. Rather, the deity is a symbolic aspect of forces that arise on a threshold between two dimensions of reality, or two dimensions of awareness. In Buddhism we speak of "relative truth," the world of appearances and forms, and "ultimate truth," the empty, spacious, nondual nature of reality. Our conventional reality of forms is understood to be the play of emptiness, lacking any inherent substantiality. Form and emptiness are interrelated as a dynamic of creative manifestation in every moment. The deity stands on this threshold as an expression of the potential for creative manifestation that can inform our life in every moment.

DIAGRAM 1

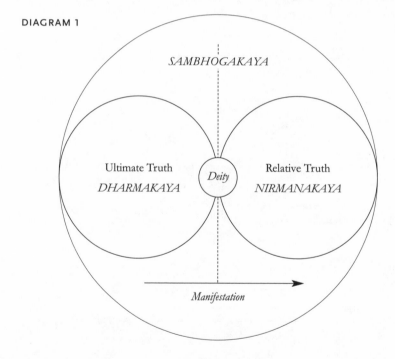

If this dynamic were to be expressed graphically, we might see it as in Diagram 1, where the interface between the two spheres of ultimate truth and relative truth is conceived as an intermediate field in which the deity manifests. In one who has fully awakened, the two spheres of

reality become the "wisdom truth body," or *dharmakaya*, and the "manifestation body," or *nirmanakaya*. The creative vitality that exists on this
threshold is the realm of *sambhogakaya*, or "complete enjoyment body,"
which is the dynamic realm within which the deity functions.

For a normal person, remaining present on this threshold of awareness is very unlikely. Our minds are too preoccupied by gross dualistic
conceptions, and too bound by our solid sense of identity. Without
training in meditation, our minds do not have the capacity to settle
into a subtle and clear enough state of awareness to open to the threshold between these two levels of truth. As a consequence, the dimension of dharmakaya becomes translated into what we might call an
"unconscious ground of being," which has many parallels to Jung's
notion of the "collective unconscious."[3]

DIAGRAM 2

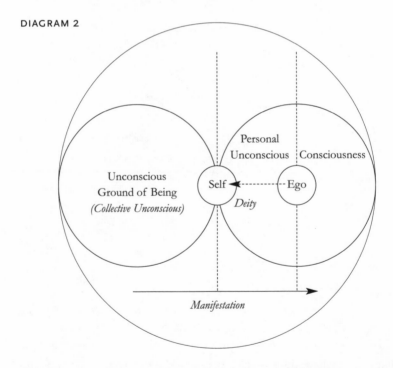

If we consider the map of the psyche expressed in Diagram 2, we see
a dynamic that reflects our normal inability to experience the subtle

awareness of dharmakaya. The left circle becomes a dimension of the
unconscious that is seen as transpersonal (i.e., outside or beyond the
personal sphere of experience), mysterious, and numinous; it corresponds to Jung's "dark background of consciousness." This gives rise
to manifestations within the unconscious of a world of archetypal
forces that underpin our instinctual and emotional lives, and emerge
across the threshold into consciousness through dreams, symbols,
visions, and peak experiences. In this world, the gods, so to speak,
become powerful unconscious forces that shape our lives. Central to
these manifestations is the archetype of the Self.

The separation that exists between our normal ego reality and that
of the Self is part of our human struggle. We are unconscious of the
source of our potential wholeness until we begin to open up some
kind of inner dialogue. Jung saw this dialogue as primary to the process
of individuation, as it is expressed through dream-work, art, writing,
and other creative processes.

For Jung, the relationship between the ego and Self deepens as we
open to the influence of the Self. From a Jungian perspective, the Self
will always remain within the unconscious as a kind of divine other,
and the separation between ego and Self will always exist (except perhaps during what the psychologist Abraham Maslow called "peak experiences"). From a Buddhist perspective, however, this separation is the
basis of a fundamental alienation from our true nature—our Buddha
nature—that can gradually be overcome. From a Buddhist perspective, our everyday sense of consciousness is a state of blindness or
ignorance (Tib. *marigpa;* literally, "not-seeing") that does not see clearly
our true nature or the nature of reality. This ignorance reinforces the
solidity of the ego, and actually separates us from direct experience of
our Buddha nature. The significant shift in awareness made possible by
Buddhist practice depends on the capacity to develop a quality of clear,
present, nondual awareness, not bound by subject/object duality. The
implication of this is that, to use Jung's language, the duality in relationship between the ego and the Self gradually disappears. Ego and
Self become reflections of the same present awareness, and are non-

dual. This is something Jung would not have considered possible.[4] In Tantra our relationship to the deity is fundamental to this process. The way in which this is actually brought about in practice will, however, vary, depending upon the level of tantra being practiced. Four levels of tantra are usually delineated: Action Tantra (*kriyatantra*); Performance Tantra (*charyatantra*); Yoga Tantra (*yogatantra*); and Highest Yoga Tantra (*anuttarayogatantra*). The two levels most frequently encountered are Action Tantra and Highest Yoga Tantra. In Action Tantra, the primary level of tantra, the deity will at first be visualized during meditation in the space immediately in front of the practitioner as the object of veneration and prayer. Placing this inner quality outside of oneself may seem dualistic, but we nevertheless need this relationship as a means of opening the gateway to dharmakaya. To clarify this, we are at first sitting in the position of the ego as our ordinary identity, looking in the direction of the arrow in Diagram 2, visualizing the deity before us as an image of the Self. This relationship is one of devotion, faith, and trust. Unless we trust our Buddha nature and begin to open to its innate knowledge and wisdom, there will be no basis in which to live our lives in a transformative way. Those who find ideas of faith, trust, and devotion hard to entertain, however, may have great difficulty with this approach.

Our Western attitude tends to view consciousness as paramount, so that if we have conscious knowledge of what is going on, we feel safe and in control. This somewhat arrogant position does not see faith or trust as acceptable. The thought of opening or surrendering to anything is antithetical to our need for the ego to predominate. Buddhism begins with a gradual shift of emphasis, acknowledging the limitations and fallibility of the ego by recognizing that our inner wisdom and insight are more powerful than the ego and the intellect. In Tantra the ego must learn to let go, and trust in the process of awakening that the deity unfolds. Thus the deity becomes the inner guru, our guide into the darkness of the unknown.

The meditation on what is called "front generation" practiced in

Action Tantra is allied to a process known as *guru yoga*, in which the guru, in the aspect of a deity, is also visualized in front of the meditator. The key to guru yoga is recognizing that the deity, the practitioner's essential nature, the guru's nature, and the wisdom of all enlightened beings are inseparable. The outer guru is considered highly significant as the vehicle that enables this nature to awaken, and within many teachings, there is great emphasis on the fact that all the realizations that arise on the spiritual path are through the blessings of the guru-deity conjunction.

Many prayers of devotion have been composed to the guru-deity in which the outer guru and deity come to be viewed as inseparably interwoven. The following prayer to Manjushri, the embodiment of the Buddhas' wisdom, is a good example:

> Homage to the guru and protector, venerable Manjushri,
> Who holds a scripture at his heart because he sees all
>     objects as they are,
> With pure and clear intelligence, free of the two obstructions,
>     like the sun free of clouds,
> Who teaches with sixty types of melody all collections of
>     sentient beings,
> Confused by the darkness of ignorance and tormented by
>     suffering in the prison of existence,
> With the love of a father for his only child,
> Whose great dragon-like proclamation of the Dharma
>     wakes them from the sleep of afflictions,
> And frees them from the shackles of Karma,
> Who holds a sword which clears away the darkness of
>     ignorance, and cuts every sprout of suffering,
> Who is pure from the very beginning, and has gone to the
>     end of the ten grounds,
> Whose physical qualities are complete, and who is the chief
>     of the Conqueror's sons,

Whose body is adorned with the one hundred and twelve
  ornaments of a Buddha,
I bow down to Manjushri in order to eliminate the darkness
  from my mind.

OM AH RA PA TSA NA DHIH

Oh kind one, having cleared away the darkness of obscurations
  from my mind,
With the brilliance of your exalted wisdom,
I beseech you to bestow the illumination of intelligence
  and wisdom,
Which realizes the meaning of the Buddha's words, and
  the treatises which explain them.[5]

Such prayers become a constant reminder of the qualities of the
guru-deity, and gradually cultivate a profound feeling of love, devotion, and veneration. As the heart increasingly opens, the blessings and
inspiration of the guru-deity are received. The heart deity is called
*yidam*, meaning, literally, "mind bound," because it is the deity at the
heart of the tantric process. This deity and the innate nature of mind
are inseparable as the root of transformation. The relationship to the
*guru yidam*, as the deity is then called, is considered sacrosanct, from the
time of initiation, and is treasured as the very heart of spiritual life.

Deepening an understanding of the particular qualities of the deity
enhances the practice of devotion. With Chenrezig (fig. 3), for example, one concentrates on the qualities of loving-kindness and compassion, imagining the deity to be like a caring parent whose sole intention
is to heal suffering. Chenrezig's white color conveys a quality of blissful peace and serenity.

Manjushri (fig. 2), the Buddha of wisdom, emphasizes the capacity
to cut through confusion and ignorance in order to develop clarity and
sharp insight into the nature of reality. Manjushri is often propitiated
at times when some aspect of our lives needs to be clarified, or when

a particular understanding is needed. Manjushri's orange color generates a fiery dynamic vitality.

Tara (fig. 4), a female deity, possesses the quality of protection;. she has the capacity to hold us with total unconditional love, and swiftly responds to whatever problems cause us distress, like a loving mother.

Vajrapani (cover) has the capacity to develop the power to be effective, or to assert our truth in life, to go beyond our limitations. His fierce dark blue appearance conveys a sense of potency that tolerates no nonsense.

At first, therefore, the relationship to the deity in Action Tantra is developed in a manner that may be seen as akin to Diagram 2. The ego is in a devotional relationship to the deity as a symbol of the Self. In this mode of practice, with the deity visualized immediately in front of the meditator, many different actions are then performed. These can include making offerings, prayers, or prostrations to the deity.

At a certain point in a meditator's practice of Action Tantra, the meditation shifts from "front generation" to what is called "self generation." This aspect of practice is also central to Highest Yoga Tantra. In the process of "self generation," a profound shift of identification is made in which the meditator begins to visualize him or herself as totally transformed into a deity.

This transformation is brought about by first dissolving all ordinary appearances, and the identification of the conventional sense of "I" into emptiness. From this sphere of emptiness, the meditator re-emerges in the aspect of the deity and its surrounding environment. If we refer to Diagram 2, the meditator is, in effect, carrying a subtle quality of awareness across the threshold from the right hand circle into the left, and then returning to the threshold between the two in the form of a deity. This leads to an identification with the rainbow-like form of the deity known as "divine pride," or "divine confidence."

Divine pride can be seen as a kind of inflation, but not as we conventionally understand the concept. Some people question the usefulness of cultivating a view of ourselves that might be considered a fantasy, or might lead us away from accepting ourselves as we are.

Indeed, for someone disposed to grandiosity and inflated fantasies, this approach may appear to reinforce such inflation, but this is a misunderstanding of the process involved.

Identification with the deity is an identification with our true nature. It becomes an idealization or inflation of the ego only if we have not first dissolved our ordinary ego identity by crossing the threshold into emptiness. Self generation as the deity in meditation brings about a gradual realignment of awareness through which the deity becomes central.

This process enables the meditator to gradually settle into awareness on the threshold between the two states of relative truth and absolute truth as seen in Diagram 1. By identifying with the form of a deity, the meditator can experience what is called "emptiness with appearance"; that is, the capacity to maintain an awareness of clarity and emptiness while holding relative appearances. According to an answer H. H. Dalai Lama once gave to a group of Westerners in Bodhgaya, this is a special capacity of deity practice. This has the effect of simulating the same potential of a Buddha for unifying these two dimensions of awareness. The understanding of emptiness enables the meditator to maintain an identification of self as deity, making, effectively, a shift from the ego-Self duality of Diagram 2 to the unification of Diagram 1.

Tantra is often called "the resultant path" because of the fundamental principle of bringing the result into the present. This means that our enlightened potential is brought into the present through the experience of the deity. The focus of our psychic makeup, which had been unconsciously alienated from our true nature, shifts to its potential reintegration. Each day, the tantric practitioner restores the relationship to the essence of his or her Buddha nature in the aspect of the deity, and, in so doing, recenters daily life. Gradually the practitioner comes to live in clarity and centeredness rather than from a place of wounding, confusion, and emotional habits. This informs every facet of life, work, leisure, looking after others, and so on. Our lives become a creative expression of the transformation of energy, like ripples radiating out from the center of a pool.

When we consider the two views expressed in the two diagrams, we are seeing two very different notions of wholeness. It is important to bear in mind that Jung's notion of wholeness is not the same as the Buddhist understanding of enlightenment or buddhahood. For Jung, wholeness is not a state of perfection, but is still within the human condition. The presence of the Self is integrated, but there is still a considerable unconscious Shadow. The difference between Diagrams 2 and 1 denotes a progression that takes place in the process of tantric practice as we move from front generation to a deepening of the experience of self generation.

Furthermore, even though we may practice the identification of divine pride as the deity, there is little value in deluding ourselves that because we can meditate on our innate potential for perfection, we have gone beyond our human fallibilities. We should not try to deny the existence of the contents of the unconscious Shadow. Jung believed that to be human is to have a Shadow, and that to deny it would lead to inflation. In Tantra there is no room for an inflated idealism that splits us from the guts of our nature, and the powerful shadowy instincts and emotions are the essential ingredients of transformation. This is the energy the tantric deity is specifically intended to evoke and transform. If we deny or suppress it, the transformation process cannot occur. The total transformation possible in Tantra requires that we include every facet of our being.

## INITIATION

A relationship with a tantric deity can germinate in a number of ways. Traditionally a disciple is led through a formal initiatory process in which the initiating lama creates an environment conducive to the awakening of the seed of the deity by direct transmission. Thus the lama empowers the disciple into recognizing and embodying his or her innate clear nature and its luminous creativity as the deity. The degree to which the initiation is effective depends upon the readiness of the disciple, the capacity of the lama, and the openness of the relationship between the two. With highly experienced lamas, the power of an initiation can be felt almost tangibly. With mature disciples, the experience of initiation can generate an almost total transformation. In the formal sense, initiation and empowerment into a deity may be repeated many times, and the experience will continue to evolve.

Following an initiation or empowerment, the disciple is usually asked to uphold the *samaya,* or commitments, to the deity. This may be viewed formally, as a requirement to perform specific meditations and rituals, but in essence, true samaya is complete adherence to innate clarity and emptiness, combined with heartfelt devotion to the sacred value of the deity as an inner creative quality. Countless practices and prayers may be performed, but if this heart connection, or clear, nondual awareness, is absent, they will be of little value.

Many high lamas fly in to Western countries, give initiations, and fly off again. The danger for Western students receiving these empowerments is that there may be little understanding of what has taken place. Our yearning for experience often draws us to the exotic and mystical, and many people are influenced by the followers of high lamas, who romanticize with gushing enthusiasm about the power of receiving initiations from such special beings. Some people are easily tempted by promises of profound and wonderful experiences, but without a proper understanding little will be gained. Receiving an initiation just because it is happening does not mean it is necessarily appropriate for everyone. However, despite this caution, an initiation from a qualified teacher is of great significance, and will open the door to the depth and vastness of tantric practice.

The relationship to a deity does not originate exclusively in this way, however. It can also arise through spontaneous revelation or vision. Because the deity is a manifestation of sambhogakaya, an aspect of our Buddha nature, we each have its latent disposition. Dharmakaya, our primordial clear-light mind (left circle of Diagram 1), is the essential nature of all archetypal forms that emerge in the domain of sambhogakaya as the pure energy of creative vision. Sambhogakaya, known as "the body of pure bliss," the "complete enjoyment body," or the "illusory body," is the realm of our fundamental vitality that has the capacity for luminous creative vision. Sambhogakaya is also described as the "purified emotional body," and is therefore at the root of our qualities of feeling.

For most of us, our experience of the vitality of sambhogakaya is not in its purified state as the deity. We do, however, experience it as creative imagination and fantasy, and the inspiration deity practices can bring. The vitality of this side of our nature is the energy that drives our inner visionary life, and that underlies our emotional passion. When our gross mind quietens through meditation, we have the potential for a deeper opening or awakening to the vitality of the deity. We may describe it or name it in different ways in different cultures, but, as Joseph Campbell comprehensively describes it, these are the masks of god.

There is much debate about the origin of the Buddhist tantras. Some people insist they are not actual teachings of the Buddha. Others assert that Tantra originated from the Hindu tradition. Neither of these views are valid, as the origins of many tantras occurred at the time of the Buddha, but only in relation to particular disciples who received initiation through vision. The similarity of some Buddhist tantras to certain Hindu tantras is partly indicative of their source in the same culture; they work towards transforming similar archetypal forces. We can also see similarities to esoteric mysteries from the Middle East, Greece, and Europe.

Many lineages of tantric deity practice originated through spontaneous revelation or vision in the sphere of sambhogakaya. Indeed, one tantric view of the Buddha's enlightenment is that he received a spontaneous awakening of a tantric mandala at the point of enlightenment. It is said that he received initiation into this mandala by the Buddhas of the realm of pure vision known as Akanishta. In tantric texts it is generally recognized that the Buddha revealed the essence of particular deities to specific practitioners, so some tantras originated while the Buddha was alive, but others appeared much later.

There are many variations of the same deity because they originated as visions in the minds of different meditators. Chenrezig, while most often in the form shown in Figure 3, also has a standing six-armed form, a standing thousand-armed form, a seated two-armed form, and another that embraces a consort. Sometimes he is white, sometimes red. Vajrayogini, or Vajravarahi (fig. 13), also has many forms originating from the visions of specific meditators. The form in Figure 13, called Naro Khacho, appeared to the Indian mahasiddha Naropa, who then initiated a lineage of practice that still continues today. Many deity lineages originated recently, and it is possible that new manifestations will emerge in the West.

However we view the origins of Tantra, it is necessary for practitioners to experience the gradual germination of an inner seed. If we naturally begin to open to and are inspired by a particular deity, this may be an important experience to notice, as it might mean this deity has a significant quality for us. We may attempt to practice deities given to us by different teachers, but if our heart does not respond and open to a deity, the practice will be of little value. When an outer initiation deeply resonates with our awakening inner process, we can be confident we are relating to a deity that is personally significant. When Westerners first encounter the tantric tradition, they sometimes want to receive many initiations, but these can become like seeds thrown upon barren ground. There is a Tibetan saying that the Indians of old practiced one deity and accomplished them all, while the Tibetans practice them all and accomplish none.

It is not the number of deities practiced that is important, but the depth and openness of our relationship to the deity. When we develop a relationship to a deity and make this the heart of our lives, there is a profound process at work. Transformation is partly dependent on the confidence, trust, and devotion we have in this relationship, and the tantric deity acts as a transformative catalyst. Eventually, the tantric practitioner opens and becomes increasingly a vehicle for the deity's true nature to manifest in the world. When the Tibetans say the Dalai Lama is an embodiment of Chenrezig, the Buddha of compassion, they mean he has fully opened to this disposition in his own psyche, and is now the perfect vehicle for its expression in the world.

Although initiation is the traditional formal method of introduction to a deity, it is not exclusive. Because the deity is intrinsically bound up with our innate nature, it can also spontaneously awaken. The psyche's natural disposition is inner vision, when our deeper nature comes through to consciousness. In this respect, initiation can happen as a natural opening. Historically, Tibetans tend to take as significant only the spontaneous visions of very high lamas, but in meditation, retreat, dreams, and visions, it is potentially possible for anyone to experience an initiatory vision.

## Eastern Deity, Western Psyche?

Many people today seek out some form of spiritual path that includes working with archetypal forces. When our own culture no longer provides the necessary myths and mysteries for transformation, however, we will often find ourselves responding to those from elsewhere. Consequently, the number of people who explore paganism, shamanism, Hinduism, the Kabbalah, and other traditions is increasing.

Although the Tibetan tradition of Tantra does not suit everyone—and there is no reason why it would—many Westerners respond to its practices with great enthusiasm. It is not unproblematic, however. A question I find myself asked time and again by those who encounter the tantric path is: How useful to Western minds are deity forms born out of an Eastern culture? Usually this question arises when people are struggling to relate to forms that feel alien, and there is often a sense that these forms are not personal enough, or that they do not fit our Western symbolic world.

This is an extremely complex question to answer because our experience is so individual. Some find they can relate to these forms with relative ease, and faith or devotion grows naturally. Others struggle with the forms, and may be unable to make a connection. Does this mean that the deity forms should be changed and made more culturally acceptable to Westerners? One opinion is that these forms are traditional and unchangeable. Others say this is open to interpretation, and that we need to relate to the essence of the form, not to its cultural coloring. We may be tempted to search for a Western equivalent, or try to form a synthesis, like merging Christ and Chenrezig, and seeing them as being of the same nature. It may be useful to make such links, but this does not address the central problem.

It is worth considering the difference between the archetype and its symbolic representation, the archetypal image. Jung recognized that an archetype will emerge in forms that are both culturally and individually flavored. The same archetype may emerge in different cultures, but in very different forms, and it may be colored by individual differences. Jung suggested that what gives an archetypal form its power and numinosity was an inner response, an inner connection. When this is missing we feel little relationship to the form, and it has little capacity to affect us.

In principle, if we are able to respond to its archetypal root, the inner connection can occur irrespective of the cultural form in which it arises. The significant breakthrough Jung made was to recognize the universality of the archetypes that lay beneath their cultural differences. Indeed, when we look at the wrathful deities within Tantra, recognizing the presence and universality of an underlying archetype can help us understand their meaning. For example, the Buddhist deity Heruka Chakrasamvara (fig. 14) has a similar archetypal root to the Hindu Shiva, the Greek Dionysus, and the Celtic Kernunos. The Dionysian cult was carried to India by the Greeks around 200 BCE, and may well have had associations with Shivaism or the tantras. The Hellenistic art of the Greeks also shaped the iconographical depictions of peaceful deities in Buddhist art, many of which were based on the youthful form of Apollo. This occurred during the Greek colonization of parts of India soon after the Buddha's lifetime.[6]

If we are familiar with a particular cultural identity of an archetype, this may cloud our capacity to respond to it in a different form. Images of Christ and the Virgin Mary, for example, are predominantly white Caucasian when depicted in paintings and sculpture. A more Middle Eastern depiction may provoke resistance. A further characteristic particular to Western taste in archetypal forms is our tendency to respond to images that are human, rather than the stylized, god-like images of the East. We tend to create gods in our own image, wanting to humanize them. Perhaps we want them to reflect our value as humans so that we can reclaim some of the power we once gave to the gods.

If you find Eastern images hard to relate to, it may be worth asking yourself where you sense the source of your reaction or resistance might be. Is it simply that the images do not come from your culture, and is this cultural preconditioning unnecessarily limiting your ability to respond to a deeper universal significance? If this is so, it can be difficult to move beyond unless you are willing to explore tantric practice and actually experience the quality of the deity. Simply changing the deity to suit Western taste is not the solution.

At one point in my work as a *thangka* (Buddhist icon) painter, I attempted to give some of the deities Western characteristics, clothing, ornaments, and so on. The effect was, in my opinion, dreadful. Rather than creating an image that inspired me, I felt I had somehow degraded the power of the image by trying to impose my human relativity onto it. I felt I was bringing the sacred down to my profane level, rather than my opening to its divinity. The tantric texts describe the deity as having a body of light, without bone structure, muscles, or the solidity that gives a sense of gravity. Humanizing the deities did not enhance their numinosity.

If we do not change the form of the deity, how then might someone who finds these images difficult begin to open to them? This leads to a further question: Can an inner relationship with a deity given to us externally grow through meditation practice?

Jung doubted the potential of imposing Eastern images upon the Western mind, and anticipated that it would not deeply affect the Western psyche. This implies that Westerners only respond to Western symbols because they are culturally consistent, because our unconscious is soaked in their presence. It also assumes there would be no latent potential in the unconscious to respond to any other cultural forms. However, Dora Kalff, a Jungian analyst who originated the therapeutic practice of sand-play, noticed how often Westerners found Eastern images more numinous, and that many Japanese she worked with saw Western images as similarly numinous.

This suggests it would be useful to go beyond cultural conditioning. It further suggests that the unconscious is not as culturally bound as consciousness when it comes to universal imagery. It may also be time to let go of the view that holds the tantric deity to be Eastern just because of its Eastern appearance. The deity's source is universal. Certainly, from a tantric perspective, the seed potential of the deity is latent in us all, irrespective of culture. The problem is whether we can go beyond the cultural overlay that may be obscuring our potential to make the connection. This does not imply that the tantric deity is the true or ultimate image of an archetype, but only that it is a particularly powerful and effective vehicle for awakening.

There is a further cultural complication, something the Tibetans would take very seriously. The ease with which most Asians take the notion of reincarnation for granted contrasts with the struggle many Westerners have in coming to terms with previous lives. Tibetans easily believe we have been born in many different cultures, and have had many kinds of rebirth in many forms, not just in human forms. From this perspective, our unconscious is steeped in influences from countless lives. It may be that those who naturally and spontaneously respond to Eastern images are reflecting some past life experience.

Can a deity imposed through meditation from outside of our culture penetrate the unconscious? Murray Cox, a psychiatrist working at Broadmoor Psychiatric Hospital, once said that the effect of a poetic metaphor was like dropping a pebble into a lake without creating ripples on the surface. It touched the bottom without disturbing the surface. So, too, the power of certain symbols is that they resonate deeply in the psyche, free from interference from the conscious mind. Many people who visited an exhibition of Tibetan thangkas in London spoke of how deeply they were affected by alien images they had not seen before and did not understand. They felt the images resonating deeply at the level of the unconscious even as their conscious minds struggled to make sense of them. It is our Western preconceptions and our need for things to make sense that often blocks our experience.

From personal experience, I have seen that when we spend time working with a particular deity form, an opening gradually occurs. People respond in different ways. For some, this may initially require being more focused on the feeling generated through the presence of the deity. For others, it may mean focusing on the vibration of the mantra, which is not dependent upon visualization for its effect. Once this quality begins to be generated and we have a feeling of the deity, the form can then begin to come to life.

While leading retreats on the deity Chenrezig I have seen some people finding the form hard to relate to. When this happens it becomes important to shift the emphasis away from the form. Focusing on the quality developed through chanting Chenrezig's mantra and opening to the feeling of the presence of Chenrezig helps a taste of the deity to awaken. Gradually this has enabled even those skeptical of the process to begin to make a connection.

A tantric deity may need to be more skillfully introduced to those who find the connection more difficult to make. This could involve more detailed explanation and amplification of the psychological meaning of the deity in order to bring it to life. In time, even an Eastern deity form can become alive, powerful, and numinous for Westerners.

The deity in Tantra is archetypal, but not all archetypal images become deities. A deity can be distinguished from other archetypal images by the power it becomes imbued with through meditation and devotional practice. A deity also carries great power behind its form because of its lineage of experience. When an archetypal image is given constant and focused meditative attention, it becomes imbued with far more power than it usually has. In this way we might turn many of our personal images into deities, but what gives them their effectiveness is the depth of concentrated awareness, devotion, and power that is projected upon them.

For those who seek a spiritual life oriented around archetypes, the lack of a living lineage of experience frequently creates obstacles. Many people in the so-called New Age world seek to develop a spiritual practice around archetypal figures of Celtic or Greek gods and goddesses. What is often lacking, however, is the lineage of experience that authenticates the quality and power of practice.

In Tantra, the deity originates through powerful visionary experience by highly evolved beings, and then acts like a channel. Lama Thubten Yeshe, an important teacher of Tantra for many Western students, once said that the deity is like a radio antenna; if we tune in, we will receive the transmission. This is aided by the power of the image and the lineage of its practice. When I attempted to paint a Westernized form of a deity, to extend the transmitter metaphor, I felt I was going off-tune, and distorting the clarity of the signal.

Over time, certain deity forms can lose their effectiveness as transmitters due to the weakening of practice and devotion that gives them their energy. As with other archetypes, the deity is a dependent arising, and manifests from emptiness into form according to our capacity to embody its quality. If we do not respond, the manifestation will be short-lived and without great effect. According to Lama Thubten Yeshe, other new forms may then appear when there is an opening for them and these may easily take a more Western aspect.

We may wish to work with archetypal images that we generate through our own creative imaginations, and these can be very important to our own experience. However, because of its specific nature, the tantric deity opens us up to a particular channel of potential. This may become extremely powerful as a style of meditation practice, but not all people will respond in this way, and our individual differences need to be valued. In this respect, Tantra is not the path for everyone.

## CHOOSING A DEITY

I am often asked how one chooses a deity for practice. This is particularly relevant for those who do not wish to become embroiled in the complexities of the guru-disciple relationship, yet still wish to practice Tantra. However, it is virtually impossible to practice Tantra without some sort of relationship with a teacher who introduces us to the various practices. Because of this, the answer to the question about deity practice lies partly in relation to the teacher.

It is often seen necessary to practice the deities within Action Tantra to develop their particular qualities. We practice Chenrezig to develop loving-kindness and compassion; Manjushri for wisdom, sharpness of intellect, and clarity of mind; and Vajrapani to develop power, the capacity to be potent, effective, and confident. Often a meditator chooses, or is told, to develop a specific practice for a period of time to cultivate the commensurate quality. Some practitioners find their relationship to one of the Action Tantra deities suits them for a long time, but when a teacher thinks it will be useful, he or she may suggest introducing a different aspect of practice.

In my own practice, I focused for many years upon one deity, which gave me the chance to deepen my relationship to this deity's quality. It enabled an increasingly devotional opening to take place that felt rich and inspirational. The deity became the heart of my life for a long time, and all I did was oriented around this center. After some time, I found that I wanted to shift the emphasis, and so I developed a deep relationship to several other Action Tantra practices. This led to a style of practice that was able to respond to particular deities when they felt appropriate in different contexts and circumstances. It also meant that when there was a need for a specific quality, there was a deity I could call upon to support it. The deity practices thus become like a resource to draw upon when needed.

In Action Tantra, the choice of deity is not as crucial as it is in Highest Yoga Tantra, nor is the relationship to a teacher so critical. The nature of Highest Yoga Tantra deity practices, their complexity and power, means the process of selection is more acute. The transformative nature of Highest Yoga Tantra practice makes the finding of a suitable deity akin to finding the correct constitutional remedy in homoeopathy. The complexity of the practices also makes it unhelpful to keep changing from one deity to another.

If we look at a deity like Yamantaka (fig. 10) and the mandala in which he stands, we see the complexity of visualization and the amount of detail that gradually needs to be learned. The process takes considerable time. Consequently, the guidance and support of a teacher is very important. Embarking on a Higher Tantra practice is a real commitment, and demands many years of study and practice.

In my own experience of choosing a Higher Tantra practice, my Tibetan teacher was willing to make a suggestion based on his own insight that I could test out in my practice. He then asked for my feedback on how I was experiencing the practice. This eventually led to a sense of clarity that I had found the right deity, which was confirmed by a growing sense of the effect of the practice. I found his willingness to enter into dialogue with me about this process more valuable than if he had stood in a place of ultimate authority and simply told me what to do.

With Higher Tantra practices, little is gained by taking any deity initiation that comes along just because a high lama is giving it. If the deity is not the practice you respond to, it can often lead to disillusionment when there is no real effectiveness. This is illustrated by the story of a monk living at Nalanda University in India soon after the Buddha's passing. He practiced the Chakrasamvara Tantra for many years, but his practice seemed to give little result, which made him increasingly frustrated. One day he was so disheartened he was ready to give up, when a *dakini*, a female deity of a different order, manifested in his room and initiated him into another practice. He quickly gained deep experiences and became enlightened in that lifetime, eventually founding the Sakya tradition of Tibetan Buddhism.

# PART II
## *The Vessel*

*Figure 5. The Inner Offering*

## THE ALCHEMICAL VESSEL OF TANTRA

NEITHER REPRESSING nor acting out our emotional and instinctual lives will resolve our problems. Repression tends to drive these forces into an unconscious Shadow, but they do not vanish. What we have actively held down eventually reemerges as sickness and disease, either psychological or physical. When the energy of the instincts and emotions is not acknowledged, integrated, or transformed, it consistently buries itself in the organs of the body. This can result in all manner of illnesses, neurotic habits, and emotional patterns, reflecting a lack of integration of the energy therein.

When we become caught in emotional patterns and repeatedly act them out, we do not transform the forces they contain, either. From a Buddhist perspective, when we are taken over by emotional and instinctual impulses and uncontrollably do what they demand, we are perpetuating the habit, simply repeating karmic patterns, which are thereby strengthened, creating more suffering and confusion. This strengthens unconscious identification with our emotions instead of transforming them, and we become possessed by the habitual tyranny of their demands. Acting out strengthens these old habits as we remain caught in the cycle of reaction, and our energy stays trapped in unhealthy, destructive, and disabling ways.

If we are possessed by the contents of our unconscious, we tend to project their fantasies and fears outside ourselves. So, as long as we live out our emotional patterns unconsciously, we will continue to blame the outside world for our suffering, and at the same time to see it as the potential source of happiness. We can project our hopes and fears outside and never have to face the fact that we create our reality from within. But in Buddhism our mind is seen as the primary creator of the reality we experience, and we can change it only by changing our inner world.

The crux of working with emotional and instinctual energy is to recognize that neither repression nor being taken over by this energy transforms it. This recognition lies at the heart of spiritual/psychological growth, and has been faced in many different ways in all the different traditions of East and West. Someone meeting the Buddhist path may assume that practicing meditation leads naturally to a solution, but the solution to the acting out/repression paradox is not that simple. A clue to the solution does, however, come from Jung's understanding of alchemy.

In the alchemical approach explored by Jung, the *prima materia*, the basic crude substance to be transformed by the work, is placed in a vessel or vase. The vessel is then sealed hermetically and the heat of the transformation process applied. The first stage of the alchemical process is known as *nigredo*, in which blackening occurs as all the dark, heavy, polluting substances rise gradually to the surface. There are many symbolic metaphors associated with this stage of the process, such as putrefaction, disintegration, and death. Though the alchemists employed the metaphor of an external chemical process as a way of disguising their art, Jung suspected they were probably aware that the true process was taking place within.

## THE BOUNDARIES OF MORALITY

Inevitably the existence of a shadowy unconscious containing unruly wild instincts and emotions gives rise to issues of moral boundaries and self-discipline. If we had no Shadow, there would be little need to consider morality, since there would be little that was not consciously integrated. Jung recognized that a natural inner expression of morality arises from a developed feeling function, which gives us a gut knowledge of what is right and wrong, without recourse to intellect.

When there is no inner feeling discrimination of what is or is not appropriate, then some outer imposition of morality is needed. When both inner and outer morality is absent, then the Shadow can possess us without restraint. Nazi medical experiments on unanesthetized patients among other forms of torture demonstrate this total lack of feeling. No person in touch with a normal feeling function could commit such atrocities and remain sane.

Thus socially determined morality holds and constrains us when we are not able to do so ourselves, when we have no internal sense of self-containment. However, true morality is a morality we are willing to actively engage in ourselves, because it arises from an inner knowledge. We are then willing to define the boundaries of the vessel of transformation and to live within them.

This process of placing ourselves into the vessel, where the vital boundaries of morality and conscious self-containment takes place, is not repression. The struggle with the forces of our untamed and instinctual Shadow begins in this environment, rather like Jacob wrestling with the angel in the desert. The forces of the unconscious are evoked and engaged with consciously in order to gradually elevate them to another level. An important feature of these boundaries is the internalization of our projections and the abandoning of acting-out, so the energy of our instincts and emotions begins to be contained consciously.

Moral boundaries are a vital part of the process of transformation for Buddhists, but must be engaged in skillfully. They are usually defined on three levels: the protection of one's own well-being—the *pratimoksha* vows; the protection of others—the bodhisattva vows; and maintaining the relationship with the higher Self, the deity, as it is released from the unconscious—the tantric vows.

We can also see these first level vows as a protection that prevents the Shadow from enacting whatever it wishes, thus potentially harming our existence by creating negative karma. The second level prevents us from harming others as the potentially destructive elements of the Shadow emerge. The third level is, however, different. It partly preserves the relationship of the Self to the forces of the deity as they begin to awaken. It protects the practitioner from being possessed by his or her own sense of power, but also protects others from the potential to abuse this power, a point particularly relevant to contemporary spiritual teachers.

When a spiritual teacher gains certain powers in relationship to the archetypal forces of the deity in his or her life, it entails a great responsibility. These powerful forces need to be safely contained in a strong vessel so they do not become subtly destructive. Often the forces of the deity living through a teacher are extremely seductive, attractive, potent, and without constraint. They are also neither moral nor immoral. If a teacher does not have a strong sense of his or her own moral boundaries—the alchemical vessel—these forces can be used for the wrong purpose; to seduce, control, and even abuse those who are most vulnerable to their power.

The tantric vows in the Tibetan tradition help prevent the tantric practitioner from using his or her psychic powers to abuse others. Recent examples of high Tibetan lamas seducing and abusing their (usually) female disciples is evidence of how hard it is for them to be able to contain themselves consistently and not to use their powers for their own ends. Their ethical boundaries are seriously questionable when abuse happens, even though this may reflect the absence of a moral constraint that results from being divorced from their cultural background on coming to the West.

Our Western relationship to rules, authority, morality, and discipline is confused. We veer between the extremes of rebellion and authoritarian dogmatism. We tend to view limits and boundaries in black and white, either feeling bound by them or fighting them violently. When we are afraid to encounter outer authority, morality, or the law face to face, we resort to underground subversion. Either we become the good child who buries his or her own feelings and identity, or we fight angrily and rebel constantly.

Guilt is also far more prevalent in the West than in the East. Consequently, in the West, morality and self-constraint often carry more emotional weight than is necessary. When we become involved in the Tibetan tradition we can easily get caught in a self-imposed rigor and strictness underlain with fear and guilt. If moral boundaries are not based on compassion and an understanding of cause and effect, but on control through guilt, they become puritanical and severe, rooted in fear, judgment, and disapproval.

People involved in spiritual traditions often see moral commitments as fixed, static, and unchanging. However, our relationship to moral precepts changes as we change, and as we get to know ourselves more deeply. Our understanding of the nature of moral boundaries must relate to the context in which they are applied. So the relative strictness of morality needs to be balanced with the changing nature of our developmental needs, and our ability to uphold them. Imposing moral boundaries may be destructive if they are inappropriate, or if we are not ready for them, but when morality arises out of wisdom, skill, and compassion, there is little danger.

Regrettably, morality can become a severe and rigorous regime that may appear righteous and pure, yet is born out of deep neurosis. Those who become fanatically moralistic are seldom aware of the unconscious malaise that drives them. The inner disposition to be severe and strict can easily be reinforced by an outer authority that demands adherence to its prescriptions. When morality is rigid and inflexible, it becomes food for any inner oppressor, the self-destructive, self-negating side of ourselves, and turns morality into unhealthy, masochistic self-punishment. If we have a destructive, moralistic side to our nature, it has no part to play in skillfully entering the vessel; it only hooks into our neurosis.

When we put ourselves into the vessel, we must observe a number of important points. The boundaries of the vessel are ultimately chosen for ourselves, not externally imposed. This is extremely important when entering into therapy or a religious discipline. If we do not make this choice personally, but on someone else's insistence, we will always be out of relationship to our will. This is far from transformative, just as morality imposed by a patriarchal order out of fear and guilt is unhealthy.

The boundaries we choose must be reasonable and not excessively tight, or they become another form of repression. There are many people who become involved in spiritual organizations and suddenly become tight, moralistic, and heavily repressive. I have seen people in religious communities who are so weighed down by moral self-denial and a pathological need for martyrdom and self-sacrifice that they are severely unhappy and depressed, believing this is their journey. This reflects a total lack of the self-acceptance and compassion that must lie at the heart of the process of transformation.

## SELF-DISCIPLINE

Self-discipline is invaluable if boundaries are to be kept for any length of time. When we lack self-discipline it is almost impossible to consistently maintain the context for a creative process of transformation. If we look at the practice of Tantra in a similar way to the creative process, the cultivation and refinement of any craft or art requires discipline and commitment. As the process unfolds, the gradual mastery which develops shapes the individual craftsperson. This channels his or her energy, and refines and transforms it. No writer, painter, carpenter, or builder can develop skill without self-discipline.

Self-discipline brings us into relationship with one of the six perfections of the bodhisattva, that of enthusiastic perseverance, which implies the willingness to engage in a process with effort and enthusiasm over a prolonged period. No material or spiritual qualities are gained without some degree of effort. Perseverance enables the practitioner to carry on and trust in the process, even when it feels hopeless. It makes it possible to face difficulties and obstacles in the path with confidence and courage, rather than giving up because it feels too hard. Self-discipline helps us remain in the vessel and not run away.

My Tibetan retreat guide described the maintenance of self-discipline over time like keeping a pot heating on a stove. If we continually remove it from the heat the pot never boils. Similarly he felt that when someone enters into the discipline of retreat, it should be maintained as rigorously as possible. In doing so the alchemical vessel will be maintained, and the "cooking" can take place. Transformation only occurs when the vessel is maintained in this way. Repeated failure to maintain boundaries weakens the capacity of transformation, which is particularly relevant in meditation retreat.

## MEDITATION RETREAT

The alchemical vessel of meditation retreat is very powerful. The Tibetan word for retreat, *samlado,* means, literally, "to sit or stay within boundaries," and the retreat situation is a place where the boundaries within which you live are defined specifically for the purpose of meditation. These boundaries may demand not speaking, not reading distracting literature like newspapers, and meeting only specific people. There may be defined geographical boundaries beyond which you do not go, and specific activities performed each day. The body, speech, and mind are placed within this context—the vessel—and whatever arises from the unconscious is what you work with. So long as you maintain your self-discipline, the energy of whatever arises is held, and transformation can take its course. This can make retreat uncomfortable, particularly over long periods.

In one retreat of over six months, I experienced weeks of powerful sexual fantasies principally resulting from the deity I was practicing, which was intended to evoke and transform such feelings. For a while I found the intensity of energy almost intolerable, but by remaining within the clearly defined retreat boundaries, and giving the energy a vehicle for its transformation in the meditation practice, the intensity eventually began to subside.

After a time the fantasies ceased, and I noticed a change had gradually taken place through the process of meditation. The wild, crazy energy that had been evoked was changing into something much freer and more blissful. The bliss was accompanied by an openness or spaciousness that enabled it to be experienced without the grasping that would turn it into sexual desire and frustration. I sensed that for the first time the wild, uncivilized rawness of my sexual energy was falling within my own control rather than my being its slave.

In retreat the practitioner enters a process that is an intense example of transformation. The practitioner is the *prima materia*, and in one sense the body is also the container in which the transformation takes place. The body is the vessel that contains the elemental forces of the unconscious; the emotions, the instincts, and their related psychological patterns and impulses. The use of deity practices and ritual sadhanas (methods of transformation) in Tantra give a focus to retreat and act as a catalyst for transformation. They provide the forces awakening within the body with a symbolic vehicle through which they can be channeled. When undertaken skillfully and with guidance, retreat can be a profound experience in which the retreat boundaries exist to support the inner process.

There are inevitable dangers with retreat, and fanatical extremism leads to trouble. If a meditator pushes too hard when he or she is not ready, the result can be disastrous. I recall a man who left the army to come and live in the Buddhist community where I once lived. He had heard that by gaining *samadhi* (Tib. *shi né*, "tranquil abiding," often called "single-pointed concentration") in meditation he could develop superhuman powers. He became utterly determined to gain this power, which takes long periods of intense, highly disciplined meditation in retreat. He prepared a room in the basement and was told by his teacher to meditate on a particular practice. Within a week of fervent pushing and squeezing, his anger and frustration were at boiling point; he burst out of retreat and made his way to the nearest pub. When last heard of, he had joined the French Foreign Legion.

## The Therapeutic Vessel

Modern therapy offers many transformative opportunities that are absent in religious forms, cultural myths, and rituals. The therapeutic context, the session, and the process of therapy can and should provide the necessary boundaries of the vessel. Whatever emotional state emerges within the session is granted the space to be experienced consciously, without judgement, explored, and potentially allowed to move on. The god or demon is freed from the darkness into the therapy room, and once there, the process of conscious integration can truly begin. Therapy, therefore, has a strong and definite moral boundary, which protects the client and holds the energy being worked with; it is not an "anything goes" situation.

Dora Kalff, the inventor of sand-play therapy, described it as a "free and secure space," a place in which boundaries are held clearly, yet the psyche is free to express what is necessary. This allows its energies to be experienced more consciously, enabling them to move or transform. The therapeutic boundary is held in a caring and nonjudging, noninvasive manner that facilitates the opening of any deep and painful experiences buried in the psyche, often from childhood.

The therapist needs to be able to provide a sense of safety and constancy, someone unafraid of the pain and chaotic emotional distress being released. The boundaries do not interfere with the experience and make it better, but are there to bring an awareness that enables a real integration and potential healing. The therapist must, as far as possible, avoid projecting his or her personal issues into the vessel, thereby confusing and clouding the transformation process.

A client came to see me who had a destructive relationship with her father, and needed to express some of the deep rage and pain in this relationship because it interfered with her marriage. At first the relationship most present in our sessions was with a father who for the first time listened to her and accepted her, giving her a chance to trust the boundaries of the therapy and gradually explore deeper feelings. As this process unfolded, the deep, dark, hateful, painful feelings long buried from childhood began to surface, feelings that had been there, deep down, but had had to be repressed to cope with their sheer force. As these feelings reemerged it became an extremely distressing time, full of guilt, anger, fear, and a strong desire to run away and avoid what was arising.

As the therapist maintaining the vessel of the therapy, it was vital I ensured the constancy and safety of the vessel. This caused the experience of the negative, hated father to become even more fully present in the session, and began to evoke many projections and hateful feelings in relation to me, the therapist. By not getting caught in the potentially destructive response of the negative father, but remaining nonjudging and accepting, the pain of the anger and rage was held and gradually integrated. It became possible to mend the split between the destructive father and the positive experience of someone who was not abusive. This made a real relationship possible for the first time that could, as it matured, heal the childhood distress and the patterns around it. Gradually it became possible for her to be who she was and be true to her nature with a solid, confident sense of worth and identity.

It is naive to assume that a total healing will take place in therapy. Someone who goes through therapy, however, may for the first time integrate traumatic experiences of childhood, rather than being overwhelmed by long-buried, powerful, destructive, and confusing emotional reactions. Once a painful emotional wound has been allowed to surface and been digested and integrated consciously, feelings such as rage and hatred can gradually make way for genuine forgiveness and acceptance.

The therapeutic context relies strongly upon the integrity of the therapist. Clearly, someone who is in danger of abusing boundaries is not a suitable person to practice therapy. There are sadly a few therapists who are not able to hold the therapeutic vessel safely. They become caught up in an abusive relationship in which they use the power imbalance of the therapy for their own unconscious ends. This is most destructive with male therapists who sexually abuse their clients; however, it is not exclusively an issue for men, and women therapists can also become caught in disempowering and abusive relationships. The Shadow side of the therapeutic world is well-charted these days, but fortunately this has not obscured the fact that therapy with skilled practitioners is extremely effective.

## The Role of the Tantric Teacher

The role of the tantric teacher is to hold the process a disciple passes through in a similar way to the psychotherapist in the therapeutic process. Teachers must be vigilant about maintaining clear and safe boundaries, as spiritual teachers are often invested with considerable power by their disciples. A teacher must be able to hold the vessel securely and not become confused with his or her own emotional needs, especially when students project all manner of fantasies onto them.

A teacher's lack of clarity about his or her own boundaries can lead to serious abuse of disciples. This can range from unconsciously taking advantage of a disciple's willingness to work for a teacher to leading a disciple into an intimate relationship. With sexual abuse, the betrayal of trust destroys the vessel and makes further transformation untenable. Once confidence in a teacher is damaged, there is little that can be done. This is a betrayal of great significance, like the abuse of children by parents. Unfortunately, the sexual abuse of a student by a teacher may not be recognized as such, particularly if the student is beguiled by the teacher and feels he or she has received some benefit from the experience. Nevertheless, the situation is still an abuse of the teacher's power over the student, no matter how a teacher attempts to justify his or her own actions. Even apparently stable relationships that grow out of the teacher-student dynamic will invariably have a power imbalance, unconscious though it may be.

The role of the tantric guru has many parallels with the master in an apprenticeship. The apprentice places a lot of power into the hands of the master when entering into a relationship, and trusts that the master will use it with integrity. Initially, as the apprentice tantric practitioner engages in the practice, the master's assistance and guidance is important. This supports the process and teaches what is needed to proceed further. As time passes and the apprentice becomes more stable in his or her practice, the immediate proximity of the teacher is less important. However, there continue to be times when the teacher is needed as a reference in the path, and as an initiator into further stages.

As the practitioner deepens the process of Tantra, the relationship to the guru as an inner process becomes more significant. This leads to a greater sense of autonomy in practice and greater trust in the practitioner's own inner capacity to contain the process. The guru on an outer level is there to gradually empower and assist in the inner process.

I found this particularly powerful once when I was in retreat in India. My retreat guide was a lama called Jampa Wangdu who had spent many years in isolated retreat, and was revered for his depth of insight and powerful practice. I had been in retreat for perhaps five months and during that time had spoken to no one. My health had begun to deteriorate and I was increasingly concerned that I was in danger. My dreams were telling me I might be going to die, and had begun to terrify me, so I was becoming increasingly depressed. My meditation was intense and I was worried that I was doing something seriously wrong.

In desperation I trudged down the mountain to visit my teacher, but was surprised that he was so casual when he saw me. He was caring and warm, but not overly concerned by the state I was in. When I explained my troubles he smiled and chuckled and said, "What are you doing down here! There are Tibetans that pray to go through what is happening to you." He reassured me that what was happening was good, "Sometimes something has to die." He believed I had enough insight to cope with my experience and should go on. Somewhat reluctantly I made my way back up the mountain, but feeling reassured by his confidence in the process and his insight into what was happening. His ease and lack of drama at a time when I felt confused and fearful held the vessel perfectly.

## ENTERING THE VESSEL

Once we have an understanding of the alchemical vessel we can place ourselves within it. This must be our own choice; no one has the right to make us enter the process, and to engage fully with the journey we then embark upon requires commitment and willingness. As we enter the vessel we must place ourselves entirely within its boundaries, including our bodies, our speech, our minds, and our emotions. No part of us can be considered outside the transformation process. We are the stuff out of which our potential awakened quality will evolve. If we consider that any part of our nature can be overlooked in this path, we are mistaken.

Our motivation in Tantra is ultimately for the welfare of all beings, to enable them also to achieve a state of wholeness, so we aim to go through total transformation. The emotions are manure out of which vital energy develops. The body is the vessel within which the process takes place. The mind is the central power of awareness without which no transformation is conceivable.

We can look at entering the vessel as something that evolves over time as we gain confidence and faith in the process. Commitment is not necessarily a sudden thing; however, there are significant points along the path where a clear and definite step must be taken. In my own experience this often occurred at particular moments when receiving teachings, taking a set of vows, or an initiation. These events may be outer markers of an inner step.

The moment of commitment and entry into the vessel can be a profound experience. Suddenly we are willing to surrender. We may see the end of one way of life, and be ready to take a step we were previously fearful of. The moments when we make this inner leap into the unknown are often marked by an acute sense of fear or doubt. This is usually a positive sign that we are taking the process seriously, and are truly engaged in the step we are taking. Once taken, there may be no turning back. There may be, however, a great sense of relief, as we can then embark upon what is truly meaningful in our lives.

I THINK I am not unusual to have grown up with a deeply entrenched split between the body and spirituality. In our culture this division is expressed as the split between matter and spirit, or, more specifically, between the body's sexuality and spirituality. It is worth considering whether this is the predisposition of all established religions, or predominantly that of the Judeo-Christian cultures of the West.

While living in the East in the Hindu and Buddhist worlds, it became apparent that within Eastern religions there are two distinct schools. One sees the relationship to the body and matter ideologically as the foundation of suffering and confusion; the other views the body and the elemental energies in nature as fundamental to the vitality of our spiritual life. These two views exemplify the difference between the exoteric and the esoteric traditions. Throughout the history of Eastern religions there have been cultural periods of Puritanism that saw the body as something to be overcome, interspersed with times of renaissance when the teachings of yogic practices flourished, focusing upon the vital energy of sexuality and eroticism.

The spirit-body split seems to be an aspect of most religions at different phases in their history in both East and West, suggesting that most religions oscillate between periods of moral conservatism and periods of liberality. Tibetan Buddhism has been no exception. Tantric teachings are often regarded by the moralistic as a form of eroticism inappropriate to genuine spirituality. Following periods of a renaissance in tantric teachings, there has often been an emphasis on moral reformation and monastic discipline to counter what was sometimes considered degenerate.

Over the past two millennia the West has elevated spirit, mind, and intellect, gradually relegating the body with its instinctual impulses and emotional turmoil into the realm of the Shadow. In Christianity, the body, its sexual needs and bodily functions, has long been associated with the devil as the source of earthly imperfections, temptation, and the sins of the flesh. We are still afflicted with this malaise today, and many people feel shame and dislike for their bodies, and for some this even leads to dissociation from inhabiting it.

It is seldom explicit in the West that the body and its emotional life are antithetical to spirituality, but it subtly influences our behavior and pervades our beliefs. The awkwardness we might experience around sexual issues, and the self-conscious discomfort around relating to the body both reflect this underlying tension. The split between spiritual purity and unruly physical needs is probably most evident in Protestant cultures, where it is fed into our consciousness as if through mother's milk.

As I grew up I learned, subliminally, to view spiritual life as the gradual denial, control, and transcendence of the body, its instincts, and emotions. As I already had a well-established, although unconscious, split between body and spirituality, when I met Buddhism this split was amplified. The view that the body and its primitive, instinctual demands are an obstacle to spirituality is fundamental to some aspects of Buddhist practice. So in my early years as a Buddhist I was taught that the body with all its filth and uncontrolled needs and impulses was to be renounced, as attachment to the body causes us to be driven time and again into suffering.

In the Indian texts traditionally taught to monks there are vivid descriptions of the foul characteristics of the body that focus particularly on women's bodies with the intention of eliminating sexual desire. The need to enable monks to quell their sexual passions by repulsion for the body is understandable. For those who are fixated on their bodies as objects worshipped for their beauty or loathed for their imperfections, however, shifting the emphasis is important. The solution for Westerners who have ambivalent relationships to their bodies is perhaps more complex than simply viewing them as things to be renounced.

A spiritual approach that emphasizes denial of the body potentially reinforces the existing split by deepening guilt and confusion in relation to the body and its instinctual needs, particularly sexuality. Many people still believe that spiritual life is best pursued by denying the body. Bodily needs and ailments are seen as obstacles to be endured, and gradually overcome for the sake of liberation. The aim of the spiritual quest from this perspective is to go beyond being bound by the limitations of the constant demands of physical and emotional life.

Even in the East this emphasis is unhealthy when taken to the extreme. When living in India I was shocked by Tibetan monks who drove themselves ruthlessly and often became seriously ill because they completely neglected their bodily needs. They would go to the Dalai Lama when they were sick and ask him for a blessing, or some holy water. His response was thankfully far more enlightened, and he would tell them to stop bothering him for blessing strings and to go and see a doctor if they were sick.

He also pleaded with his senior monks not to eat so badly. Many were getting sick and dying, particularly of heart problems and diabetes. His example is refreshingly pragmatic and clearly recognizes the need to respect and value the body. Some of my fellow Westerners, however, praised the virtue of the dedicated monks who had totally renounced their physical needs. When practitioners fail to respect their bodies, then fall ill and refuse to deal with it realistically, this form of renunciation is a serious mistake.

Living in spiritual communities among people dedicated to a spiritual life, I realized how out of touch we were with our bodies, and how resistant we were to looking after ourselves. This was generally condemned as being self-indulgent and unwholesome. Because we saw our emotional and instinctual life as something to be controlled and repressed, it became trapped in our bodies. Many of us had tense, stiff, armored postures, and a dogged determination to endure any discomfort.

There was a subtle competitive pride in the degree of stoicism we could endure. This was in some ways admirable, since we sincerely believed such values were necessary for our training in self-discipline, and that enduring the hardships of the spiritual path was a great virtue. Our models were Tibetans, who, as we learned, were so dedicated to their spiritual practices that they never stopped to take care of their physical needs, even at the cost of their lives.

There is a need in the West for a more disciplined, less cosseted and indulgent lifestyle. Cultivating a spiritual discipline is a valuable process that most of us can usefully pass through at some point in our journey, but Westerners tend not to. When we do, however, there are some serious hazards that may eventually manifest. While few of us enter a severe regime of self-discipline, the denial, disregard, and general abuse of the body in our daily lives is evident everywhere. We increasingly suffer the psychosomatic symptoms of chronic emotional stress in our high-pressure culture and polluted environment. Modern science and medicine still have little understanding of the nature of the psychosomatic process, and split the two for diagnostic purposes. If in our spiritual life we continue this split and perpetuate the abuse and denial of the body, we do so at our own risk.

When we control or repress our emotional and instinctual life in order to become more spiritually correct, it does not simply dissipate and disappear. It remains held in the unconscious and buried in the body, stored in every cell in the muscles, ligaments, organs, blood, and tissues. The body becomes a shadowy manifestation of the unconscious that erupts in symptoms that reflect our emotional imbalance. Appreciating the significance of this makes it necessary to listen to our own body as a profound source of insight.

The body and the unconscious are almost synonymous, and what we need to free in ourselves is almost always held somewhere in the body. For those who have a poor relationship to the body, spirituality becomes ungrounded and out of touch with a vital source of energy.

The greater the degree of denial of what takes place in the body, the more likely it is to strike back with something critical. Sickness brings us back into relationship to our bodies, the earth, and our Shadow, especially when we have a disposition to escape into an elevated view of the mind and spirit.

The energy of some people's sexuality, aggression, or rage may have been buried since childhood as too dangerous to be allowed expression. This often results in a chronic lack of vitality, the power to be effective in life, and the freedom to express sexual passions in intimate relationships. To reconnect with and liberate the force of these wild, raw emotions and instincts is vital if such people are to become healthy. These instincts embody a crucial source of vitality and creativity to help us live more effectively. However, allowing these powerful forces to come to life may be extremely frightening, as they can feel potentially overwhelming and destructive.

A familiar protection from our inner life is to disconnect from the body. This can be a vital and natural mechanism to protect us from trauma, emotional and physical shock. It will also protect us from being overwhelmed by inner forces that feel dangerous and uncontrollable. However, the emotions and instincts held in our bodies are a crucial source of vitality in our lives, and if our spirituality perpetuates the habit of dismissing them and dissociating from the body, we are likely to exacerbate damage to the psyche.

In my work as a psychotherapist I frequently encounter people whose spirituality is disconnected from their bodies, often because of some traumatic experience in early life. Some wish to stay in this disembodied state because incarnating is too fearful, particularly for those who have experienced sexual abuse. Others become disembodied when they are caught in their intellect as a way to protect themselves from their emotional life and feelings. Unfortunately it also makes their spirituality heady, idealistic, and ungrounded, and it is important for these people that the spiritual process address the split and not simply exacerbate it.

Renunciation ought not to split us off from the body, but when this happens it is an expression of avoidance. An awareness of the "truth of suffering" in Buddhism arises from being truly incarnate and feeling the nature of suffering; it should not remain just an intellectual concept. Renouncing the "cause of suffering" does not mean leaving the body, but changing the way we relate to its pleasures and distresses. So we need to learn how to live with distress in a new way, free of the grasping and aversion that is our usual response to pain. This is the only "true path" to a genuine healing and "cessation of suffering."

When I began my studies of Buddhist Tantra, it became increasingly apparent that herein lay an entirely different view of the body and its energy. In Tantra the vital energy of the body and emotions is seen as an essential ingredient; far from being abandoned, the body is actually valued for its elemental nature. To develop fully the experiences of the spiritual path, we must awaken and transform the emotional and sexual energies of the body.

The Western obsession with physical exercise and workouts has turned into a cult of the body beautiful, which has little or no relationship to the release and transformation of emotional energy. Meanwhile, for thousands of years in the East, there has been a sophisticated tradition of working with the body. The yogic traditions of both Hinduism and Buddhism are based on an understanding that the subtle energies within the body are to be freed and transformed, and there are physical exercises specifically designed to open up the energy in the body to free its blocks and defilements. Some of these practices have become familiar to us through the various forms of yoga now available in the West.

I was once instructed by one of my Tibetan teachers to spend an extensive period in retreat performing one such system of exercises. These were specifically designed to purify the energy trapped in the physical body, and I performed some simple physical activities daily for many months. Sometimes the pain of release and movement of energy were excruciating, at other times the exercise would lead to an almost unbearable ecstasy. If I had been aware of the powerful effect of these simple exercises I might never have begun. When I finally emerged from the process it was apparent that something had changed in my body. I was convinced of the effectiveness of this kind of practice to cleanse the energy in the body, and the vital part the body plays in our spiritual path.

It is important for anyone practicing meditation in the West to place awareness firmly back in relation to feeling and the body. Buddhist meditation is supposed to transform the emotions and feelings in the body by remaining in relation to them, and experiencing them in a different way, with clear awareness. Avoidance by attempting to transcend body and feelings is not the way to transform and heal this relationship. Those who engage in meditation and do not face up to this are likely to deceive themselves into believing they have dealt with emotional problems when all they have done is temporarily dissociate from them.

Our habitual tendency to fly into ungrounded, intellectual spirituality can only be countered by reconnecting with body and feelings. When we are willing to incarnate into the body and relate to our feelings, rather than wanting to be elsewhere, it enables us to acknowledge the value of our humanness with compassion and acceptance. We can begin to free and heal the dis-ease that is held in our bodies, liberating its energy as a source of vitality, love, and joy.

Our relationship to our sexuality is of crucial significance, and the ambivalent relationship to sexuality in the West seldom gives it the respect and understanding it requires. The guilt and confusion some people feel around sexuality ranges between complete inhibition and repression to compulsive gratification of sexual needs. When our sexual energy is blocked or disrupted, we lose relationship to the creative vitality of the psyche, and it remains trapped in destructive patterns. Our sexual energy is one of the most important aspects of our physical, emotional, and spiritual life. Creativity and sexuality are inextricably related, and when they are frustrated, blocked, and denied, they subtly affect every aspect of our lives.

In Tantra it is understood that this energy needs a vehicle for its release and transformation, and in tantric practice our emotional and sexual energy are at the heart of the process of transformation. This has unsurprisingly led to widespread misunderstanding and confusion about the nature of tantric practice. Regrettably, the popularized distortion of Tantra as a sophisticated and mystical way to improve sex emphasizes the erotic aspect of Tantra, but fails to place it within its true context. The practice of Tantra is a profound process in which the sexual dimension is a small facet, albeit a significant one. Awakening sexual energy through Tantra is an inner process, the result of specific yogic practices. The outer sexual act is inevitably altered, but this is not the primary intention.

From a tantric perspective the intimate relationship between spiritual awakening and the body has always been central, and the body is viewed as a vehicle for the underlying forces that are being cultivated and transformed. For this reason there are specific tantric precepts that specify not harming or abusing the body in order that practice not be hindered. Certain tantras describe how being born into a human body with its elements and energies is the most auspicious birth one can receive. It is said that only with these qualities is it possible to practice Tantra and attain full buddhahood within one lifetime.

## REAWAKENING BODY SENSE

From my experience as a psychotherapist and a meditation teacher it has become clear that reawakening body sense is vital before we can go deeper into our experience. Meditation that is not grounded in the body perpetuates dissociation. Some Westerners believe that meditation is a kind of transcendence that can free us from our relationship with the body, but from a Buddhist viewpoint this is a mistake. The fundamental Buddhist practice of meditation aims to bring about an awareness of whatever arises. For the many Westerners who have poor relationships to their bodies, meditation can become just a mental activity with little or no awareness of a basic presence in the body. We meditate often in the head.

It is useful to look at a meditation that restores a subtle body awareness before diving into the meditation introduced later. This is also useful for those with busy minds who find it difficult to settle into a quiet awareness. Meditation on feeling and sensation in the body can help to settle the mind in a way that other meditations do not, and also gives a fresh way of relating to emotions and painful feelings that may otherwise be hard to cope with. When we have greater openness to physical pains and distress, our capacity to hold them increases. So often it is our struggle with pain that makes it less manageable. We push it away, not wanting it, or we become caught in it and identified with it. Neither habit enables pain to move and heal.

Developing a quality of presence that allows and accepts body feelings without becoming stuck in them enables healing of both physical and emotional distress. This awareness does not judge or discriminate; it allows and openly accepts what is there. We can call it a kind of "nonstick" attitude that does not get pulled into and lost in feeling. However, this awareness does not split away from feeling or try to separate from it. Feeling is experienced fully but with clear awareness.

The following meditation introduces a way of cultivating this quality of presence as a forerunner for the meditation that follows later.

> Sit in a comfortable position, with a straight back and if possible with legs crossed. Your hands rest upon your knees or in your lap. You can choose to sit with your eyes closed or slightly open.

> Gradually allow your awareness to focus upon the sensations of the rising and falling of the breath. Relax as much as you can during the out-breath, and settle deeply into your body. Check that you are not holding tension anywhere in your body. You may need to do this for some time before moving on to the next stage.

> When your mind has begun to quieten, slowly shift the focus of your attention to the crown of your head. Become aware

of the subtle sensations and feelings there. You may feel heat
or tingling, tension or pain. Remain with whatever sensations arise.

Gradually sweep your awareness down your face to your jaw
and round to your ears. Again, spend some time waking up
your awareness of any sensations and feelings. Do not ana-
lyze them or do anything with them, just let them be there
with clear open awareness.

After a few minutes slowly shift your attention to the back of
your head and remain there with the sensations and feelings.
After a few minutes gradually sweep down to your neck and
throat; then to your shoulders; along your right shoulder and
down your right arm to your hand; then to your left shoulder and down your left arm to your hand; from your shoulders slowly sweep down your back to the base of your spine
feeling your bottom on the seat; again from your shoulders
sweep down the front of your body; from your right hip
sweep along your right leg to the foot; then from your left
hip sweep along the left leg to the foot.

Once you reach your feet gradually reverse the process and
sweep back up through your body to the crown. Give yourself plenty of time to really awaken any areas of your body
that may be dull or blank.

Once you reach the crown make another sweep back down
the body returning to the feet.

Finally from the feet allow your awareness to slowly spread
to encompass your entire body. Remain with this awareness
and watch the arising and passing of sensations and feelings.
As much as possible simply allow any painful sensations to

be there and soften around them. Accept them with a quiet, open, nonjudgmental presence.

While sitting with quiet awareness, allow your breath to flow as if every cell of your body were breathing. You can imagine that your skin is like a permeable membrane allowing your whole body to breathe. As you become aware of sensations moving through your body, simply let them go where they need to go. Do the same with any emotions that arise; leave them alone with clarity and openness.

Remain for as long as you wish with this quality of presence. Try to ensure that your center of gravity and awareness remain deeply in your body and do not simply rise to your head. Whenever your mind becomes busy, restore awareness with the breath and return to the presence of sensation and feeling. Any tension that arises will cause agitation in the mind. With awareness, allow yourself to relax and let go.

In time this meditation can bring a profound relaxation. While painful sensations of body discomfort or tension will still arise, they can release and shift through this practice, eventually leading to a very subtle sense of feeling that becomes increasingly blissful. For those who are unfamiliar with their bodies, the gradual return to relationship with the life of the body and its feelings is of great importance. Anyone who has a tendency to be ungrounded will also find this meditation useful.

Meditation on the subtle presence within body sensation and feeling will at first still be a dualistic awareness. The subject/object duality allows us to witness with bare attention whatever is arising. However, over time, a shift of awareness takes place. The duality of witnessing awareness and objective sensation suddenly disappears, leaving a presence in sensation that no longer distinguishes a cognizing consciousness as separate from sensation. Sensor and sensation are no longer split, and identification with the ego also stops. On the basis of this meditation practice it is possible to shift the focus of attention to an awareness of the natural state of clarity called *Mahamudra*.

## THE PRIMA MATERIA

As WE ENTER the alchemical vessel in the process of transform-
tion, we must include every facet of our nature. The body, with
its emotional and instinctual life, is at the heart of this process. However, the tantric path introduces a radically new way of understanding
what underlies most if not all of the mental and emotional processes
within the body. Perhaps the most significant ingredient of the tantric
process is the nature of subtle energy.

The consideration of subtle energy separates Tantra from almost
every other school of Buddhism. It is called *lung* in Tibetan, which is
often translated as "energy-wind." While in Sutra teaching the primary
concern is the nature of the mind and its functioning, the focus in
Tantra shifts to this underlying subtle energy. In the West this phenomenon is little understood within conventional medicine and science, and there is as yet no empirical means of measuring, quantifying,
or validating subtle energy. This does not imply there has been no
knowledge historically of something equivalent to it, but in scientific
circles its sources would not usually be considered credible.

Jung believed that the alchemists of the Middle Ages discovered a
phenomenon similar to subtle energy as they sought to resolve the paradox of good and evil presented by Christianity. They believed that
the polarities of Christ's absolute brightness and perfection, in contrast to the Devil's darkness and unacceptability, created a paradoxical
split in man's nature that had to be healed. According to Jung, healing
this split was vital to integrating the shadowy side of our nature, and

the alchemical opus of transformation embodied the resolution. The essential principle shared by all alchemical traditions, whether Greek, Arabic, European, or Eastern, is transformation of a primordial basic material, the *prima materia*, into its potential purified state.

The *prima materia* was a metaphor for the devil, lead, Saturn, Satan, chaos, and the instinctual basis of our being, also called the *massa confusa*. The *prima materia*—which is also a metaphor for the individual alchemist with all his untamed emotional and instinctual forces—is placed into the vessel at the beginning of the process. The alchemists believed that through the alchemical process the dark forces would emerge as impurities in the first stage, the *nigredo.* In subsequent stages the substance is dissolved and separated, coagulated, materialized, and finally brought to the state of completion as the *lapis*, or Philosopher's Stone.

This goal of the alchemical process, the lapis or gold, was also represented as the Hermaphrodite or the Androgyne, the alchemists' metaphors for Christ. Thus, through this metaphorical process, the alchemists resolved the conflict of good and evil. They considered evil as the primitive initial state of a phenomenon that can gradually be freed from darkness and chaos, until it is brought into a refined state as the alchemists' gold or the Philosopher's Stone.

Far from being absolute states of irreconcilable opposites, the alchemist saw good and evil as stages in a process of evolution and transformation. They were part of a continuum. The alchemical symbol of this transformation process was Spirit Mercurius, paradoxical in nature, both good and evil, light and dark, masculine and feminine, solid and liquid, fiery and watery. His mercurial nature holds together vital paradoxes as he shifts from one state to another. Mercurius is the archetypal image of process in psychological terms. It is this paradoxical nature that enables change to take place.

In their obscure way the alchemists had found a resolution to the paradox of good and evil in the deity Spirit Mercurius. While it is unlikely they understood their process in psychological terms, Jung recognized that they had indeed found a powerful metaphor for the transformation of the individual psyche. Mercurius is the symbolic expression of an essential ingredient in our psyche that can be in different states of evolution; at one time gross, dark, leaden, and heavy, and at another pure and bright. The heart of these states is of the same essential nature, but they manifest differently according to conditions.

Jung explored this phenomenon in two ways. One related to his concept of libido; the other spoke specifically of spirit in the alchemical sense. He said, "The hallmarks of spirit are first, the principle of spontaneous movement and activity; second, the spontaneous capacity to produce images independently of sense perception; and third, the autonomous and sovereign manipulation of these images."[7] He described the alchemical view of spirit as "a subtle, volatile, active and vivifying essence . . . an immaterial substance . . . the vehicle of psychic phenomena or even of life itself."[8] This sense of spirit conveys an idea of something that exists in a subtle way, and is the underlying basis for a range of psychic experiences.

Jung's view of spirit suggests a phenomenon present in the psyche of each individual, giving rise to the power of imagination. Indeed he saw it as the substance, or vivifying essence, of the psyche's imaginative gift to create and manipulate images. There is also the important sense of spirit as a kind of deity when he writes "[I]n keeping with its original wind nature, spirit is always an active, winged, swift moving being as that which vivifies, stimulates, incites, and inspires."[9]

There is a lack of clarity in the West about the meaning of the terms "spirit" and "soul," and they are often used to describe the same phenomenon. Jung's connection between spirit and a volatile wind makes an important link to the Eastern concept of subtle energy. The Eastern systems of healing and spiritual practice, which specifically use subtle energy as the basis of their understanding, have been in existence for hundreds of years. Though the pre-Christian religions of Europe may well have known about subtle energy, recent history does not take it into account. However, to understand the process of Tantra it is of vital significance.

In the Tibetan tantric tradition this substance of transformation personified by the alchemist's Spirit Mercurius is called *lung,* or "energy-wind." Eastern traditions have long recognized that energy-wind underlies the functioning of all physical and mental processes. In Yoga it is called *prana,* and in shiatsu and acupuncture it is called *chi* or *qi.* From this point, I will use the terms energy-wind, subtle body, and vitality to refer to the same phenomenon.

## THE TANTRIC ENERGY-WIND

Energy-wind is central to every aspect of transformation in Tantra, whereas the exoteric Sutra teachings deal mainly with the psychological and philosophical aspects of the mind and its functions. The esoteric tantric teachings focus specifically upon the underlying energy of the body, mind, and emotions. According to the tantric view, the emotional life of the psyche has its basis in the energy-winds, and the energy-wind body or subtle body is often called "the emotional body." We experience its presence directly and immediately whenever we experience intense emotions.

The feelings of anger that leave us hot and agitated, the sadness and grief that cause aching physical pain, or the feelings of excitement and inspiration of being in love, are all easily recognizable states of energy. We know this from our experience, but we seldom choose to see them just as energy in a certain condition. Yet all these emotions are simply the expression of the energy-winds, as they become stimulated within the psyche.

Western scientific and psychological research has still not fully explained the interface between the mind or consciousness and the workings of the physical, neurological body. We know there is a direct connection, but the actual causal mechanism of consciousness remains a mystery. In the East this connection has been explained and understood for thousands of years, although not in a way that Western science can objectively validate.

We have three constitutional aspects; the physical body, consciousness, and the energy-wind body, which facilitates an interface between the other two. The energy-wind body is instrumental in translating physical experience into consciousness, and vice versa. Because of the intimate relationship between energy-wind and consciousness, every experience of consciousness has a corresponding associated energy-wind. Their relationship is like the relationship between a horse and its rider, symbolized by the Tibetans as the *lungta,* or "wind horse" (fig. 6). The flaming jewel symbolizes consciousness, and the horse symbolizes the energy-wind. When the energy-wind is gross and agitated, the consciousness riding upon it will also be agitated; when it is soft and smooth, the quality of consciousness corresponds.

The mind therefore has degrees of subtlety relating directly to the degrees of subtlety of the energy-wind. The mind is seen as having three levels of subtlety, beginning with gross consciousness, moving deeper into subtle consciousness, and deeper into extremely subtle consciousness. These three levels of consciousness have intimately related corresponding energy-winds, of gross, subtle, and extremely subtle.

Gross consciousness/energy-wind corresponds to normal daily awareness with its emotional life and thought processes. Subtle consciousness/energy-wind relates to inner subtle feelings and emotional undercurrents, the contents of which are considered the unconscious, as in Jung's personal unconscious. The extremely subtle consciousness/energy-wind relates to the clear light nature of the mind. This is the aspect of consciousness that is our innate wisdom, or Buddha nature. This consciousness/energy-wind is primordially pure and empty of relative dualistic confusion. It is the deepest level of awareness, the one that takes us beyond the personal into relationship with the essential nature of reality. Energetically, we are entering a dimension of the vital forces that are the fundamental undercurrents of life. Their archetypal nature makes this akin to Jung's collective unconscious.

The subtlest aspect of this energy-wind is also known as the "life-supporting wind." It is inseparable from consciousness, and accompanies it at the time of conception when it enters a fertilized egg. Even if the egg is fertilized, life has not truly begun until this energy-wind and consciousness combination enters it. Just as Jung described spirit as the vehicle of life itself, so, too, the life-supporting wind can be seen as the vehicle of consciousness and life.

At present, our bodies are the basis for the pain, sickness, and discomfort we constantly experience in our lives (Diagram 3). Our consciousness is currently the basis for the turmoil, busyness, and confusion of our normal waking awareness. The subtle energy-wind body is the vehicle for the unpredictability and diversity of our emotional lives, as well as governing the subtle physical experience of feelings and sensations that are constantly pervading our bodies.

DIAGRAM 3

|  | GROSS BODY | SUBTLE BODY | CONSCIOUSNESS |
|---|---|---|---|
| HUMAN CONDITION | Pain Sickness Discomfort | Blocked Toxic Unbalanced | Confusion Worry Busy thinking Fantasy |
| BUDDHAHOOD | Vehicle of manifestation Nirmanakaya (Emanation Body) | Purified Blissful Balanced Sambhogakaya (Enjoyment Body) | Clarity Openness Dharmakaya (Wisdom Body) |

When our state of mind is disturbed and agitated by some emotional turmoil, worries, or anxieties, the energy body is equally disturbed and agitated. When the mind is racing with excited thoughts and ideas the corresponding energy-winds are equally excited. The underlying base of *namtok*, or "discursive thoughts," that constantly disturb the mind and stop it from quietening, is agitated energy-wind.

When our mind is calm and stable, pervaded by ease, or feelings of love and happiness, the energy-winds directly correspond. In meditation, as the mind is gradually able to settle and quieten, the energy-winds also settle. Similarly, if we allow our energy-winds to be healed, calmed, or soothed, there is a direct corresponding effect on our quality of mind. This is also intimately connected with the corresponding physical and physiological changes. If for example we are emotionally distressed, this passes through into our nervous system, affecting our digestion, breathing, heart rate, and so on. If we attempt to suppress the disturbed nature of these energy-winds, rather than being subdued and eliminated they become absorbed into the body and affect our physical health.

The energy-winds are considered the primary phenomena to be transformed through tantric meditation. Tantra emphasizes freeing this energy underlying mental activity, the emotions, and instinctual reactions, from its blocked and disturbed state. We are unable to experience the innate potential of our energy-wind body because of its relative state of dis-ease. Only when it has been freed from the blocks, defilements, and imbalances that affect it so radically will the bliss that is its essential nature be experienced.

The energy-wind body in someone still bound by ignorance and emotional disturbances shares the characteristics of the *prima materia* to be transformed by tantric alchemy. In Tantra, the distinction of energy in its defiled or purified state is not seen as the split between good and evil, but between ignorance and wisdom. Evil is not an absolute, rather it is energy-wind in a defiled state, which can be refined and purified into its awakened potential. Because our energy-winds may be disturbed, blocked, and polluted, they manifest behavior that is potentially unwholesome, but as these energies are freed from this defiled state, their innate quality is released—a bliss that is full of deep peace and love.

This innate bliss is not something that arises through transcending our emotional life, but through its transformation. While currently these energy-winds are the source of pain, distress, and sickness, when they are freed and transformed that same vitality turns into the bliss, joy, and love of enlightenment. In buddhahood, the body, energy-wind, and consciousness are still present, but they have been radically transformed through the process.

The physical body of a Buddha remains bound by the limitations defined by the human condition. Physically, they still die, require food, and have normal basic functions. However, the condition of a Buddha's subtle energy body radically shifts the way in which a Buddha can live in the gross body. Many human limitations can be transcended because of the extraordinary powers and abilities given by a purified energy body.

## MANIFESTATIONS OF ENERGY-WIND

The energy-winds are fundamental to many different manifestations (Diagram 4). In their disturbed state they are the basis for the constant internal gossip the Tibetans call *namtok*. The worried mind runs endlessly through plans and fantasies as a result of disturbed energy-wind. Our emotional life and the effect this has upon the health of the subtle energies are well recognized by the complementary healing world. In shiatsu, even the quality of our voice can be used as a diagnostic tool to understand what organs are affected.

The interaction between the subtle body and our gross physical body accounts for many of the psychosomatic disorders we experience. We can see the causality between repressed emotion and its effect upon the physical body through the nature of energy-winds. Strong emotions such as fear or anger can become lodged in different organs in the body, causing dis-ease in those places.

The energy-winds also play a significant role in our sensory experience. The functioning of the five sense consciousnesses is intimately connected to the energy-winds that govern each sense. When these energy-winds are stimulated they can manifest positively or negatively. Overstimulation can be unpleasant, but indulging in one sense can also result from energy imbalances, as in the case of an addiction.

There are two manifestations of energy-wind that are highly significant in the practice of Tantra. Our dream world is a manifestation of the subtle energy body emerging during sleep, and the manifestation of energy-winds closely associated with the dream body is our capacity for inner vision and fantasy. Thus our ability to create fantasies and experience visionary images is a direct result of the condition of the energy-winds.

By recognizing these symptomatic manifestations of energy-wind we can see the possibility of healing potentially taking place. For example, meditation helps clear the discursive chatter that aggravates the busy mind, and this has a direct influence over the condition of the energy-winds.

Through voice and sound, using mantra and chanting, it is possible to attune the energy-winds to a healthier vibration. The health of the subtle energy body can be treated through approaches such as acupuncture or homeopathy, and the gross physical body can be helped constitutionally through exercise, yoga, healthy diet, and so on, all of which indirectly change the state of the energy-winds. We can also use the senses for healing through sound, sight, smell, and so on.

Dream life has been a royal road in Jungian analysis for many years. In tantric practice the dream state is used as a means to meditate during sleep, the development of which is known as "lucid dreaming." The power of inner vision has been used for many years in the arts and modern psychotherapy to help free and transform the subtle energy through symbolic expression. This use of visualization is perhaps the dimension of healing most developed in the practice of Tantra.

## VISUALIZATION AND ACTIVE IMAGINATION

The energy-wind body and our imagination and fantasy have an intimate relationship. We could say that the luminosity of energy-wind *is* the vehicle of imagination in the same way that Jung described the nature of spirit as "the spontaneous capacity to produce images independently of sense perception." One implication of this is that our imaginative life, our fantasies, will reflect the relative state of subtle levels of the energy-winds. This is a key element in healing the energy

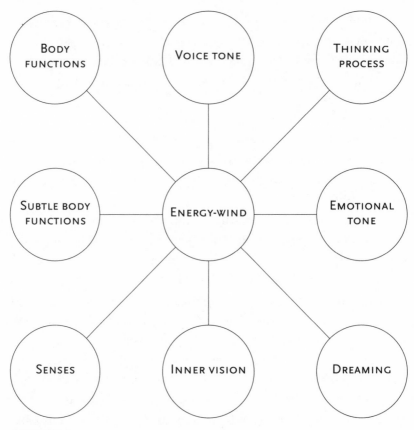

DIAGRAM 4

body using both active imagination and visualization, and also in see-ing the significance of dreams as an expression of the relative condi-tion of the energy-winds.

Active imagination used by the therapy world is a direct mechanism for activating an expression of the energy of the psyche. The essential principle of active imagination is a free yet contained process in which the unconscious is enabled to fantasize at will around a theme. Having used guided imagery extensively in workshops for many years, I have found it to be a most extraordinary process. I have grown to deeply respect the ability of the unconscious to express its inner world in a subtle and profound way when it is given a vehicle to do so. Active imagination is a rich source of insight, and with experience its profound symbolic language becomes increasingly accessible as a means to dialogue with the unconscious. The symbol is one of the main languages of the energy-wind, and its free expression gives a vehicle for insight and creative transformation.

The intimate link between energy-wind and imagination may also throw light upon the subtle effects of fantasy and visual imagery from films, television and advertising. Disturbing, violent, or frightening films and images can have a particularly agitating affect on our energy, making it difficult to pacify. This contributes subtly but significantly to the level of emotional stress in which we live.

The image-creating capacity of energy-wind is also fundamental to the effectiveness of inner vision and visualization. However, visualization is different from active imagination and fantasy. Unlike active imagination, visualization focuses upon specific images that are generated consciously; whereas active imagination allows spontaneity of images, visualization does not. In Tantra, the power of visualization is principally used in the generation or invocation of deities, and inner vision is central to different complex rituals. The inner visualized aspect of ritual is usually considered more important than the outer physical activity.

In Highest Yoga Tantra, the visualization used in the process of self-transformation has two phases; the "creation" or "generation stage" (Tib. *kyerim*), and the "completion stage" (Tib. *tsogrim*). In the generation stage, a practitioner cultivates a visualized form of self as a deity standing within an intricately detailed mandala. This self-transformation is repeated time and again, day after day, for long periods. For example, a meditator spends hours generating the detailed visualization of the deity Yamantaka (fig. 10) complete with all his attributes. With continuous practice the power of visualization develops sufficiently to be able to maintain an awareness of the deity's complexity for a long time.

Repeated self-generation, or self-transformation, into a deity has a gradual maturational effect on the nature and health of the subtle energy. With increasing refinement, deeper and subtler practices are possible as developed in the completion stage. Here the energy body is temporarily isolated from the physical body within the central channel so that it can be purified and transformed.

This gradually leads to a Buddha's *sambhogakaya*, or "purified energy body," which acts as a creative vitality enabling the capacity to manifest constant activity. One of the most important attributes of this body is its manifestation in the aspect of deities, which act as channels for the transmission of particular qualities. Unlike other Buddhist traditions, much tantric practice is specifically focused on the cultivation of the sambhogakaya through the power of visualization. This is only possible because of the luminosity of energy-wind and its capacity to create images.

## THE POWER OF MANTRA

Perhaps the most extraordinary practice developed in Tantra is created by the power of sound. Mantra is the manifestation of pure sound as a direct and immediate expression of the energy-winds. Tantra is often called *Mantrayana,* to emphasize the significance of mantra, and "mantra" actually means "mind protection," reflecting its capacity to protect the mind from gross conceptual disturbance. The agitation and internal chatter of the mind is one of its most destructive characteristics, but mantra has the ability to cut through this chatter and address its underlying energy-winds.

The origin of mantra is a pure sound that arises directly from the primordial nature of the mind/subtle energy-wind combination. In India pure sound is expressed in Sanskrit, often seen as an undefiled language unlike English, which has become heavily polluted with time. Sanskrit was never used as a colloquial language, but always for spiritual purposes, and the alphabet of Sanskrit syllables is considered to be the root of all speech.

From the tantric perspective, all phenomena originate from seed sounds or seed syllables, which can be seen as their innate vibration. This applies particularly to visualization in tantric meditation, where visualized forms often emerge from seed syllables. Thus, the deity is a manifestation of both sound and energy-wind. So we visualize the deity Chenrezig emerging from the seed syllable HRIH, Manjushri from the syllable DHIH, and Tara from the syllable TAM. When visualizing the generation of Chenrezig, we imagine a lotus and moon disc lying flat, and upon this, a white syllable HRIH that suddenly transforms into the aspect of Chenrezig.

*HRIH*          *DHIH*          *TAM*

A mantra is an extension of this principle. Sanskrit phrases which carry specific meaning and sound resonance are associated with specific archetypal forms, or particular symbolic activities. The mantra of Chenrezig is OM MANI PADME HUM, sometimes translated as "the jewel within the lotus," *mani* meaning "jewel" and *padma,* "lotus." This mantra has a resonant vibration of the deity Chenrezig, and, when it is recited or chanted, it begins to attune the energy-winds to that frequency. Gradually this activates the natural vibration of Chenrezig within the practitioner's energy body. Over time this clears and heals the energy-winds, gradually transforming them into this vibration. Slowly the meditator's energy body is transformed and emerges as the deity.

There are many mantras relating to the different deity forms and tantric activities. Although some mantras can be translated specifically, this is not universal. Many mantras are groups of syllables that have a particular vibration but that are untranslatable; for example, the mantra of Manjushri, OM AH RA PA TSA NA DHIH.

Some mantras are extremely powerful. If used skillfully they can be very valuable in practice; if used unskillfully they can become destructive and dangerous. Milarepa, the famous Tibetan yogi, for example, used a powerful mantra given him by a tantric shaman to destroy thirty-seven of his relatives. He had sworn to avenge the actions of his uncle, who had evicted his mother from her home. In a more positive way, however, when one of my Tibetan lamas was suffering from a huge boil on his neck, his teacher used a particular mantra to heal him. The lama spent a few minutes reciting the mantra and then blew upon the boil. This was so powerful it blew the infection off his neck.

Mantras have the power to heal, to dispel interfering negative forces that may harm us, to cleanse negative energy in the environment, and to heal the land. Mantras can be used peacefully to enrich and increase our vitality. We can use them to invoke wonderful deity qualities, or wrathfully use their power for protection or destruction.

Almost all deity practice is combined with mantra, and when carried out skillfully and with a clear motivation, this can be extraordinary. If someone has a poor relationship to the symbolic form of a particular deity, using the mantra can help the person connect to the experience of the deity through a direct taste of its vitality in the sound. This can awaken a sense of the deity's quality that gradually brings the visualized form to life.

❖❖ ——————————————————————————

THE ALCHEMICAL VESSEL is the context in which the forces released from the darkness can be held. However, transformation will seldom occur within this vessel without a particular quality of consciousness. When a tantric practitioner enters the vessel, a special awareness is needed to remain present, alert, and conscious to the energy generated as the life of the unconscious is activated. Without awareness there is unlikely to be transformation or integration. Instead we will find ourselves pulled into emotional habits and will be easily overwhelmed.

One of the central obstacles to the effectiveness of any developmental path arises from a lack of awareness. This goes along with and often reflects a damaged and undeveloped sense of self-identity. From a psychological perspective, the ego is the focus of basic awareness, and, in this respect, far from being an obstacle to spirituality that must be transcended, the ego is a vital first step. Before going beyond the ego, or in the Buddhist sense recognizing its emptiness, we must first establish a clear experience of what the ego is; otherwise we will negate the wrong thing. The stability of the ego is directly related to our capacity to maintain conscious awareness and to have cultivated a stable threshold between consciousness and the unconscious. It gives us a sense of continuity and individuality. Before embarking on the path of Tantra, this normal stability must have been developed.

With a weak or wounded ego, the experiences of the spiritual path will not have a stable foundation in which to be grounded and integrated. Powerful spiritual experience can then become overwhelming or destructive. A stable ego identity is imperative in personal growth, so that we are not constantly blown around by unconscious emotional turbulence, and are able to gain clarity and focus our awareness.

Many of the Mahayana Buddhist texts on mind training can be seen as ways to develop a stronger ego. This is well expressed in the verses describing how to cultivate a heroic ego standpoint in relation to potential emotional problems, or disturbing conceptions that can overwhelm and dominate us. In Shantideva's *Guide to the Bodhisattva's Way of Life,* the author emphasizes developing a strong attitude of mind towards the arising of such disturbances.

> And how shall I ever have happiness
> If, in a net of attachment within my mind,
> There dwell the guardians of the prison
>     of cyclic existence,
> These (disturbing conceptions) that become
>     my butchers and tormentors in hell?
>
> Therefore as long as this enemy is not slain
>     before my very eyes,
> I shall never give up exerting myself (towards that end) . . .
>
> If I find myself amidst a crowd of disturbing conceptions,
> I shall endure them in a thousand ways;
> Like a lion among foxes,
> I will not be affected by this disturbing host.

. . . . . . . . . .

> Just as an old warrior approaches
> The swords of an enemy upon the battlefront,
> So shall I avoid the weapons of disturbing conceptions
> And skillfully bind this enemy.

If someone dropped a sword during a battle,
They would immediately pick it up out of fear.
Likewise, if I lose the weapon of mindfulness
I should quickly retrieve it, being afraid of hell.[10]

Adopting a warrior-like stance towards emotional problems arising from the unconscious can be very powerful. Strengthening our capacity for awareness and mindfulness is perhaps the single most important quality we need when confronted by powerful unconscious emotional habits or disturbing conceptions. No matter how much we know about our patterns and habits, if we have no mindfulness, we also have no capacity to make a choice as to whether they dominate us, or we act in a different way.

In the *Guide to the Bodhisattva's Way of Life*, this quality of mindfulness is partly cultivated by a fear of the karmic consequence of being overwhelmed by the unconscious. However, it is questionable whether standing in an aggressively heroic stance in relation to the unconscious actually transforms and eliminates these forces. By so doing we may simply consolidate a disposition to repress and control our emotions in order to avoid them, thereby deepening the Shadow. Nevertheless, only when the ego is stabilized and free of unconscious disturbing conceptions can we move towards letting go of the tendency to grasp at the ego as a solid self-identity.

By definition, what lies below the level of consciousness is unconscious and shadowy. The Shadow, as Jung called the repressed side of our nature, in particular is kept in the dark by fear and denial. It lives in the darkness we create by our unwillingness to go beneath the surface and shine a light on what may be there. As long as we are unprepared or unwilling to look at ourselves, our Shadow has the perfect condition in which to intensify and grow. When we are unaware of the emotional and instinctual patterns and habits that lie within our unconscious, they are able to emerge, overwhelm, dominate, and potentially extinguish conscious clarity and awareness. When this happens we lose the conscious capacity for choice. The unconscious has control over us, and our normal ego identity becomes completely identified with the force of an emotional reaction.

In the practice of Tantra, as with other alchemical processes, the shadowy, chaotic, wild, and fearful side of our nature is of primary importance in transformation. Our Shadow holds much of the vitality that is needed for our spiritual path, and so long as it is not faced honestly, we delude ourselves into believing we are truly changing. A spiritual path that cannot address the forces of the unconscious is only able to split us into good and evil. We then have a desire to transcend and repress one for the sake of the other. Such a dualistic approach is not the aim of Tantra. The essential principle of this path is to evoke and transform, so the vitality bound up in the unconscious is freed by becoming aware of its essential nature. Therefore, if we are to free ourselves from the more disruptive effects of the unconscious, we must gradually cultivate a quality of awareness that is able to remain clear and stable.

According to Jung, the emotional patterns that constitute shadowy material within the unconscious tend to cluster together, often around particular instinctual needs, or emotional traumas. He named these "complexes," and defined them as "psychic entities that have escaped from the control of consciousness and split off from it, to lead a separate existence in the dark sphere of the psyche, whence they may at any time hinder or help conscious performance."

In their negative form, complexes are incompatible with consciousness, and arise when our buttons are pushed. At such times their energy dominates the ego. We experience identification with the complex to the point where its emotional content is totally overwhelming. Our entire personality is transformed in a matter of moments, often at times when we least wish or expect it. We may, for example, suddenly find ourselves behaving like a hurt, needy, or raging infant. Dominated by this emotional force, we may feel we can do almost nothing to pull ourselves out of it.

In their positive aspect, some complexes are an important aid in our lives, and may give us qualities such as the capacity to mother. Positive aspects tend not to lead to distress; however, it is their negative or destructive side that is considered important to heal in psychotherapy in order to transform our emotional state. When we have internalized a negative and destructive experience of the mother, for example, this can have an extremely detrimental effect on our sense of worth, or our confidence. It may also damage our ability to be a loving, supportive, caring parent.

The Buddhist view of karmic patterns, their dynamic and emotional tone, is closely allied to the complex. *Karma* literally means "action," and refers to our actions of body, speech, and mind, which leave a latent potential energy in the unconscious. When the right conditions arise, this potential ripens in the form of habitual patterns of emotional reaction. These reactions may be positive or negative, and contain a high level of emotional charge. They easily become habitual ways of reacting to our pain and suffering, or our pleasures, which keep us set into repetitive emotional cycles.

As long as we remain unconscious of their nature, we will respond again and again without any apparent choice or conscious control. In the case of positive and pleasurable habits this may be to our advantage, like knowing how to obtain what we need in our lives, how to look after our families, or how to avoid danger. However, with negative emotional habits, we are likely to become trapped in destructive patterns, repeating the cycle of emotional pain and reaction in a vain attempt to free ourselves from it.

While we are controlled by our habitual emotional responses—our conditioning—there is no freedom, and we waste so much potential energy locked in destructive patterns. Unconscious forces motivate our lives, apparently without any choice. It is as though we have no alternative response, and our emotional energy remains caught in a vicious cycle of pain and reactiveness. When we are trapped in this way, our energy feels out of control and unable to be freed into a healthier state. We become compulsive, narrow, and fixed in our responses to life, caught in neurotic, limiting, emotional habits.

There is a saying in Buddhism that first we replace old negative habits with new positive ones, and then we get rid of habits altogether. This may sound simple, but is clearly no easy task, not least because initially our habits are so unconscious. At first our negative emotional patterns will trouble us because they take us over and completely distort our conscious state. As we become more familiar with them we may be able to see what lies at their emotional core. Only then can we discover the innate beliefs living in their heart, which shape the whole of our lives, how we view ourselves, and how we limit our potential. These core beliefs are often extremely destructive and form the emotional basis of our wounded sense of "I," held onto so solidly. Only when they are released are we ultimately freed from the emotional patterns that surround them.

At first the only way to free ourselves from our habitual emotional patterns is to name them or give them a face; to face them. This is the vital beginning of a process of liberation, which the psychotherapeutic world calls "disidentification." When we give our inner demons a face and a name we are more able to recognize their presence when they arise. While they are unnamed or unrecognized, they control us; we become identified with them and are enslaved by their power. By naming them we gain some distance, some ability to disidentify and free our sense of self from their domination. Then they are no longer shapeless, tyrannizing monsters, and we will therefore feel more in control and less vulnerable to the unconscious. While they are unconscious, emotional patterns remain virtually autonomous forces within us, and their energy can become increasingly unhealthy and draining. As we are less pulled into their habitual compulsion we also regain much of our vitality, and our sense of self begins to separate from identification with our emotional traumas. We begin to awaken from an unconscious, undifferentiated, prereflective state into conscious awareness.

Roberto Assagioli, a contemporary of Jung's, introduced the notion of the "sub-personality" as a way of giving faces to our complexes. Through knowing our emotional patterns as sub-personalities we may recognize the frightened insecure child, the crippling criticizing judge, the harsh disapproving parent, the fanatical tyrannical controller, the eternal victim, the idealistic dreamer, and so on. Our inner characters are like the actors in an internal play. We may discover that we have powerful creative forces in us that have been blocked and frustrated. We may also discover that we are dominated or tyrannized by particular emotional habits that feel beyond our control.

The forces clustered together in the unconscious often seem to follow archetypal themes shared by us all. This imbues our personal inner drama with a quality that can feel even more potent and uncontrollable. When we are touching aspects of the collective drama of the human condition, we live out patterns in our lives that have been lived out by generation after generation. The aspects of our personal drama may reflect archetypal themes and motifs that have unfolded time and again, expressed in myths and legends. In our culture we have many myths of change and transformation that deeply inform the psyche of the way in which healing can take place. When we are willing to take the psyche seriously, and listen to its symbolic expression, we can gain greater clarity and insight into the forces that influence us. We will no longer be victims of the unconscious.

Jung recognized that at the heart of the negative complex was often a trauma that generated deeply rooted beliefs about ourselves. When a complex is active we experience within it a powerful emotional sense of "I" which feels solid, true and unchangeable. We may feel worthless, unlovable, unwanted, not good enough, or deserted and terrified, in a way that gives a vivid feeling of "I." This "I" is the wounded ego that we cling to as if it were an absolute entity. Holding onto such a negative belief gives a feeling of solidity and identity, painful though it may be, when no positive belief has developed. This is nevertheless a fabrication that was usually generated through traumatic experiences in infancy and childhood. It is the basis of what in Buddhism would be called "ego-grasping," clinging to a truly existent ego.

In Buddhist psychology, there is no developmental model of the processes that unfold in childhood, as it assumes that the development of the ego has already been established. For this reason many Eastern teachers do not easily understand the nature of the wounding that often happens to Westerners as we grow up. They are surprised by how much damage has occurred to our sense of identity.

Perhaps the most useful aspect of Western psychotherapeutic understanding that could be integrated into Buddhist practice is the knowledge of child development. This throws light on how the ego develops, and the potential wounding that can occur. Only when this is fully recognized can much of what Buddhist practice offers to personal development be skillfully integrated. Without an understanding of developmental pathology, it is easy to cover deep emotional wounds with a veneer of meditation and practice. Many Westerners need a psychotherapeutic approach to working with personal issues alongside conventional Buddhist practice. This is particularly important as a foundation for Buddhist practice, so that the ego and its wounding can be addressed from the start.

Recognizing and naming emotional patterns enables us to disidentify, so that our sense of self can be freed from the tyranny of their power. This rescues consciousness and the ego from drowning in the power of the unconscious. At the heart of these emotional patterns lie fundamental wounded ego beliefs from which emerge all the other emotional reactions that cluster around them. When we are taken over by an emotional pattern, we become identified with its core belief. We may suddenly feel hopeless, unlovable, or impotent, and have no separation from this view. As we learn to disidentify, we are able to begin to separate awareness from identification with our wounded emotional beliefs that are the root of suffering. A stable functioning ego-identity needs an awareness that is not continually overwhelmed by unconscious emotional forces. From a Buddhist viewpoint, the ego is not a complex phenomenon; it is merely a subjective focus of awareness that can be held at all times, even when the emotional life of the unconscious is powerfully active.

Once we have gained this capacity to remain conscious, we can shift the way in which we relate to emotional problems. Facing and naming our emotional karmic patterns and habits begins to free us from their power and domination, which enables us to cultivate a more stable and constant sense of identity, vital for any deeper spiritual transformation. However, to completely transform and liberate the energy bound up in these patterns eventually requires a subtler approach. Having stabilized our sense of ego identity through the development of consciousness, it is possible to gradually go deeper into what we have hitherto called the unconscious.

*Figure 6. Wind Horse* (Lungta)

# PART III
## *The Process*

*Figure 7. Heruka Vajrasattva*

_Liberation in Clarity_ **10**

## Form and Emptiness

WHEN FIRST ENCOUNTERING TANTRA, we might think that tantric practice is just concerned with complicated visualizations and rituals. This obscures the fact that there are also important tantric meditations with the simplicity of Vipashyana and Zen. There are principally two ways in which the tantras approach transformation. One is the path of transformation relating to the complexities of form, appearance, and relative truth. The other is the path of clarity, simplicity, emptiness, and formlessness; the path of ultimate truth. These correspond to the Sutra paths of method, or skillful means, and wisdom.

While these two paths can be understood to focus upon different dimensions of reality, in practice they are impossible to separate. Though at first they may be considered as two distinct processes of transformation, the intention of Tantra is to bring about their unification. Working within the dimension of relative truth, method, and form creates _rupakaya_, a Buddha's "form body." Working in the dimension of absolute truth, or the wisdom of emptiness, cultivates _dharmakaya_, the "wisdom body" of a Buddha.

Transformation within the dimension of form has two avenues. Both work with deity practice, but in radically different ways. The first uses peaceful healing visualizations for cleansing and purifying the blocked energy in the psyche, such as the practice of Action Tantra. The second deals more directly with the archetypal forces of the unconscious, and can be described as transformation through wrathful deity practice. This approach is found mainly in Highest Yoga Tantra, and works with the principle that energy needs a vehicle, catalyst, or channel for its transformation. Both these approaches require a direct insight into the nature of reality, without which the forms of the deities will become bound in dualistic misunderstanding. This insight is gained through practices that develop an awareness of clarity and emptiness.

Insight into the underlying nature of reality is developed in Tantra through the practice of *Mahamudra*. Mahamudra focuses upon the innate clarity and emptiness of the mind as the causal ground of all phenomena. Mahamudra develops a quality of awareness that goes beyond the limitations and complexities of appearance. This is vital if we are not to become caught in the form of tantric practice, as if it were an absolute truth. Mahamudra practice is also significant as an approach to transformation where the energy of the instincts and emotions is liberated into openness and clarity. Without first developing clarity in meditation, no deity practice will be beneficial. Therefore we will consider this first.

Meditation upon the mind's innate clarity enables us to relate to our experiences from a new perspective, particularly with our emotional lives. Once we develop the ability to name our emotional patterns, we have greater freedom to make choices, and not to get so caught in their power. To become liberated from them altogether requires a more subtle level of awareness that addresses their underlying nature. To develop this awareness we must go through a number of stages, beginning with the cultivation of bare awareness.

## DEVELOPING BARE AWARENESS

While we are driven by emotional patterns, much of our vitality is bound by them, caught in unproductive, limiting, and often destructive vicious circles. Whenever these patterns are touched by some event in our lives it can be exhausting and painful as we struggle to regain equilibrium. We may even be dominated by forces we feel utterly powerless to overcome. We may have found strategies to compensate for or anesthetize our distress and sense of limitation, but we still fail to release the creative vitality that is innate within the unconscious, untapped and caught in neurotic habits.

If we can crack these patterns, we liberate new potentials for growth and creativity. Rather than feeling dissatisfied and frustrated by our limitations and fears we can awaken resources we perhaps did not realize we had. The contents of the unconscious and the Shadow, far from being garbage to be abandoned, are rich manure out of which something vital can grow. This is the stuff out of which our awakened potential emerges, as the energy of the psyche begins to flow more freely and creatively.

We begin to make the habitual patterns in which our energy is trapped more conscious through naming and giving a face to them. Disidentification from these emotional habits gives a degree of liberation, stabilizes the ego, and enables us to have a more objective relationship to our feelings and emotions so that they do not dominate our reality.

Western psychotherapy recognizes that we need to stay with our feelings and emotions with awareness in order to heal them. From this place of awareness we may then be able to describe and explain how they affect us. We may follow the story of our emotional life and learn much about ourselves. What the therapeutic world is increasingly beginning to value also is the use of what in the meditation world is called "bare awareness" or "bare attention" as a means of cultivating a much simpler healing relationship with feelings. Bare awareness is a quality of mind that is free of the conceptual chatter that labels, analyzes, and evaluates. It is a quiet, unintrusive, impartial attention that does not interfere with whatever arises and passes through awareness.

Most of the time our struggle with emotions and feelings is that we fear they will become too much to bear. Healing may involve some expression or catharsis to free the distress being held in. Strong emotions such as rage and anger cannot always be dealt with through more subtle approaches. As we develop bare awareness, however, it becomes possible to gain a safe proximity to strong feelings such that we do not drown in the power of emotional distress. While remaining in touch with the depth of feeling, with acceptance, and without grasping or pushing away, we can watch the energy of our emotions shift and begin to heal.

Bare awareness is not easy to develop and maintain because of the mind's disposition to be constantly preoccupied by thoughts. We easily lose attention because our mind is so busy. When we do, our emotional life can creep up on us and take us over. Without mindfulness, the capacity to maintain attention, disidentification is very difficult, and bare awareness even more so. Through meditation it is possible to cultivate a quiet, unintrusive awareness that greatly strengthens our capacity to remain with our feelings. We simply allow their presence without judging them, or needing to make them different.

The early stage of meditation focuses attention and cultivates mindfulness. Mindfulness is our capacity to watch and remain conscious as emotions, feelings, and thoughts arise. We may begin in meditation by observing the breath and gradually quietening the mind from the constant discursive chatter that interrupts our attention. In time a quality of bare awareness is established free from the conceptual confusion that discriminates and evaluates what arises and parcels it up in conceptual boxes of good or bad. Furthermore, this quiet awareness does not become pulled into the contents of mental activity and drown in their confusion.

Once this capacity to remain mindful and witness what is happening unintrusively is stable, disidentification becomes stronger. The temptation to be pulled into emotions and feelings weakens, yet we can remain present with them. To take this process further, however, we must gradually deepen the quality of attention to a more subtle level.

## SUBTLE PRESENCE

To transform our emotional lives more deeply, we need to become aware of the underlying processes that occur on a subtle level. Only then do we become conscious of the broader field of feeling that is present beneath the emotional patterns we get caught in. This requires a willingness to remain with emotions, and gradually to open awareness to the broader feeling context in which they arise. Having cultivated bare awareness, it is possible to allow a gradual relaxation of focus. Bare awareness begins to open to a more subtle, less focused, spacious quality. This awareness is perhaps more appropriately called a quality of "subtle presence" within feeling. It is an awareness of the underlying, subtle, feeling ground within the body out of which strong, more focused emotions become manifest, sometimes called a "felt-sense."

During strong emotions, the underlying subtle ground of feeling is usually lost. We effectively go unconscious. Subtle presence brings us back into this underlying ground so we can liberate the energy that is arising before it becomes strong focused emotion. To recognize how this is possible within meditation, however, we need to explore a different concept of the unconscious.

Jung, together with Freud, was largely responsible for bringing us the concept of an unconscious, a concept that has given Western understanding an invaluable map of the psyche to explain psychological processes. The view of the psyche most familiar in the Western psychotherapy world considers a threshold between consciousness and the unconscious. As I said in Chapter 3, this threshold is necessary for psychological health and a stable identity, and needs to have been developed as a precursor to meditation.

The unconscious is a realm beyond the reach of normal consciousness, that which contains aspects of ourselves in potential. According to this view, we cannot know directly the contents of the unconscious except when they break through into consciousness, either supporting or disrupting conscious functioning. According to Jung, unconscious contents tend to have an autonomy that gives them the power to potentially dominate consciousness. "The unconscious is a mental condition of which no ego is aware. It is only by indirect means that we eventually become conscious of the existence of the unconscious. We can observe *its* manifestations..."[11] While this explanation helps us understand how we are influenced by forces in the unconscious that are preconscious, it tends to create an artificial division between consciousness and the unconscious. From a Buddhist point of view this does not serve us when we are considering the process of meditation.

This view of the psyche presents us with a question: Is it possible to cross the threshold to the unconscious and remain conscious? Unfortunately Jung seems to have had a somewhat skeptical view of Westerners' ability to use meditation. He thought that meditation led to a state of mind that ceased to have a focus on consciousness, and thus was effectively unconscious. "To us consciousness is inconceivable without an ego... If there is no ego there is no-body to be conscious of anything."[12] He considered meditation to be an "introverted tendency" that may not be appropriate for Western psychological development. Indeed, as I said earlier, for someone who has a poorly developed ego, meditation may be hazardous.

For us to consider meditation as a valid means to develop awareness we need to recognize two points in particular. First, a map of the psyche that divides consciousness and the unconscious cannot serve to explain what takes place. Second, we need to review the assumption that there can be no awareness without an ego focus. In practice, this is not the case.

The tantric view of the psyche sees the unconscious in a different way, and offers a map of the psyche that is not a structure, but rather an interactive process on different levels of subtlety. The unconscious is a more subtle level of consciousness that needs a cultivated awareness to make it accessible. It is unconscious because we are normally caught up in a gross level of busy consciousness, preoccupied by the powerful influences arising from outside and within. As a subtle level of awareness, the unconscious is constantly in relationship to the environment through body feeling as a perceptual sensor, continually receiving and transmitting subtle experiences. Can we be aware of this happening? When we enter a room full of people, for example, we receive considerably more than we are conscious of. We may then find ourselves responding in ways that surprise us, because we are unaware of what caused it.

Through a gradually cultivated meditation practice, normal awareness can become more subtle, more refined, and less dominated by discursive thoughts. As this quality of awareness deepens, it enables access to subtle levels of consciousness and sense perception. Far from losing conscious awareness, the focus becomes more subtle, and yet at the same time more open and spacious. This subtle awareness is more diffused and able to take in a more spacious context of the processes out of which our conventional focused consciousness emerges. When we are caught and focused on the gross reactive perceptual process of consciousness, we are generally unable to recognize subtle levels of experience.

The meditations that cultivate a subtle presence enable us to remain with the underlying energy that gives rise to emotions in a completely different way. Meditation is not a means to transcend or avoid our feelings by rising above them, or disengaging from them. Buddhist meditation is the cultivation of a present and clear awareness of the underlying processes of all that is arising into consciousness. This includes body feeling, sensation, and sensory experiences, as well as mental phenomena like thoughts and images. If we seek transcendence, we are probably running away from the presence of our feelings and sensations, and losing our relationship with the environment. There is a similar danger of using meditative absorption, cultivating deep states of focused awareness, as a means to inhibit and dissociate from feelings.

The subtle habit of contracting around pain and pleasure keeps us bound in a cycle of suffering. This begins on a subtle level when we cling and tighten, so that before we have any conscious choice, we have unconsciously created the conditions to become dominated by our emotional reactions. When we contract around an experience in any way, we create suffering, and the strength of tightening determines how much we suffer. This disposition to grasp and tighten around our experiences creates samsara—the cycle of suffering existence—not the actual experiences.

Liberation arises through being utterly present within feelings and seeing their true nature. When we are able to stay clear, present, and unclinging, our experience of reality changes on increasingly subtle levels. Instead of compulsively reacting to emotional disturbances as they arise, by grabbing at them, or pushing them away, we begin to let them be as they are. By remaining totally open and free of the discriminating judgments that make us contract, we can allow the natural unfolding of emotion and feeling. We begin to let it move through and free itself on a subtle level.

This quality of awareness leads to a different understanding of the contents of the unconscious. When we let go of the idea of the unconscious as a location and see it as a process of subtle consciousness, our understanding changes. The contents of the unconscious are not autonomous entities with any kind of permanence; they are habitual responses to the present situation. They are also not so locked in time and structure as to make our relationship with them dualistic. When we look at the subtle underlying nature of our emotional complexes, they exhibit a progression that develops and emerges, becomes more potent, and then decays and passes. Our past traumas can be healed through experiencing their emotional energy in the present and responding to it directly and openly. Even in the therapeutic context this is the principal way to heal emotional traumas where interpretation and analysis may not do so.

Once we have cultivated our capacity to remain with the underlying subtle processes of the emergence of feelings, emotions, and other sensory phenomena with clear, "non-stick" presence, we can go gradually deeper. We will still experience a subtle duality of subjective awareness in relation to phenomena as they arise, but now our awareness has moved to a more subtle level. The potential for this subtle presence to allow emotional energy to move and transform is now much enhanced. This also softens the solidity of the ego, as awareness becomes increasingly open and spacious. We will gradually lose the sense of separateness that creates such a clear subject-object duality. Contrary to the view that we would lose consciousness, in practice the quality of a subjective witness has simply become more subtle.

## CULTIVATING NONDUAL PRESENCE

The gradual cultivation in meditation of a subtle level of presence enables a significant shift in relationship to feeling and emotion within the body. We do not lose consciousness as the focus of awareness opens and becomes more diffused. Instead we are able to take in a broader field of perceptual experience that is able to apprehend far more subtle processes taking place. We will, furthermore, be decreasing gradually the sense of split between our solid sense of identity and our environment. This will in turn increase our sensitivity, which can have its positive as well as its disturbing effects when too much sensitivity opens us to experiences that are hard to cope with. Softening our boundaries may from one perspective be seen as a regressive step towards a loss of self or merging with the surroundings. It should be borne in mind, however, that this follows a prior strengthening of the sense of self and the cultivation of clear self-awareness.

As a process of deepening awareness, there remains, however, a subtle duality. The sense of self and a subtle focus of presence still creates a separation from the world of feelings, emotions, and sensory experiences. From a Buddhist viewpoint, this duality, subtle though it may be, is still the root of the creation of suffering and confusion. We still retain the seeds of ego-grasping and the holding of consciousness and the ego as inherently existent phenomena. There remains the existential point of anxiety as to the nature of the self and its existence. Only when we move into a state of nonduality do we truly start to relinquish this instinctual habit. When we are able to settle in nondual presence, the emotional and feeling life that arises no longer pulls the mind into a subject-object duality. In this quality of presence the emotions are, as it says in Mahamudra teachings, purified in their own nature, like clouds arising in the sky and vaporizing in a matter of moments because there are no conditions to support them.

When pain, despair, grief, and so on arise with nondual presence, the energy is felt fully but without identification and without objectification. There is simply the capacity to remain clear and open in the eeling without reacting from ego identification. With a subtle presence we may become aware of the disposition to struggle with pain, to fight it, contract around it, split off from it. By developing clear, nondual presence we can find a capacity to come back to a natural openness and clarity in the pain. There is nothing more to be done than simply allow the feelings to be there in clarity. One could see this as a kind of surrender.

This is particularly effective for dealing with depression or grief; letting the feeling be without losing consciousness, but also without fighting it. This allows us to be with the emerging emotions in a way that does not interfere with their natural process of release. It is also a remarkable way of being with pain in the body in a way that liberates the underlying energy caught in contraction. As a therapeutic approach this will also be a powerful way to face and transform feelings of fear, despair, and annihilation when we are ready to do so.

What differentiates this process from the "bare awareness" that witnesses the emotions, and from "subtle presence" that stays with the underlying feeling ground, is that the separation between awareness and feeling falls away. All emotions arise as an expression of clear nondual presence. So long as we remain in that presence of clarity, it is possible for emotion to be in its natural condition, without splitting into the subject/object duality. In this spacious emptiness of clarity, emotions may still arise, but nothing prevents them from being released into their own nature, which is empty of inherent existence. They are liberated in clarity.

## MAHAMUDRA

The meditation that cultivates this subtle nondual presence in tantra is called *Mahamudra*. Mahamudra is based on the understanding that the essential nature of mind is primordially pure and clear. This clarity of consciousness is usually lost and obscured by the emotional chaos and conceptual internal gossip that fills our awareness. When we watch waves thrashing around on the surface of the ocean, we cannot see that underneath the water is clear blue-green and unobstructed by the surface chaos. The waves may emerge from this blue-green water, but they obscure its underlying nature. In the same way, thoughts, images, and emotions emerge from the mind's natural clarity, but they obscure our awareness of it. Once we restore clarity through meditation, we can begin to relate to any appearance that comes into our field of awareness in a different way.

In a state of clarity, dualistic separation does not occur, and all appearances arise like a reflection in a mirror. They are not other than clarity, and cannot disturb or obscure its nature. In the Ganges Mahamudra Instructions, the Indian mahasiddha Tilopa says:

> In space, shapes and colors form,
> But neither by black nor white is space tinged.
> From the Self-mind all things emerge, the mind
> By virtues and by vices is not stained.[13]

The mind's clarity is not disturbed by the arising of emotions, thoughts, images, sounds, or sights. Once we can retain this natural spacious presence, the tendency to discriminate and engage with phenomena ceases, and we no longer create the duality of mind and object. At this point the difference between becoming lost in our feelings, with the consequent loss of awareness, and the state of clarity is most obvious. In both states there is no separation, but in the former there is no presence of clarity, because we have gone unconscious; there is no awareness at all.

The practice of Mahamudra relies upon a view of the mind that takes the ocean as a metaphor. The turbulent waters buffet anything floating on the surface. We mostly live on the ocean surface, and are pulled into the emotional currents that wash around just beneath it. We have little or no access to the deeper clarity. If we sink just below the surface the buffeting decreases, but there are powerful currents that pull in all directions, and a strong swell that rises and falls, lifting to the surface and back again. Underlying the surface turbulence, powerful currents flow back and forth like winds beneath the ocean. Submariners speak of sinking through these currents, which gradually become weaker and less disturbing as they descend. Close to the ocean bed they sometimes describe entering a realm they call the clear element. Here all comes to rest in stillness and there is quiet calm.

The practice of Mahamudra is simple, but not easy, because the normal condition of the mind is not easy to change. As soon as we sit and begin to meditate we are immediately confronted by the mental busyness going on just below our surface activity. Gradually as we persevere we become more aware of the undercurrents that wash our mind back and forth. In time the mind settles and is able to remain more and more in a quality of presence that is increasingly aware of the ebbs and flows of energy in the body. Deeper still the mind comes to a point of quiet spaciousness that remains clear and free of disturbance. In the Ganges Mahamudra Instructions, Tilopa says:

> At first the Yogi feels his mind
> Is tumbling like a waterfall;
> In mid-course, like the Ganges,
> It flows on slow and gentle;
> In the end, it is a great
> Vast ocean, where the Lights
> Of son and mother merge as one.[14]

There are many styles of meditation using different objects of focus, but with Mahamudra, the focus of meditation is the innate clarity of the mind. The aim is to bring our awareness totally into the present moment, gradually shifting the focus of attention just onto the natural quality of awareness itself. There may be a number of useful stages in this process because it is not easy to immediately become aware of the clarity of the mind itself. It is useful to begin by observing the arising and falling of the breath to enable the mind to settle. Gradually attention can be shifted to the arising and passing of thoughts or

images. By remaining alert to the presence of a thought process and
not becoming caught up in its actual content, we can see its passing.

The thoughts themselves have no other origin than the mind, and as
they pass they lead us back into awareness of the mind itself. In the
quiet space that is left when a thought process fades, before another
begins, there is the clarity of the mind itself. This sounds simple, but
is by no means easy! Our mind has a habit of being constantly engaged
in an internal dialogue (Tib. *namtok*). We normally allow this endless
discursive chatter to go on unchecked, freely stirring up feelings, fantasies, plans, and worries, which, if we stop and investigate them, are
mostly a waste of energy.

Once we have begun to bring the mind into a more clarified state,
free of discursive chatter, we can move to a deeper, more subtle level
of awareness. When the mind has quieted it slowly becomes possible
to settle in its natural clarity as a presence within whatever is arising.
Thoughts may arise but not interfere with the experience of clarity,
like fish swimming through water. As our awareness settles more
deeply, the subject-object duality increasingly dissolves into a state of
natural clarity and nondual presence. Eventually the disposition to split
awareness from its objects ceases. At this time relative appearances do
not disturb the mind's clarity. They do not give rise to the conceptual
discrimination that creates a solidification of forms and consciousness
as separate.

The following basic introduction to Mahamudra meditation is for
cultivating an awareness of the mind's innate nature, specifically developing four essential qualities of quiet, present, openness, and clarity.
"Quiet" means settling and being free of distracting thoughts; "present" means we recognize the significance of being utterly present, in
relationship to what is happening, not caught in past or future, and not
split off, disengaged, or "spaced out." "Openness" means being
relaxed, spacious, and accepting, remaining loose and natural, not clinging to anything; and, finally, "clarity" means being sharp, alert, and not
sluggish or dull.

## THE BASIC MAHAMUDRA METHOD

Sit with a straight back (preferably in a cross-legged posture, as this helps the mind to stabilize) with your eyes partly closed and ensuring your body is relaxed. To aid this relaxation spend a few moments sweeping your attention through your body to check there is no tension held in your shoulders, neck, abdomen, and so on. (Relaxation is vital to this meditation.)

Begin to stabilize your awareness by placing it upon the rise and fall of the breath in the body, not merely at the nostrils. Remain focused on the sensation of the breath as it comes and goes, so that whenever your awareness drifts to any thoughts you try to bring it back. Maintain this process for some time until your energy begins to relax, and a degree of stability is gained. In the beginning it may be necessary to just do this for most of the meditation.

As this mindfulness of the breath becomes easier, gradually turn your attention to the passing of thoughts and images through your mind, but without engaging in them. Simply allow them to come and go, like watching a car passing down the road without getting into it. You do not totally lose awareness of the breath, and can turn to it at any point to stabilize your mind. Gradually you become more conscious that these thoughts are transitory; they emerge from the mind itself, and so they return to it. Try to hold your attention on the passing or fading of these thoughts, listening or watching for the moment that is left as the thought ceases.

At the moment a thought fades, there, in that instant, you experience the mind's natural clarity; a moment of clear, quiet, present awareness before the next thought arises. Remaining loose and natural in your attention, let go into the moment of clarity and gradually expand it. The more relaxed you are, the better you will be able to rest in this state of clear awareness. Stay with this meditation for some minutes, but do not allow your mind to become tight or tired.

Another way to shift attention to the mind's clarity is to start by being aware of the arising and passing of thoughts. Then shift the focus of attention, and turn your awareness around gradually to be aware of the mind that is watching the thoughts. The resulting clarity is not affected by the thoughts, and simply remains clear as they come and go, like fish swimming through water.

Slowly, a deeper and more stable experience of the mind's clarity grows, and it becomes increasingly possible to sustain this clarity throughout the day. In the beginning it is best to meditate for periods no longer than about twenty minutes. By meditating in short sessions the mind does not become tight, as it may if we try longer. As the depth of relaxation and quiet increases, the mind becomes more blissful and we can meditate for longer periods.

It is most important with this meditation upon the mind's clarity to cultivate a deep quality of relaxation, as a tense mind or body causes much mental gossip. We sometimes use the word "concentration" to describe the quality of awareness developed in meditation, but this is not what is needed here. Concentration tends to give us the idea of squeezing a lot into a small space. The Tibetans use the word *shi né* (Skt. *samadhi*), which literally means "tranquil abiding," a state where the mind rests naturally upon the object of meditation, without tension or excessive effort.

When we are deeply relaxed the mind settles in its natural clarity; and, like allowing dust to settle in a room, it is only possible to let the mind settle by not fussing around. We must let ourselves be loose and natural without trying to do anything, free from worries about whether we are getting it right or not. There is nothing to achieve, nowhere to go, and no goals, just resting in clarity. However, a major obstacle to a clear alert meditation is sluggishness, which must be overcome if the mind is not to become dull.

We learn to simply stay with whatever is happening in the present. After a while, even when things arise in the mind they do not obstruct clear awareness. Sounds come and go and we hear them, but we do not get caught up in concepts about them. Images come and go without becoming distracting fantasies; they dissolve back into clarity. We learn to be with our feelings and emotions, without judgment and analysis, without pushing them away or becoming absorbed into them and thereby losing our clarity. Instead, we look straight into the energy of the emotion itself, freeing the mind of all discursive thoughts that are fluttering around.

At first, Mahamudra helps to cultivate the quality of bare awareness that watches emotions as they arise. As this stabilizes we gradually and subtly turn our attention around to simply rest in clarity. This gradually leads to subtle presence, and finally nondual presence. At this point the subject/object distinction falls away and we are left with an open state of being with whatever arises without discrimination.

## PURIFYING ENERGY-WINDS INTO CLARITY

When we are able to remain with nondual presence in emotions and feelings as they arise, their nature starts to change as the energy-winds upon which they ride are slowly released.

Although the practice of Mahamudra focuses on the mind, it does not divorce us from the body. Having led numerous meditation retreats and worked with people in the therapeutic context, I have become increasingly aware that many of us have little or no relationship with our bodies. Our awareness tends to be caught in the head, which is where we then focus meditation. Consequently the present awareness brought about by Mahamudra does not engage the subtle energy in the body. It is as though we are split off from our bodies, yet still believe we are meditating correctly.

In order to practice Mahamudra, we must be present in our body energy, not in our heads, so we may need to approach this practice from a different direction. Rather than attempting to bring awareness directly to the clarity of the mind, we can follow an indirect route that brings us first into relationship with the body, its feelings and sensations. These are a direct manifestation of the energy-winds that circulate through the body carrying consciousness. We can re-inhabit our bodies by starting our meditation with a slow sweep through the subtle feelings and sensations, beginning at the crown and descending from there. (See text for meditation, p. 83.) Repeating this process until we have a stable awareness of the body's energy makes it possible to simply rest, with quiet attention to all that arises. This relaxed bare awareness enables the energy in the body to move as and when it needs to.

Once this bare feeling/sensation awareness is stabilized, we need to turn our attention to the mind that is aware of the sensation. This requires a subtle opening of awareness to shift simply to the clarity of the mind itself. This can be done in a way that allows the presence in the body to remain central to awareness. Then the meditation is no longer in the head, and brings together the feeling of the subtle energy-winds with clarity. Meditating in this way helps us become more grounded and present, rather than "spaced out," disconnected from reality.

This approach keeps our awareness present with what is happening in our bodies, because of the presence of energy-winds. With clear and present awareness we are able to remain with whatever feelings arise in the body, and to relate to them differently. According to Tantra, the underlying energy-wind is able to move and balance by maintaining a subtle awareness that does not tighten around pain or distress in the body. We can then begin to release emotional traumas that have been held energetically within the body for years and have damaged our health. Because the innate nature of the energy-wind is blissful, this open relaxed awareness also gradually releases that potential bliss, which leads to profound inner satisfaction and joy pervading the body.

At first there will be a subtle duality between the subjective subtle presence and the objective energy-wind feeling tone. However, because of the pervasive nature of the energy-winds, the quality of presence can swiftly shift to one in which this duality disappears. Eventually the experience of clarity becomes inseparably pervaded by the feeling nature of the energy-wind.

Healing in this way takes courage and a willingness to stay with what is there and not run away. We must accept ourselves with our dis-ease, and be prepared to remain with it over time. As we learn to trust this process the results can be dramatic. We may for the first time not feel overwhelmed by the distress of powerful emotions, which leads to liberation from the patterns of reactiveness living around them. Mahamudra meditation eventually brings a greater confidence in our capacity to live with our pains, fears, and distress without their dominating us.

## THE FRUITS OF MAHAMUDRA

To understand the fruit of Mahamudra, we must first understand the "causal mind" in Tantra, sometimes called the "Self-mind," or the "mind of clear light." Understanding causal mind is essential if we are to realize our potential to recognize the difference between ignorance that clings to phenomena as inherently existent, and the wisdom that recognizes their true nature.

In Tantra, all relative appearances emerge from—or, we could say, are generated by—causal mind. This extremely subtle quality of mind is primordially pure, empty of inherent existence, and uncontaminated by the appearances of relative phenomena. We seldom experience this quality of mind except at special moments such as the moment of death, when it is called "the clear light of death." We may also experience it during sleep, as deep, dreamless sleep, but for most of us this mind is inaccessible.

Because we are unaware of its nature we fail to recognize that all appearances are its manifestations, and instead believe phenomena to be solid and substantially self-existent. In other words, we think the material reality out there is real and solid. Consequently we could say the causal mind is the source of samsara, the relative world of suffering and confusion.

If we recognize the nature of causal mind as clear and empty, we see all the relative appearances that arise within it are likewise mere appearance without substantiality. They exist as relative phenomena, but have no ultimate or inherent existence. The aim of Mahamudra is to gradually awaken the awareness of causal mind, our mind's extremely subtle clarity and emptiness. Although we say this is a quality of mind, perhaps it is more appropriate to say there is no mind at all in this state, as the conventional relative duality of mind has disappeared. There is simply presence; but no person present, no mind, no phenomena.

The deeper our Mahamudra meditation becomes, the more subtle our awareness, and the greater the quality of relaxation and bliss. As our mind becomes subtler, the closer our awareness is to the experience of clear light (Tib. *osel*), which usually manifests as the energy-winds enter the heart chakra. In the completion stage of Highest Yoga Tantra, this entry to the heart chakra is facilitated by yogic practices, but with Mahamudra this can happen spontaneously as the quality of meditation deepens.

When in the Ganges Mahamudra Instructions Tilopa says ". . . the lights of son and mother merge as one," "the light of the mother" refers to our innate clear light, which is an ever-present pervasive universal wisdom of nonduality. "The light of the son" is our personal insight as it deepens towards universal wisdom. When they merge as one, it is as if our individual awareness becomes like a drop of water dissolving into the ocean of universal nonduality, the nature of all reality. This is called the "ocean of dharmakaya." It is symbolized in Tantra as the goddess Prajnaparamita, in Taoism as the goddess Kwan Yin, and in Gnosticism as the goddess Sophia. She is the wisdom of emptiness that is the birthplace of all universal reality, the Great Mother, and the Ground of Being.

Thus, the practice of Mahamudra leads to profound insight into the unified nature of all universal reality, the quality known as dharmakaya. The mind of clear light becomes dharmakaya by an extremely subtle shift of perception, the sudden disappearance of subtle dualistic appearance. Initially in meditation, even in clear light, there remains a very subtle dualistic impression. Suddenly this disappears and the mind dissolves into emptiness, like water into water.

Dharmakaya is the ground of all reality, and all relative appearances emerge from this underlying clarity and emptiness. The appearances that arise as our relative world do not obscure or taint this essential nature, just as form does not obstruct space itself. Appearances and emptiness are of the same nature; or, as it says in the *Heart Sutra*, "Form is emptiness, emptiness is form."

So long as we are unable to experience directly the nature of dharmakaya, it becomes a numinous mystery upon which we can project all manner of spiritual beliefs. We may see it as God, Brahman, universal consciousness, and countless other conceptions of what remains a mystery. It is the root of archetypal potential as the "dark background of consciousness," like Jung's collective unconscious.[15] We are once again left with a duality between consciousness and the unconscious or the unknown. However, as Jung points out, "Consciousness in our sense of the word is rated a definitely inferior condition, the state of *avidya* (ignorance) . . . ."[16]

The practice of Mahamudra eventually leads to a unification of two qualities of awareness, one retaining relative appearances and the other their underlying clarity and emptiness. In Mahamudra meditation the form of normal relative appearances does not obstruct clarity. Appearances are seen as illusory, like a mirage or a rainbow.

A fundamental characteristic of a Buddha's achievement is the unification of these two levels of reality, relative truth and ultimate truth. In actuality these two levels of truth are inseparable, and the ignorance we suffer derives from our inability to recognize this fact. Tantra and the practice of Mahamudra enable a meditator to cultivate a quality of emptiness with appearance. This is the ability to stand on the threshold between relative and absolute truth where, moment by moment, appearances arise in dharmakaya as the play of emptiness.

*Figure 8. Amitayus*

Action Tantra is particularly valuable in bringing us into relationship with the sacred in our lives. Even in Buddhism, the emphasis on philosophy can sometimes seem arid, devoid of the inspirational moisture felt in relation to what we value as sacred. When we emphasize emptiness, the significance of relative form is often hard to recognize. It may also be hard to see the value of cultivating the feeling side of our spirituality. Where is the place to express prayer, devotion, and the deep feelings of inspiration, awe, and joy that a relationship to the sacred can evoke? Are these mere superstitions to be abandoned?

We have a curious ambivalence to the sacred in the West, particularly within Protestant cultures. In Europe, during the Reformation, the symbolic richness that ornamented our churches was eradicated, leaving them plain and stark. Though many people like and respond to this simple absence of adornment, others feel the lack of the mystery and symbolism that resonates deeply in the unconscious. What the Protestant Reformation was attempting to overcome was the power of the symbolic archetypal world upon the human psyche. It was a threat to the authority of the Christian message.

Growing up in a Protestant culture is in this respect very different to growing up in a Catholic culture, and people who meet Buddhism from these two different backgrounds respond differently to the richness of the tantric world, its symbolism and ritual. Some find it too cluttered and complicated, and yearn for the simplicity of Zen. Others may have an aversion toward sacred symbols and devotional expression and seek out a practice that has no form, no relationship to anything other than emptiness. For these people, the tantric path may seem impossible to relate to. Involvement in a world that requires a relationship to the sacred that manifests in a rich diversity of symbolism may not be easy, particularly if that relationship involves some form of devotion, faith, and commitment. This is an important consideration if we are to relate to the relative dimension of the sacred in our spiritual life.

An understanding of emptiness and an experience of nonduality are not the only intention of Buddhist practice. A Buddha's enlightened state unifies relative and absolute truth, which gives the ability to manifest constantly in the dimension of form for the welfare of sentient beings. We develop our relationship to the sacred within this relative dimension of reality. If we overlook the significance of relative truth, we lose some of the richness that comes through an appreciation of the sacred. Emptiness alone is sacred, insofar as its experience profoundly affects our lives. It is the sacred mystery that underlies every aspect of Buddhist practice. However, it is often easier to understand the nature of ultimate truth than it is to comprehend and then live creatively with relative truth.

Inhabiting relative truth and not seeking to abandon a relationship to its meaning lies at the heart of the bodhisattva's journey. Though relative truth brings us into relationship with all that may be seen as the cause of suffering, how can the bodhisattva abandon sentient beings by seeking personal liberation? The bodhisattva manifests in an embodied form to serve sentient beings through dynamic love and compassion, and that compassion will not allow the abandonment of active participation in relative truth for the sake of a disembodied nirvana.

In Tantra, our relationship to the dimensions of form and the manifestation of Buddha activity is cultivated with great skill, devotion, and beauty. Learning to live with the world of relative truth requires kill and understanding, and the threshold between relative and

absolute is subtle and mysterious. It is a place of dynamic cr
where form comes into being as the spontaneous expression of
ness. This threshold is also the place of the sacred in its archetypal and
symbolic manifestations. On this threshold we come into relationship
with the power of "archetypal intent," the forces that can shape our
lives. The tantric deity occupies a central position on this threshold as
a personification of that intent. While this threshold remains unconscious it will remain akin to Jung's notion of the collective unconscious
(Diagram 2). Awakening our relationship to the sacred on this level
has a profound influence upon our lives, because the deity is the vehicle or channel through which the power of dharmakaya manifests
(Diagram 1). The dynamic energy present here is a creative and vivifying force, the inspiration that Tibetans call the *jinlab*, the "blessing"
of the deity.

We need to see dharmakaya as a kind of imminence to understand
this dynamic, not just as a negation or absence of relative form. The
relationship between dharmakaya and relative form is dynamic and
creative, and when we open to it there is a flow from one to the other
across the threshold. We can also say that when we bring our awareness
to a certain quality of presence in the momentary arising of phenomena on that threshold, we experience the vitality of creation. We experience with clarity the appearances of our relative world in their
fleeting, transitory nature.

The deity is an expression of the power of this manifestation, and
the symbolic attributes of each deity are part of that archetypal potential. Chenrezig is an expression of enlightened compassion, Manjushri
of wisdom and clarity of intellect, and Vajrapani of the innate power
and effectiveness of enlightened activity. The deity offers the potential
to open to dharmakaya, and to embody these qualities through the
power of its inspiration.

We need both wisdom and devotion to open this gateway and
receive the inspiration of the deity. The quality of devotion and the
feelings generated in relation to the deity are the moisture that lubri-
cates the spiritual journey. With devotion, the qualities and insights of

the path are said to flow down like rain, but without it our practice will be arid and devoid of heart. Devotion brings inspiration, and then our lives are filled with meaning, vitality, and profound bliss.

Our relationship to the deity is formed around *samaya*, literally meaning "commitment." Formally, this is samaya to the practice of the deity in a systematized way, and an outer commitment to the guru. When tantric practitioners uphold this samaya, they are required to perform daily recitations and prayers. This is, however, a somewhat simplistic understanding of the meaning of samaya.

The "samaya being" (or "samaya deity") truly touches our hearts, enabling us to awaken devotion. No number of formal recitations can replace the absence of deep heartfelt connection. When this inner bond is made, it only diminishes if we ignore it or fail to maintain an opening to it. Maintaining this connection is part of the discipline of meditation practice. This deep heart connection of devotion is perhaps the true meaning of the word *religio*, "to bind," from which the word "religion" is derived. In Sanskrit, the word *yoga* has a similar meaning: "to yoke, link, or make a deep inner connection." Ultimately this bond, not the system of practices, is the crucial aspect of samaya, and the deity is known as the *yidam*, or "mind bound deity," to signify this profound heart connection.

When this deep connection awakens, it naturally encourages trust and faith, which increasingly strengthens the power of refuge and prayer. The tantric practitioner learns to surrender self-will to the deity on a very subtle level, and the deity becomes the inner guru as the root of insight and trust. This devotional relationship is the source of the blessing of the deity.

Words such as "surrender," "devotion," "trust," and "blessings" are not easy for all of us to relate to, as they echo the Christian idea of relationship to God as an external benevolent power who can bestow blessings or punishment. However, the very different idea of "blessing" in Tantra is a way of describing the effect of a profound inner relationship. We must recognize that the deity we are awakening is not just the innate potential within our own continuum. It is also a channel for powerful forces. The deity is not an external god, even though, in some Hindu traditions and among the uneducated Tibetan laypeople living in the mountains, the deity is seen this way. The Dalai Lama is then seen as the incarnation of a god, Chenrezig, in human form. The deity is not a god, but this does not mean it is not a powerful force and source of inspiration.

Deities like Chenrezig or Manjushri are very powerful because their forms have been charged with power through many meditators' experiences. This experience is then passed down through a lineage of initiation that remains unbroken. Unlike many other archetypal images, the tantric deity has become a symbol of immense power and vitality because of continuous meditation. Any image given enough devoted concentration will become potent, and Jung's comment—"In the East they have taken the essence of our capacity to fantasize and turned it into a powerful religion"—is certainly true. This is in part the result of the devotional relationship, but it is also the effect of the development of deep concentration. However, in the West we are mostly unfamiliar with the mind's capacity to take a particular symbolic form and imbue it with power.

The development of samadhi is important for the eventual effectiveness of tantric practice. As we saw earlier, samadhi denotes the capacity of the mind to remain unmoving and settled upon an object for long periods of time. In the Tibetan tradition, the measure of the attainment of samadhi is said to be about four hours without a flicker. Samadhi is a powerful state of mind, and, when focused upon a deity form, has a profound effect. In meditation upon a deity—Chenrezig, for example—a tangible presence of the deity is generated. When highly developed meditators cultivate this practice, the form of the deity becomes highly charged, taking Jung's concept of numinosity onto another level.

The deity as a manifestation of dharmakaya is no conventional archetype, though we may be familiar with the energy and charge that a symbol brings when it awakens. This is often quite brief and cannot be sustained, in part because we are not able to hold the presence in awareness for long. From my own sense of visionary experiences that have arisen in my life as an artist, their power lasts for a while and then fades. If we could enter into samadhi in relation to a vision as it arises, it would have an entirely different effect, like turning a water tap on a fraction for a few moments in comparison to a tap fully opened continually.

In Action Tantra the relationship to the deity is first practiced as if it were external to us; it is usually visualized in front of us, or on top of the head. During meditation, this visualization is brought into our hearts as a reminder that the deity is actually a manifestation of our own true nature. As a tantric practitioner deepens the meditative relationship to the deity, a greater presence of its quality arises. This is felt as a quality pervading every cell of our bodies, our consciousness, and the environment. Although in Action Tantra the deity is generated or invoked in visualization, the actual quality of the deity is present and pervasive at all times, as, ultimately, the deity pervades our lives, regardless of our awareness of it. The practice of Action Tantra awakens awareness of that presence through symbolic generation. Once this is truly understood, the symbolic process becomes less vital, because we are always in relationship to the sacred.

The use of mantra is an intrinsic aspect of the process of awakening the deity in all the tantras. Mantra recitation, whether chanted or recited silently on the breath, can be profound, because mantra, as a form of pure sound, can free the mind of its confused discursive thinking. Mantra directly affects the energy-winds upon which the mind rides, and generates specific qualities according to the mantra used. Gradually the recitation of a particular mantra attunes the energy-wind to its natural frequency, and so subtly but directly influences the quality of consciousness. Over time this has a deeply purifying and transformative effect.

In Action Tantra, the mantras associated with each deity are usually considered peaceful. As the root sound out of which the deity manifests, the effect of reciting the mantra activates its quality within the nervous system. Combining mantra with deity visualization is a dramatic and powerful way of healing and purifying the energy-wind body, and therefore the interface between consciousness and the gross body. Mantra is often used to assist in healing physical disorders and clearing emotional problems. When simply used as a general aid to healing, mantra recitation affects subtle levels of the psyche and radically changes the way we feel.

To generate a real taste of the deity it is usual to spend time in retreat working with a particular deity and mantra practice. Meditators are often required to recite a specific number of mantras, perhaps one hundred thousand, and these are usually counted with a *mala,* or rosary. The actual number of mantras counted is ultimately less important than the quality of meditation. If one has strong samadhi and great devotion, very few mantras need be recited for a strong effect.

The more a tantric practitioner opens to the quality of the deity in Action Tantra practice, the more whole and centered he or she feels in all areas of life. There is an increasing sense of the presence of the deity as the heart and focus of life, and all life's activities center around this deep inner connection to the sacred. Work, relationships, and creativity increasingly become expressions of this connection as vehicles for the deity to engage in the world. This helps us understand how the Dalai Lama is said to be the incarnation of Chenrezig. He has awakened this quality in himself and become a vehicle for it in every aspect of his life. When this occurs, the sacred and the worldly are not split apart, but live intimately in relationship, one within the other.

## MUDRA

The more we contact the body's natural creative expression, the more we begin to understand its potential. However, there is an aspect of Tantra called *mudra* that has often remained unexplored and seldom fully understood by Westerners. In its simplest sense, mudra, often translated as "gesture," is the symbolic language of the body. We most often encounter mudra in the various iconographical forms of the Buddhas and deities.

For a thangka painter, many years of study are required to begin to grasp the significance of the deity mudras. Every deity sits or stands with arms, hands, legs, and feet in various positions, each of which has deep symbolic significance. The tilt of the body and the expressions of the face can also be seen as aspects of mudra with specific meaning. As we have seen, the innate clarity of the mind is Mahamudra, or "great symbol." With mudra, the sexual embrace of certain deities is known as the "secret mudra."

Mudra is understood on several different levels, which, as with all symbols in Tantra, can be outer, inner, or secret. The outer level is a symbolic language expressed through the body. Mudra performed physically has, on an inner level, a distinct effect on our energetic feeling sense. If we actually perform certain mudras with clarity of awareness, we can begin to discover the nature of this subtle energetic movement.

The intimate relationship between the mind, body, and energy-winds comes into play in the expression of mudra, and can be felt when performing them. The "earth-touching" or "earth-witness" mudra of the Buddha (fig. 1) feels stabilizing and grounding. The "mudra of bestowing sublime realization" expressed by Tara (fig. 4) gives a sense of openness and generosity. The "mudra of fearlessness" expressed by the Buddha Amoghasiddhi brings a powerful sense of our ability to create boundaries and say "No!" And anyone familiar with the sitting posture in meditation is aware of the sense of circularity and centering of having the hands placed in the lap in the "equipoise" mudra of Amitayus (fig. 8).

These mudras are simple examples of a language that becomes richer and more complex as we delve further. The deity forms visualized in Tantra are static iconographical postures that we begin to see as extremely complex. If we can see these forms as fixed frames in an unfolding movement of expression, we enter an entirely different relationship to mudra. Although the deity is visualized in a static form, this does not suggest that the deity, as an aspect of the subtle energy body, is a static phenomenon.

When we see mudra as a process of movement, we begin to understand it as a kind of dance or play of the symbolic expression of the body, which has a direct relationship to the life of the subtle energy-wind body. When this process is brought alive in movement, its effect is remarkable. However, most of our body language is limited to set characteristic habits and mannerisms that express our psychological make-up. Many psychologists and therapists have studied body language and body armor, and recognize the damaging effect of body structures that become stuck. Our normal mudras tend to express both stuck dysfunction as well as the natural healthy expression of who we are. With the practice of movement, we can free our body language and liberate its innate creative life.

There is a growing interest in the West in this area of expression, and there are many historical antecedents in the East of this creative and ritualized process. In Indonesian dance and movement, a meditative language has been developed to a highly sophisticated degree, and the culture of dance in India is likewise highly refined. The Lama dances in Tibet and the Nepalese Newari deity dances are living examples of tantric movement and mudra.

When we bring alive the body's innate language through movement and mudra, we tap into a rich creative source within ourselves. We discover a new language when we understand the significance of mudra and its effect on our energy-winds and their psychological and emotional components. Movement and mudra are powerful ways of liberating the energy that gets caught in unhealthy patterns in the body, and are a valuable counterbalance to sitting meditation. Mudra and movement free the blocked, stagnant energy that can develop through protracted sitting. It helps us inhabit our bodies fully and freely, and enables us to embody our emotional life in a way that helps it move through and heal, rather than becoming stuck and unhealthy.

As we express ourselves more freely and creatively in movement, we can liberate our natural capacity to embody our inner language of feeling and expression. As this deepens, we can then begin to include the awareness of ourselves as the deity. Movement as the deity enhances our natural expression and aids the maintenance of "divine pride" as the deity in all activities in our lives. Increasingly we become a vehicle for vitality of the deity expressed through the body. The presence of the deity will in turn have a purifying effect on the energy-wind body. This process counters the disposition to separate or split our daily experience of the body from our potential to embody the deity. We become increasingly comfortable in our bodies and our feeling lives, so that every activity becomes an expression of mudra.

Action Tantra emphasizes actions expressed through visualization and ritual, and many specific activities are ritually performed in a combination of samadhi, mantra, and mudra. Samadhi refers to a quality of awareness that is fully present and aware of the process unfolding, whether it is ritual movement or visualization. Without this quality of concentration little is gained, as the mind is distracted and wandering.

The power of mantra in tantric practice contrasts with our conventional lack of awareness of the power of speech and sound. Western languages have become polluted and lost much of their power, but Sanskrit retains the roots of the power of sound, as it is used specifically for spiritual purposes. Sanskrit mantras therefore have the potential to tap into the source of that power within our own nervous system, which is why Tantra is often called Mantrayana, or Secret Mantra. Mantra used alongside mudra has a direct influence on the underlying energy-winds, and we can perhaps call mantra "the mudra of speech." Mantra, mudra, and movement together help focus the mind's awareness, and directly invoke a quality of energy that influences our experience of what is taking place. The pure sound of mantra with its associated deity manifestation is powerful, and subtly affects the energies being transformed in ritual and movement.

It is increasingly evident when working with creative movement during meditation retreats that it is extremely valuable for the development and embodiment of the deity. Movement complements static meditation, and is invaluable in clearing toxic energy caused by prolonged sitting. It enables an expression of emotion and feeling that embodies, transforms, and liberates its energy. When mudra movement is used with silent mantra practice, it powerfully affects our developing awareness of self as deity that connects immediately to the energy-winds. Through movement we can genuinely begin to embody the deity, although this may be a new approach to the practice of Tantra as yet unexplored by most Westerners. When guided skillfully by someone adept in recognizing areas of difficulty, its effectiveness can be extraordinary.

The combination of samadhi, mantra, and mudra is a powerful language for the creative expression of mind, speech, and body, which in Tantra are seen as a manifestation of the activity of the deity that is awakening within. If we awaken the mudra and movement of the body, our natural expression becomes increasingly creative, alive, and healthy, thereby enriching the power and vitality of our creative potential as an expression of the deity in all that we do.

## THE CREATION OF SACRED SPACE

The combined practices of deity invocation, reciting mantra, and the creative expression of ritual or movement in Action Tantra requires a context in which healing and transformation can take place. This is the sacred space that contains and protects our relationship to the source of healing and inspiration. The meditator invokes the presence of the deity within this sacred space. This is often formalized as the temple or meditation room, where sacred images are present that provide a focus for symbolic rituals or practices such as offerings and prostrations.

However, sacred space can be anywhere, as long as there is awareness of the boundaries within which the sacred is present. This space should be protected from those who do not appreciate or understand what we are doing. The sacredness of our relationship to the deity in Tantra may need to be secret, especially in a culture that has little understanding. Other people's disregard can damage our relationship by not taking it seriously or respecting it, so tantric practitioners often become hidden practitioners, emphasizing visualization rather than an external show of ritual and practice.

The creation of sacred space in Action Tantra is also important for purification. Much emphasis is placed upon rituals associated with cleaning, washing, and maintaining a clean body and environment for spiritual practice. Cleaning the sacred space in which we live or meditate in order to generate a healthy environment can be beneficial both practically and as a mind training. How we enter and leave that space, and the people we allow into it then become important. In Buddhist countries we often see protecting guardians at the entrances of temples, and people removing their shoes and making prostrations to the Buddhas as they enter. These rituals become natural expressions of respect for the sanctity of the place where we enter into relationship to the divine in the aspect of the Buddhas.

Perhaps the most crucial area of sacred space in Action Tantra relates to retreat. If we are to awaken the quality of a particular deity, cultivating a relationship during retreat is important. Retreat can provide a more concentrated experience of the quality of a deity so that it becomes more deeply felt within our nervous systems. It may enable an opening to the deity not experienced in daily life. During retreat the creation and maintenance of sacred space is considered very carefully.

Action Tantra requires certain specific conditions to produce the best results. Some of these have to do with the environment, and others relate to how we treat the body, speech, and mind. First, the environment needs to be clean and tidy, free of any dirt or clutter. Cleansing the space with incense and sprinkling water helps clear away negative energy. Creating a protection circle to prevent interferences is also important. This can be generated through visualization, or by literally creating a physical boundary. Sometimes it is useful to mark these boundaries with stones or specific objects. We should never underestimate the psychological value and effectiveness of creating a circle of protection. People and elemental interferences should be prevented from transgressing the retreat boundaries.

During one of my long retreats in the Himalayas, I spent some time at the beginning of the retreat creating a protection circle. One of my lamas recommended that I actually place special stones at certain places to symbolize guardians. Part of my retreat boundary was to ensure no one came into my enclosure other than the friend bringing me food. About three months into the retreat I was comfortably settled in my hermitage. However, one morning I was sitting in meditation when a voice broke into my silence, and I heard what appeared to be angry shouts from someone who had come close to my small stone shack with its little enclosed courtyard. I heard rocks being kicked around, and suddenly a fierce, turbaned Indian shepherd known as a Gadhi broke through my wooden gate and entered the courtyard.

I was incredibly shaken by this sudden intrusion, as he was probably the first person I had seen in months other than the friend who used to bring me food every ten days. I had also been in silence. Reluctantly I left my meditation and made a feeble attempt to challenge him, but I was terrified. I felt he was like some kind of powerful destructive demon that had smashed into my retreat space. So much for my protection!

After I gave him a few tokens of peace—a bucket of water and some matches—I discovered that he had brought his flock of goats and parked them right outside my shack. The noise they were making and the damage they could do to my roof as they clambered over it was very disturbing. He was clearly angry at my presence there, and had even kicked away all of my guardian stones. A curious coincidence. I decided I had to do something to clear my retreat space and restore its sanctity.

That night I made many prayers and offerings to a Dharma protector called Mahakala, a wrathful manifestation of the Buddha Chenrezig, and a powerful guardian of sacred space. While I could get used to the presence of someone around my hut, it was psychic protection I needed in my particularly vulnerable state. In the middle of the night I awoke to a ferocious clattering of hailstones upon my tin roof and a terrible storm blowing across the mountain. It felt as if something very powerful was happening outside. I suddenly remembered the Gadhi sitting huddled under his blanket and thought I would not wish to be in his shoes. I heard a call the shepherds make across the mountains as a kind of communication to each other, a haunting wail in the night. When I awoke next morning the shepherd and his flock were nowhere to be seen, and silence had returned to my sanctuary. I had been made acutely aware of my fragility up on the mountain, the vulnerability and sensitivity that retreat brings, and of the power of the Buddhas to protect.

The way we relate to our bodies is considered important in Action Tantra practice, especially in retreat. Washing each morning and wearing clean clothes are important aspects of purification, as is the food we eat. A vegetarian diet is essential so that the body is not contaminated with animal products, and it is traditional to abstain from spices and strong foods such as garlic or onions, because they affect the energy-winds in a detrimental way. Alcohol and intoxicants are obviously out of the question.

The sacred space of retreat also involves boundaries around what we do with body, speech, and mind. When reciting mantras it is important to remain silent otherwise, so the quality of energy generated does not become lost or polluted. We also abstain from any activities that increase distraction, like meeting certain people, playing music, or reading newspapers. Once these conditions are created, the retreat space is a wonderfully contained environment to settle into. Having cleared out the distractions and interferences that normally pull us outside ourselves, we are left with the inner process. Unfortunately this is where the real work begins, and we discover just how hard it is to tame our wild mind.

Sacred space is of great importance in our private lives, particularly in a culture where there is little appreciation of the sacred. We inhabit an environment that is often unhealthy, hostile, and chaotic, especially in cities, and creating sacred space provides a sanctuary in which to rest and regenerate. If this is not easy physically, then at least we need to create it internally and temporally. Spending a small amount of time daily meditating on the deity that is our heart connection radically alters how we experience the day.

One of the most delightful things to see in Hindu and Buddhist countries is the expression of ritual devotion in daily life. Watching a Brahmin by the river Ganges touch a few drops of water to his forehead and spend a moment in quiet prayer, or a Balinese girl offer a few grains of rice and a flower to a shrine in the corner of the garden, is beautiful and natural. We have mostly lost this capacity of linking the spiritual to the mundane so that one is ever present in the other. Action Tantra brings this back into our lives.

It is important to consider that our motivation and wisdom are vital components in how we use sacred space. Ultimately there is no distinction between one space and another, as sacredness depends upon our perception and how we personally imbue it with meaning. To cling too dogmatically to sacred space as an absolute can lead to all manner of confusion, conflict, and misunderstanding, and if notions of sacredness become too dualistic, we are missing the point. I have seen people become tense and hostile around what they claim is the correct way to behave in sacred space, which defeats the meaning of what is sacred. Becoming overprecious about sacred space is just another kind of clinging. If, for example, someone destroys a Buddha statue, it in no way damages the essential meaning of what it represents.

This does not negate the value and power of generating and respecting sacred space. There are times in our lives when protection is necessary, and those things we value and hold as sacred need to be respected. This may be partly to protect the growing sprouts of our inner experience, and to create an environment in which meditation practice can grow. Once our meditation practice has matured, our ability to retain an inner awareness of the sacred need not discriminat between the toilet and the temple.

## THE NATURE OF RITUAL

The practice of Action Tantra introduces us to ways in which we can begin to dialogue creatively with the sacred. As in Action Tantra, the development of ritual is emphasized. Ritual, however, is easily misunderstood, and some people have much resistance to participating in what seem like pointless charades. Seeing others engage in rituals that seem to demonstrate a blindness or ignorance of what they are doing exacerbates this.

It can be hard for people who find devotion difficult to fathom what others get from their ritual. Many years ago I recall watching Burmese people throwing buckets of water over statues of the Buddha in Rangoon and thinking, "What on earth do they think they are doing!" Seeing Thai people in Bangkok kneeling in front of a Buddha statue with a label saying "Offerings to this Buddha will help cultivate wealth" also made me highly skeptical. Nevertheless, when understood, ritual is a profound and highly creative process that can be transformative.

Perhaps the most important feature of any ritualized practice is our motivation. Because Tantra belongs to the Mahayana path, there is an implicit recognition that bodhichitta is the primary intention. Whatever rituals are performed are intended to awaken the practitioner to the highest potential of being able to benefit others. If this intention is absent, then these rituals bring only limited result or benefit. The science of ritual is highly developed in Action Tantra, and is oriented towards opening a channel to the deity so that a dialogue or exchange can flow. This dialogue is with our innate nature as the source of healing and insight.

Many rituals focus upon the relationship between the ego and the Self, to use Jung's language, where the Self becomes the deity (see Diagram 2, p. 40). There are three primary types of ritual; making offerings, prostrations, and prayers, all of which place the ego in a deferential relation to the deity. These rituals enhance the growth of an open, devotional receptivity towards the deity as the source of blessing and inspiration. Rituals range from simple to extremely elaborate, but the principle of supplication and homage is the same.

Visualization is emphasized in Action Tantra rituals and even more so in those of Highest Yoga Tantra, so external forms are not needed, as the inner visualized process is considered paramount. Ritual offerings can therefore be externally simple or even absent, but the inner vision is vast and elaborate, so we may offer a simple bowl of water to the Buddhas externally, while internally we imagine a vast array of wonderful delights.

The most common example of visualized offerings is a series of eight offerings made time and again during the practice of the sadhana, which follow a form derived from the old Indian custom of making offerings to a visiting dignitary like a *raja*, or king. The eight offerings are water for washing, drinking water, flowers, incense, lamps, perfumed anointing oils, food, and music. They are visualized as offering goddesses manifesting and offering beautiful vessels with water, vast bouquets of flowers, ornate perfume vessels, fragrant incense, butter lamps, delicious food, and wonderful music.

Being creative with these visualizations can inspire and develop our spiritual practice, but without understanding there is little benefit. With the right understanding and clear motivation, the value of making offerings is immeasurable. Rather than having an impoverished and narrow attitude, our experience can be liberating and enriching, enabling a generosity of heart that then pervades other aspects of life.

There are complex rituals of burning offerings where many symbolic substances are offered to a fire deity. Each substance has a particular symbolic significance for the development of specific spiritual qualities. There is also an offering, known as "the mandala offering," in which a visualized creation of the entire universe is offered to represent every aspect of our lives surrendered to the Buddhas. A simple ritual is offering a single stick of incense to the Buddhas.

The depth of meaning inherent in the creation of offerings requires much study, and it is a profound and highly significant aspect of the tantric path. In my years of study and practice of Tibetan Buddhism,

I have been greatly inspired by the devotion and skill that Tibetans put into their offerings. They have developed a unique style, full of rich symbolism, something Westerners do not always fully appreciate.

The Tibetan cultural flavor of ritual does not easily translate into Western culture. We have much to learn about how to be creative and, as Lama Thubten Yeshe always supported, how to find our own expression of these practices. Tibetan culture shaped the Buddhism that came from India, so there is no reason why we should not too generate our own flavor of practice. However, whatever we do develop in this way is, as it has always been, for the purpose ultimately of accumulating the necessary vitality or energy to practice and awaken to our full potential.

## THE ACCUMULATION OF VITALITY

In Mahayana Buddhism great emphasis is placed upon the accumulation of *sonam*, or "merit." This is traditionally seen as the individual gaining a store of virtue in order to receive a positive, ripening result. According to the principle of karma, if we create the causes we will reap the result. What differentiates merit from other positive karma is its motivation and goal. Merit is the cause for enlightenment, and is therefore seen as taking us beyond the cycle of existence. When ordinary positive karma ripens, it is still within the cycle of birth and death—samsara. But the primary motivation that enables the accumulation of merit is bodhichitta, and the bodhisattva's actions are solely oriented towards eventual buddhahood for the welfare of others.

Although this process might sound materialistic or self-conscious, it is nonetheless important to understand its significance. Within the Sutra teachings, the accumulation of merit is seen as the cause for generating the "form body," or *rupakaya*, of a Buddha. According to the Sutra path, merit is accumulated through practicing generosity, morality, enthusiastic perseverance, patience, concentration, and wisdom over a prolonged period. The texts indicate that it takes a bodhisattva many lifetimes to make sufficient accumulation to become a Buddha.

Tantra generally, and Action Tantra in particular, has a distinct approach to the accumulation of merit that reflects its unique practice. The form body has two components. One is the "manifestation body," or *nirmanakaya*, which is essentially the normal physical body. The other is the *sambhogakaya*, or "illusory body," which is seen as the transformation and purification of the subtle energy-wind body. Although the Sutra teachings mention the sambhogakaya, the notion of subtle energy is not considered. In Tantra, however, the consideration of energy-wind contributes to a wholly different understanding of merit.

The accumulation of merit directly develops and enhances the essential power and vitality of the energy-wind body. Through tantric practice the subtle body becomes increasingly healthy, vibrant, and powerful in facilitating certain inner experiences. As the energy body grows in strength, its ability to generate the presence of the deity increases. No realizations of the path are possible without this accumulation of personal vitality, and the practice of Tantra is so designed that this happens sufficiently quickly to facilitate attaining the sambhogakaya of a Buddha even within one lifetime.

We can see the vitality generated in practice as a kind of power. Power is often scorned as something to be avoided in spiritual circles, yet secretly it may be wished for. We are often afraid of owning or embodying our power because we are afraid of its consequences. We think having personal power will be viewed as simply inflating the ego. Inflation in its true sense can indeed be seen as taking in the power of the divine to inspire. However, when we ignore or deny personal power because we are afraid, it is driven into the Shadow. Once split off from conscious acknowledgement, power is then even more destructive and abusive. When we fail to own our power, it comes out unconsciously, underlying many of our actions.

Owning our power is truly acknowledging and being responsible for our capacity to be effective. The development of the energy body enhances this capacity, and awakens the potential for specific powers called *siddhis* to arise. Some spiritual traditions see these siddhis as the goal, because they are signs of personal power. But in Buddhist Tantra they are considered incidental by-products of the path, the main point of accumulating merit being to gain the illusory body of a Buddha. This body then facilitates a Buddha's constant capacity to manifest for the welfare of others.

Ritual practices performed in relation to the deity in Action Tantra accumulate and enhance the vitality of the subtle body. These rituals may be physically performed or mentally visualized. Usually it is the inner mental process that is important. Foremost of the practices that accumulate merit is ritual offering.

Another practice used to generate the vitality and power of the energy body is prostrations. Devoted practitioners often perform these ritual acts of homage to the deity many thousands of times. They are seen as a powerful preliminary to our relationship with the deity. Many Tibetans prostrate across vast distances of Tibet on pilgrimage to holy places, performing prostrations before reliquaries, holy objects, or shrines in powerful sacred places is considered of great benefit. At the Mahabodhi stupa in Bodhgaya, the place in India where the Buddha attained enlightenment, it is usual to see many practitioners making thousands of prostrations. Having performed many thousands of prostrations in this place myself, I can vouch for the power of the process.

If we wish to gradually develop our minds and cultivate qualities that are meaningful on our journey, accumulating vitality is crucial. In Greek mythology it was necessary to pay the ferryman a talent or token to cross the river Styx. This token is symbolic of our personal power. If we have no inner resources, we are unable to go forward on the journey, and we are unable to cross the river. If we have no energy or inspiration, little is gained when we try to perform a spiritual practice. The greatest hindrance is a lack of vitality, and for this reason the accumulation of personal vitality is crucial in the early stages of practice.

The accumulation of merit is focused within the deity practice in Tantra. Without merit, little is experienced in terms of the results of practice. To enter the process of Highest Yoga Tantra this preliminary accumulation is crucial, so great emphasis is placed upon performing *ngondro*, or "preliminary practices," which act as a purification and accumulation of vitality. Most of these preliminary practices are contained within Action Tantra, and many years are devoted to cultivating the foundation for later, Higher Tantra practice. When these preliminaries are developed sufficiently, there are few obstacles to later experiences; without them, all manner of difficulties can arise.

*Figure 9. The Healing Vase*

✦ ✦

In Maitreya's *Uttaratantra*, Buddha nature is described as being like a golden statue wrapped in filthy rags. Our innate potential is to awaken this nature, like discovering a precious jewel buried in the depths of the earth. Buddha nature is primordially pure, but obscured by karmic debris accumulated over countless lifetimes. Purification is fundamental to the release of this potential from its obscurations and is seen as a vital preliminary to the practice of Tantra. It is often said that if we purify karmic obstructions sufficiently, this innate primordial nature will manifest spontaneously.

We might think that the concept of purification implies a dualism between that which is impure, and therefore undesired, and that which is pure and desired. This may also seem to contradict the essential meaning of Buddha nature, which is that all phenomena, whether pure or impure, are empty of inherent existence. It is our ignorance and dualistic thinking that judges and discriminates one from the other. This implies that the primary obscuration to be purified is dualistic thinking and its consequences.

The ultimate purification is indeed the realization of emptiness experienced moment by moment. However, because attention in Tantra is focused upon the energy-winds, purification on this level helps to clear the underlying obstructions that prevent an experience of nonduality. It is defiled energy-winds that are the underlying or hidden cause of dualistic ignorance.

While the conventional language of Tantra speaks of purification, we can equally see this as a process of healing. In Action Tantra, healing and purification are a significant aspect of the relationship to the deity through visualizations and mantra recitations. Its effectiveness arises from the intimate relationship between visualization, mantra, and the energy-winds. Approaching the healing process is relatively simple and extremely powerful if practiced with strong concentration, clarity, and an appreciation of the quality of the deity. Even after a brief period of mantra recitation the effect can be dramatic; the mind feels clearer and the energy in the body smoother and more fluid.

The process of healing visualization begins by generating or invoking the presence of the deity to be practiced. The deity is usually visualized either in the space in front of the meditator, or a few centimeters above the crown of the head. The meditator often makes certain prayers and perhaps offerings as a preliminary practice to establish an open receptive relationship with the deity.

Although traditionally this is done formally, through the recitation of the sadhana, the important thing is to make a personal connection. The disadvantage with reciting traditional prayers in an unfamiliar language can be that they may not generate the feeling of openness and devotion that needs to be present for the practice to be effective. A personal style that includes our own particular life issues, problems, emotional distresses, and sicknesses as part of this process may be important to include in our reflections. We may wish to clear certain obstacles or limitations, or to cultivate qualities to help us, but when we do not make this personal link the practice can be dry and without feeling.

Healing and purification visualizations are usually of light and blissful nectar washing through the body, visualized as the practitioner simultaneously recites the mantra of the deity. This gradually cleanses, heals, or purifies the energy-winds, freeing them from blocked, sick, tired, toxic states. It can be helpful to imagine the sickness, emotional blocks or hindrances leaving the body as black substances. Visualizations of this kind are increasingly common in the Western healing world, particularly when working with diseases such as cancer. There are relatively few dangers, and these visualizations are simple to learn.

Increasingly, our health, both physical and psychological, is affected by the environments in which we live and work. The intensity of emotional stress from work will invariably leave a residue within our nervous systems. The energetic quality of city life is often extremely unhealthy. Pollution pervades our world and feeds into our bodies through the air, our food, and our water. All these conditions contribute to a toxicity in our subtle energy that is extremely detrimental. Finding a simple way to clear this toxicity is important for our general state of health, as a way to prevent more severe illness. The purification practices of Action Tantra, while not clearing all the gross effects of pollution in our bodies, will certainly help to clear toxic energy arising from stress.

One of the most powerful purification and healing deity practices is Heruka Vajrasattva (fig. 7), who is visualized seated upon the crown of the head. Nectar and light are imagined pouring from the heart of Vajrasattva through the crown of the meditator's head and, as this descends into the body, all the dark, toxic, and sick energy is driven out as unclean black substances. Impure energy and sickness can be visualized driven out through the lower orifices, or as though filling a bottle so that they flow up and out through the mouth, ears, and nose. We can also imagine that the dark, depressed energy is dispelled suddenly, like an explosion of light filling a dark room.

After the cleansing and purification visualization, the positive attributes of the deity are then visualized entering the body in the form of light or nectar. Visualizing being endowed with the qualities we need in our lives is a valuable process of empowerment and can also be important in healing our wounded sense of self.

Meditating on the deity Chenrezig (fig. 3), the Buddha of compassion, helps cultivate a more loving, accepting and caring sense of self-worth. Chenrezig is generally visualized seated in the space in front of the practitioner at the level of the forehead. While reciting the mantra of Chenrezig, OM MANI PADME HUM, we visualize light coming from his body and heart into our bodies and hearts. This is particularly good for generating compassion and loving-kindness for self and others, as well as being a purification meditation. Chenrezig is described in the Buddhist texts as smiling compassionately, like a loving parent smiling on his only child. Cultivating this sense of unconditional acceptance towards oneself and then others through meditation can be very healing.

Sometimes Chenrezig is visualized in the heart chakra, with light and nectar filling the body and radiating out to the world as a source of love and acceptance that can heal others. This visualization helps cultivate confidence that this healing source is an aspect of our own nature, not something external. It also helps to open our hearts to be more responsive and caring towards others. This visualization is extremely useful in healing relationships that are problematic, or full of conflict and anger, by helping clear the negative conceptions that block clear communication.

Eastern teachers are surprised to hear of the deep emotional wounding Westerners experience in relation to their parents. I have often found the practice of Green Tara (fig. 4) very powerful, when developed carefully, for people who have emotional difficulties in relation to their mothers. When we have a damaged sense of the mother, we can draw on the archetypal quality of Tara as a way to heal by reflecting deeply on the qualities we wish for in the archetypal mother as we visualize Tara and recite her mantra. To imagine our own mothers as present at the same time and to visualize healing in these relationships is also helpful.

However, this practice may bring up painful feelings that need to be allowed and given space to heal. Only then can we begin to move closer to forgiveness and compassion and away from anger and resentment. When someone I work with has a deeply wounded sense of their inner child, I often suggest they visualize holding this child in their arms or on their lap while healing light comes from Tara in the space in front of them. This visualization can be adapted if you wish to aid the healing of someone close to you. Visualizing the person in your heart, or seated in front of you, and sending them healing light while reciting Tara's mantra enables healing for someone who is ill or in need of emotional support.

The following meditation on Chenrezig gives clear instructions on the process of visualization. If you wish to explore this meditation, you will need to find a quiet space and a short period of uninterrupted time. Sit in a comfortable position, preferably with your legs crossed and back straight. If this proves difficult, use a comfortable upright chair, place your feet squarely on the floor, and place your right hand in your left on your lap.

> With your eyes closed, spend time simply becoming aware of your breath rising and falling in order to quieten your mind. After some minutes, visualize arising in the space before you, at the level of the forehead and about three feet away, a small white lotus flower with eight petals, open and radiant with light, and about the size of the palm of your hand. In its center sits a small circular moon disc lying flat, like a cushion. In the center of this moon disc, visualize a small shaft of white light-energy, and imagine this is, in essence, your own higher Self, your Buddha nature. It radiates light out in all directions, filling space out into the universe.

> From dharmakaya, the omniscient wisdom of all the Buddhas, this light invokes the essence of enlightened compassion and wisdom in the aspect of a snowfall of billions of tiny white Chenrezigs. They are gradually drawn forth and dissolve into the shaft of light, making it very powerful, radiant, and vibrant. Suddenly this shaft of light transforms into the aspect of Chenrezig, who is white, has four arms, and is seated in the full lotus posture arms. The first two hold a lapis lazuli with palms together at the heart, the second right hand holds a crystal rosary, and the second left hand the stem of a lotus flower. He is dressed in silken robes and gold ornaments, is surrounded by an aura of light, and smiles with narrow compassionate eyes.

> Imagine that Chenrezig is the essence of the love, wisdom, and compassion that is your innate Buddha nature, inseparable

from the universal compassion of all the divine beings, saints, and Buddhas of all traditions. Consider that Chenrezig radiates love and total acceptance, irrespective of your faults and difficulties, like a loving parent for his only child.

Spend a few moments considering what is currently distressing you, what obstacle, sickness, or emotional problems you may have. Also think about what you need to develop in yourself, such as strength, self-confidence, courage, openness, or love. Imagine that light-energy and nectar begins to radiate into you from Chenrezig, cleansing and healing any sickness or blocked energy, freeing you from emotional pains and filling your entire body with blissful radiant energy spreading to every cell and atom and giving you the qualities you wish for. Visualize that any sick, blocked energy is washed through you and leaves your body in the form of black substances.

As you visualize this, recite quietly the mantra of Chenrezig: OM MANI PADME HUM.

Keep repeating this mantra as you visualize the light and energy cleansing and healing you, for as long as twenty minutes if you wish. When you end the recitation, let yourself settle quietly into the quality of awareness that remains, free of thoughts. Spend some time allowing yourself to relax into the all-pervasive warm, blissful, and radiant energy. After some minutes imagine that Chenrezig comes to the crown of your head and, becoming smaller, descends to become seated in your heart chakra. He remains there as the essence of your own Buddha nature and the source of love, wisdom, and unconditional compassion towards you and all others.

It is then possible to imagine the same light and energy of loving-kindness and compassion radiates out from your heart, totally opening your heart to all beings around you. Visualize, if you wish, all those you work with and live among, particularly those you have problems with, or fear and dislike. Send them love and acceptance and a healing light to fulfill their wishes and free them from their distress and problems, while again reciting the mantra OM MANI PADME HUM.

An alternative meditation has Chenrezig upon the crown of your head. You visualize nectar descending like a waterfall or shower, washing and cleansing all the energy in your body. This meditation can be simplified with great effect. The following meditation is a basic cleansing meditation utilizing a healing vase (fig. 9), which is often used to clear away life hindrances.

Sit in a comfortable, quiet position and spend a few moments sweeping your body to be sure you are not holding tension anywhere. Bring your attention to the rising and falling of the breath and allow your mind to settle for some minutes. Then visualize a small white lotus with a pink complexion arising just above the crown of your head. In its center is a circular moon disc, upon which stands a beautiful golden healing vase, and within which grows a small peach tree, a symbol of longevity, the tree of life.

Imagine that radiant light shines out from the vase in all directions, drawing forth love, compassion, and wisdom from the enlightened awareness of all holy beings. This is in the form of nectar-energy, which is then absorbed back into the vase. At the same time, the light draws forth all the healing energy of all of the elements, herbs, and minerals on the entire planet, also absorbing them back into the vase in the form of nectar and light-energy.

The vase fills to overflowing with radiant, inexhaustible, life-giving nectar, which begins to flow down through the lotus. It descends onto the crown of your head and starts to wash down through your body until every atom and cell is cleansed. It washes down the outside of your body like a shower. Imagine that any dark, sick, blocked energy is gradually washed away and leaves your body through your lower orifices in the form of black substances, which descend into the ground and are totally absorbed and transformed. While doing this visualization you can repeat constantly to yourself the three Sanskrit syllables OM AH HUM, which symbolize the purified body, speech, and mind of the enlightened ones.

Spend some minutes absorbed in the awareness of your entire body free of any dark, blocked energy or sickness and filled with radiant, blissful nectar that penetrates every cell. Then visualize that the vase melts into light and dissolves into you, so that its wisdom energy pervades every cell of your body.

This visualization is particularly associated with the deity Amitayus (fig. 8), practiced for the generation of long life.

With good concentration, these practices can have a profound effect psychologically, energetically, and physically. They can be a powerful way to address the accumulation of toxic stress that comes from our increasingly pressured lives. Psychologically they can help us to gradually develop a deeper sense of self-worth and acceptance. These practices are also an effective way to enhance and cultivate our personal vitality.

Having spent long periods in intensive retreat using similar visualizations, I have been greatly inspired by some of the effects that occur. These practices can work in surprising ways to shift our emotional and physical wellbeing. To develop confidence in this process, it is necessary to spend time in actual practice, as no amount of intellectual study can give us this experience.

As healing or purification takes place, many signs occur which we must consider carefully, as they may easily be misunderstood. There may be strong movements of energy in the body where blocked emotions are released, sometimes with great cathartic effect. At other times emotional and physical healing takes the form of sudden illnesses, vomiting, skin eruptions of boils and spots, or intense pain in various parts of the body that shift quite suddenly.

Dreams show signs of powerful disturbances, or images of excreting and purifying. Tibetan literature contains many descriptions of the dream signs that occur when healing and purification is taking place. If none of these signs occur, however, it does not mean purification is not happening. Often the effect is more on the level of a deepening of inner strength and clarity, or feeling more centered and whole. However, there is always the danger of expectation with any meditation practice, and to expect results or signs is a great hindrance.

We will sense the difference as the energy-wind of our subtle body begins to be freed of blocks and toxicity and our vitality returns. We may experience a shift in the general level of energy in our daily lives as we feel healthier and more deeply satisfied emotionally. It may also affect our sexual and creative vitality as we open up to our inner resources. According to the tantric tradition, the innate potential of our energy body when freed from defilement is great bliss (Tib. *de chen*). If we are able to tap into this inner healing source, we access a wellspring that affects our entire lives.

*Figure 10. Yamantaka*

THE PRINCIPLE at work in Highest Yoga Tantra, the highest level of Tantra, is subtly different from Action Tantra. Here the deity is considered a catalyst of transformation, and may be likened to a homeopathic remedy whose nature is constitutionally resonant with each individual's disposition. The deity is an innate aspect of the practitioner's consciousness and acts as a seed potential for transformation. When this seed is activated, it acts as a catalyst to transform the energy of the psyche from within.

Homeopathy is based on the principle that "like cures like," and we could say that, in a similar way, the deity needs to be of a corresponding disposition archetypally to the forces being transformed. The transformation of sexuality, aggression, or desire requires a catalyst that resonates with the same disposition, and the deity practiced emphasizes the transformation of these particular qualities.

The relationship to the deity as the root of transformation is initiated in a similar manner to Action Tantra; initiation is through the action of a teacher. The process of empowerment is more complex, but the essence is the same; the teacher introduces disciples into the deity appropriate for each disciple's particular needs.

The method of meditation used in Highest Yoga Tantra differs from Action Tantra. The meditator visualizes total transformation into the deity, rather than visualizing the deity in front of them or above the head. To enable this transformation it is necessary first to dissolve normal ego identification into emptiness and then to reemerge as the deity.

This facilitates two things. First, it enables the meditator to center reality in the Self as the deity in meditation by letting go of normal ego identification. Second, it enables identification with an image personifying the forces held in the unconscious, forces that need a vehicle to bring about transformation.

In this way the energy to be transformed is gradually activated and brought to the surface. When this kind of practice is carried out in retreat conditions, the use of mantra recitation adds power to the evocation of the archetypal energies one is going to transform. As these energies are activated they may be experienced as anger, hatred, frustration, and aggression, or lust, passion, and erotic fantasy, according to the nature of the deity.

As these feelings arise they have an object—the deity—on which to focus. Focusing on the deity harnesses the feelings and gives them a meaningful symbol to identify with. The effect is to transform the energy itself into the aspect of the deity. While holding the deity and its forces in consciousness, the meditator also recognizes that the deity has the nature of light and lacks any inherent self-existence or substantiality. This combination of identification with the deity, or divine pride, as well as the wisdom and clarity that realizes its empty nature, powerfully transforms the underlying emotions and their instincts.

Doing this kind of practice requires much skill, understanding, and faith in the transformative process. There must also be a clear knowledge of the vessel in which the process takes place, as the boundaries of transformation are vital to contain the forces of the "god being released from the darkness." This is why the practitioner first undergoes an initiation into the deity that—together with the upholding of various vows and commitments—safeguards the practitioner and those around him or her. The initiation puts the practitioner into the vessel, making a sacred place in which to undergo the transformation. It is helpful to have confidence in a spiritual guide who has experienced the practice and who supports and holds the process taking place, similar to the alchemist and the apprentice, or the therapist and the client.

There is little benefit if Higher Tantra is entered into frivolously and without faith, skill, or understanding. When not given a suitable basis in which to emerge, the forces of the unconscious bite back; not maintaining the vessel brings little transformation as the energies become lost and wasted, or destructive. Being unprepared to enter the vessel and then unskillful in maintaining the intensity of practice breaks down the threshold of the unconscious, causing psychological problems.

I have personally known a number of practitioners with a disposition to psychosis who went over the edge by pushing too hard in meditation. These casualties of what—if practiced properly—can be a profound process, require a great deal of assistance to make it back across the threshold. Sadly, such assistance is seldom available even from Tibetan teachers, as they have little or no skill in psychotherapy. There is a serious need for Western practitioners to gain skills to assist such people.

When we honor the forces of the unconscious in the aspect of the deity, they can be respected and understood and safely allowed into our lives. They are returned to the temple rather than pushed underground into the Shadow of our so-called civilized persona, where they become our diseases. When we engage with the potent, wild, instinctual side of our nature in a healthy way, it begins to be transformed. The deities that act as vehicles for transformation are potent and often fierce archetypal images, not the peaceful deities of Action Tantra. For example, Yamantaka (fig. 10), Heruka Chakrasamvara (fig. 14), and Vajrayogini (fig. 13) all exhibit demonic characteristics and are depicted with the heads of demons, or snarling, with fangs and ferocious eyes. They are adorned with skulls, severed heads, and animal skins.

The relationship to the deity in Highest Yoga Tantra can radically reorient the roots of the practitioner's life in a profound way. As a path of transformation it is demanding, but the fruits can be extremely rewarding as the experience of the deity becomes increasingly alive in all areas of creative life. The deity becomes the center and heart of meaning and inspiration in the same way that Jung spoke of the Self as the archetype of meaning.

The wrathful forms of Higher Tantra are powerful forces for transformation when understood fully. The deity brings into direct awareness a constant manifestation of potent instinctual forces of the
unconscious that can be both creative and destructive. Using the deity
as a channel, the archetypal forces that underlie our lives are incarnated
into relative form within the individual in a healthy way, rather than
becoming destructive.

## THE GENERATION STAGE

There are two stages of practice in Highest Yoga Tantra—*kyerim*, the
creation, or generation, stage, and *tsogrim*, the completion, or
fulfillment, stage. The generation stage is oriented around the sadhana
practice, or method of accomplishment, in which the practitioner
passes through a daily process of self-generation as the deity within the
mandala or sacred place. The sadhana is a sequence of visualizations
that the meditator gradually integrates into his or her mind so it
becomes increasingly spontaneous. A meditator once likened it to a
tape loop that goes round and round until it becomes integrated. Like
an accelerating car, the sadhana slowly picks up speed of its own
accord.

The sadhana usually begins with complex and detailed descriptions
of the process of visualization, which may take several hours to complete. As the mind becomes more and more attuned to this sadhana,
the meditator graduates to a simpler form with less detail, yet following the same essential process. Eventually, a brief sadhana is sufficient
to generate the full complexity of the practice. A meditator who has
integrated the sadhana fully into his or her continuum can then go
beyond its form, but the process may take many years. At this stage the
deity is well established and awakened in the meditator.

A particular characteristic of the generation stage cultivated in the
sadhana can be described as a death transformation. The concept of
transformation through a death may be familiar from Western psychology, as it is the kind of experience people go through during crit-

ical periods of crisis. The old sense of identity gradually dies and— following a period of deep transformation—reemerges. From a psychological perspective, reemergence often involves a radical shift in perception, as the ego has been reborn in a different way.

This process of death and transformation obviously occurs at the actual time of death, together with the dissolution of the sense of self. In the East it is readily accepted that some sort of rebirth and the reemergence of a sense of identity follow death. In Highest Yoga Tantra teachings, the process of death and reemergence is described in detail, with a clear understanding of how the energy body and the consciousness progress through the evolution of death, intermediate state, and rebirth. It is also recognized that we can experience a process in meditation that is virtually the same as actual death, except that consciousness does not leave the body. Within the generation stage, these three phases of death, intermediate stage, and rebirth are experienced as a visualized simulation of what will take place during the completion stage and, later, at the actual time of death.

Each of the three phases enables a particular characteristic of a Buddha to be developed. The death dissolution is transformed into the experience of dharmakaya. The intermediate state, or *bardo*, leads to the development of sambhogakaya, or the "illusory body," and rebirth develops the quality of nirmanakaya. To understand this more clearly, we must first know the actual process that, according to Tantra, takes place at the time of death.

When we are about to die, the energy-winds in the body decrease their function, gradually fading from gross to subtle. As they fade, they absorb into the central channel from which they originated. The energy-wind of the earth element absorbs first, then water, fire, and air. The signs of death are a weakening of the body, a drying of liquids, loss of heat, and deterioration in sight, hearing, digestion, and so on, which are all supported by energy-wind. Eventually these energy-winds absorb into the heart chakra, and the internal experience is of becoming unconscious.

On a subtle level, however, a process is still taking place even when a person is clinically dead. The energy-winds become increasingly subtle as they cease to function, and eventually only the subtlest energy-wind, called the "life supporting wind," remains. This is the energy-wind associated with the extremely subtle consciousness called the "clear light of death," which abides in the heart chakra. The dying person enters the clear light of death, which is experienced as the bright light often described by those who have been through a near-death experience. Following the clear light of death, consciousness, together with its extremely subtle life supporting wind, usually leaves the body.

The extremely subtle consciousness- or life-supporting wind enters the intermediate stage, *bardo*, where it has a subtle volatile nature, like the Western concept of spirit (see the description of *prima materia*, p. 88). This subtle body can manifest different appearances, although these are imperceptible except to those with an acute clairvoyance. After a period of time there is a powerful karmic pull, like an instinct to be reborn. The intermediate stage being is drawn towards a new life during a moment of conception between two beings with whom the intermediate stage being has a strong karmic relationship. Contrary to some thinking, there is no volition in this process, except in the cases of a few highly evolved meditators who have developed a subtlety of awareness. According to the Buddhist view, what draws us into the next life is the power of our karma, mostly set in motion during the last moments of the present life. In this way, the extremely subtle consciousness/life supporting wind combination enters a new body.

In the generation stage, the evolution of these three phases is simulated in meditation. The dissolution of energy-winds in the early phase before death is followed through a visualization technique. The meditator visualizes that all relative appearances melt into light and dissolve into the body, which then also melts into light and dissolves into a syllable at the heart, such as HUM. As the HUM dissolves, all relative appearance of self and phenomena disappear into the clarity of emptiness.

*HUM*

This replicates an experience similar to the extremely subtle mind of clear light that arises at the time of death, when all the elements and energy-winds absorb into the heart chakra. At this point the meditator practices Mahamudra in order to deepen the experience of clear light and emptiness. After a visualized dissolution, meditating on Mahamudra enables an experience of clarity that is not always possible at other times. This may only be a simulation, but it generates a spacious openness without dualistic appearances like that of dharmakaya. It creates a mental image of dharmakaya that gradually becomes a direct insight. This experience of meditation resembles the transformation of the clear light of death into dharmakaya, and completes the first stage of transforming death into the means to realize dharmakaya.

Much of the symbolism of Higher Tantra deities is associated with this death transformation, principally the frequent use of skulls and bone ornaments. The skull symbolizes the wisdom that is generated through the clear light of death. We can see the skull as the result of stripping away the conventional identity of the flesh. This identity is the basis for the ego and persona. In the dissolution into the clear light of death, all worldly identity is cleansed and purified. The skull is therefore clean and bare in its uncontrived starkness. In the same way, our innate nature is laid bare, and we are purified of all dualistic identity in the clear light of death.

After resting in the emptiness of dharmakaya, meditation moves to the second phase of death evolution. The meditator's subtle identity begins to re-manifest, with the subtle energy-wind/mind combination visualized in the aspect of a seed syllable HUM, or a similar image. This seed syllable is like an original sound syllable, usually visualized in

Sanskrit. It represents the emergence of the energy-wind/mind combination into the intermediate state when consciousness leaves the
body after death. During meditation this extremely subtle energy-
wind/mind has been freed of all previous dualistic identity through
the process of dissolution into dharmakaya. The previous ego conception has effectively died, and the subtle energy-wind has thereby
been purified into the sambhogakaya, or "illusory body," of a Buddha.
This completes the second stage of transforming the intermediate
stage into the means to realize sambhogakaya.

At this point our intention to reincarnate or return to conventional
reality is important. Why do we wish to be here in embodied form?
What is our motivation and purpose in reincarnating? In the sadhana
we generate the thought: "I must take rebirth for the welfare and
benefit of all sentient beings to help free them from the cycle of existence." This bodhichitta motivation fundamental to Tantra is crucial;
it is considered the only purpose for incarnating. The meditator is being
asked to take his or her reasons for incarnating seriously. The third
phase in this process then begins. This is the actual self-generation, in
which the meditator visualizes being born, arising as the deity standing
within the celestial mansion of a mandala. By doing so, he or she transforms rebirth into the means to achieve nirmanakaya, a Buddha's
"emanation body."

If we return for a moment to Diagram 1, this process becomes
clearer. The focus of identity, the sense of "I," normally central to the
right-hand circle must be shifted to centralize awareness in the deity on
the threshold between the two circles. For this shift to happen, a death
must first occur that takes us totally into the left-hand circle, where the
ego dies or dissolves into emptiness. On returning to relative awareness, the deity enables the meditator to stand in the position of the
interface.

Once the meditator has arisen in the aspect of the deity, this experience must be gradually stabilized. The experience of the deity then
grows with clearer appearance and a deeper feeling of divine pride. In
the generation stage a significant aspect of the practice is the cultiva-

tion of samadhi, or tranquil abiding. The measure of having attained the generation stage is said to be holding in awareness the entire form of the deity with its surrounding mandala without disturbance for a prolonged period.

This is a painstaking and lengthy process of recreating the appearance of the deity in meditation time and again, usually in retreat, so that eventually it can be held steadily. Once a meditator has attained this degree of concentration, transformation through the power of the deity can be rapid. With the aid of mantra recitation associated with the deity, this experience is deepened and stabilized.

Over time, meditators become constantly aware of the nature of the deity within the continuum and experience the deity's associated blissful quality both during and outside of meditation. As this meditation deepens and stabilizes, the energy-wind body is profoundly affected, becoming purified of blocks and emotional defilements. As described earlier, movement can enhance this experience and greatly aid the cultivation of a sense of divine pride.

The generation stage of Highest Yoga Tantra is considered a potent means of accumulating personal vitality or merit, primarily because of the self-generation as the deity. As the subtle energy body becomes increasingly purified and awakened, its nature matures in potency. However, the final purification and transformation takes place in the completion stage.

*Figure 11. Mahakala*

*The Symbol of Transformation*

✦✦

THE OBSCURE and sometimes frightening appearance of Higher Tantra deities is not easy to understand. When Colonel Francis Younghusband visited Tibet in 1904, his first response as a Christian was to think the Tibetans were demon worshipers. The wrathful deities of Higher Tantra are indeed often demonic in appearance. To understand their effectiveness as symbols of transformation requires a deeper insight into their psychological significance and the power of archetypes and their images.

Within the commentaries given on the various tantric deities are some interpretations of their meanings and complex symbolic characteristics. Their various symbolic attributes and implements are given specific meaning relating to that which is being transformed or generated. The specific nature of this meaning, however, still leaves the potential for greater intuitive interpretation in a more creative way.

However, this understanding is seldom written in the commentaries and is only gathered through experience, or by finding a teacher with deep intuitive insight into the nature of the deity. There is still much to explore from the psychological perspective we are familiar with in the West. To gain a deeper sense of the workings of these profound and complex deity forms it is useful to bridge our understanding, particularly through the insight of Jung, into the symbolic process of transformation.

In *Symbols of Transformation*, Jung explored the way the instinctual forces that affect our emotional and physical lives are rooted in the archetypal depth of the unconscious.[17] These primordial patterns, or archetypes, are inherent in our human condition, shaping our lives. He realized that the obstruction of this archetypal energy was a key factor in psychological disorder and emerged in all manner of aberrant behavior. When the archetypal intent of the instincts is blocked, it builds up and emerges in neurotic patterns of behavior that are an apparent outlet for the energy; hence, as he said, "The gods have become our diseases." He saw that his patients' compulsive and ritualistic behaviors and fantasy lives were a metaphorical release of neurotic energy. To give two examples, blocked rage at parental figures and authority is sometimes expressed through vandalism, and the need to rid oneself of bad feeling after having been sexually abused may manifest as compulsive washing.

Jung saw, however, that if the energy, or libido, of the psyche is given a suitable channel, it can be freed from its neurotic, destructive nature and transformed. He recognized that the symbolic life of the psyche was a natural channel to transform this energy.[18] When a symbol or symbolic theme is of the right order, it can hook the energy of particular emotional and instinctual forces and thereby elevate them to healthier states. There is, in Jung's view, a direct relationship between the progression of the symbolic life of the psyche and the transformation of the underlying energy. Thus, as blocked instinctual energy is freed through some form of creative expression, the nature of its symbolic life changes and evolves, gradually becoming healthier.

In Tantra, the instinctual forces of the unconscious are seen as the powerful, wild effects of energy-wind. This energy is given a vehicle or channel through the practice of the deity. The archetypal forces associated with the deity are activated or awakened in the meditator and gradually given a vehicle for transformation. The deity is said to be like a *simbu,* or woodworm, that feeds off the very thing that gives birth to it—namely, the archetypal instincts that are to be transformed.

From an archetypal perspective, these deities focus in two primary directions. One group deals particularly with the transformation of the destructive Shadow, and the other with the relationship between the archetypal masculine and feminine.

## THE ARCHETYPAL SHADOW

Working with the forces of the unconscious and the Shadow is taken to its deepest level in the Highest Yoga Tantras. The deities involved are powerful, demonic, and wrathful, which makes them easy for Westerners to misunderstand. As we move into the domain of the archetypal Shadow we might think the archetypal images used in Tantra are specific or unique to the East; but if we look more closely at our Western backgrounds we can make meaningful links.

In the West our particular notions of good and evil have favored the Shadow. Shadow and evil have always been tied to darkness and the underworld, the realm of demons, goblins, spirits, snakes, serpents, wolves, bats, and werewolves. There are numerous creatures that evoke the sense of cold, dark, sinister, haunted places; the realm where humans go at their peril.

Here dwell the archetypal figures of the masculine Shadow—the Devil, Satan, the vampire, the black magician, the black knight, and the destructive, dark father. We see them as cruel, cold and powerful, consuming light, blood, and goodness. They are fearsome, living in the dark, feeding on it, moving under its cloak, and protected by its cover. Those who cling to light do not enter this domain for fear of destruction. Because we fear the forces of the underworld, they must be kept at bay by repression and control. However, this keeps them powerful and shadowy.

Many of these underworld archetypal images also convey sexuality, not just the sense of demonic and destructive evil. The devil is often connected to tales of sexual rites performed by naked women. Vampires and werewolves link soul-devouring, blood-draining, and biting with power and possession through sexuality. Many of the modern, cult-horror-movie characters have this sinister, sexual, devouring, and violent nature, where the fear of being seduced and overpowered by a demonic and evil yet sexual force is played upon. This may titillate a morbid and thrilling fascination for primitive forces within us. However, although seeing sexual violence in a film may stimulate this side of our Shadow, it is unlikely to transform it.

The alchemists conjured archetypal images of Shadow in a subtly different way, as it was projected into their "opus." They drew on images of Saturn, lead, the Abyssinian, the savage, or the gorilla. Many of these images still live with us in our racial prejudices and attitudes towards animals such as gorillas and wolves, which never live up to their savage reputations. These images on the one hand convey the sense of the heavy, leaden prima materia that is to be transformed in the work. They also convey the link to our own instincts as the forces to be released from the darkness. These are the instinctual forces that the alchemists saw no longer had a means for transformation within Christianity.

As Christianity became an increasingly powerful patriarchal, political authority, the emphasis placed upon theological and intellectual doctrine deepened the rift between religion and nature, including the instinctual, emotional aspects of life. This was most evident during various periods of missionary zeal to convert so-called savages throughout various regions of the New World. The failure to respect and value indigenous cultures, which had their own spiritual roots, was largely a reflection of the fear of the significance of the forces of nature in man.

In aboriginal cultures, spirituality is intimately connected to one's relationship with nature and the feminine principle, forms of spiritual power that have never found a comfortable place in Christian theology, especially the Protestant church. The pre-Christian religions in Europe were more closely allied to matter, the earth, and the body, which, in the eyes of patriarchal theology, were impure, unclean, and dark. Old folklore was connected to the goddess and nature, with natural magic and the healing arts, together with the body, sexuality, and fertility, all of which have often been feared as witchery. Natural lore does not conform to masculine, spiritual, moral laws or authority. It has its own laws, which are inspired by the rhythm of the seasons, the moon, the body, and the psyche, not by spiritual authority or control.

Eventually the power of the old natural religions—with their local rites and festivals, most of which were associated with the goddess, fertility, and farming—became subsumed under a Christian cloak. This translated them into a form that has today all but lost the connection to its origins. The patriarchal religious establishment's poor relationship to the feminine has had the effect of driving the feminine principle, nature, matter, and the body into the Christian Shadow. Out of fear and ignorance they have been condemned as witchery in allegiance with the devil. Healers, herbalists, and midwives became feared evil sorceresses and black witches, associated with black cats, frogs, toads, and spiders, all images of the dark mother.

The nature gods and their rites of passage and myths of transformation were also cast into the Christian Shadow. This is particularly important because the nature gods— Dionysus, Pan, Kernunos, and their retinues—were major figures in the mysteries of the natural religions. They were the consorts of the goddess, the symbol of the creative, fertilizing forces of the male principle in nature. Half human and half beast, representing their unified relationship with nature and the instincts, they were the perfect basis for the image of the Christian devil. Horned and often cloven-hoofed, they embodied instinctual forces feared by Christian authority and so became its Shadow.

Christ has many parallels to Dionysus; both are the sacrificed god, the vine on the cross, the god worshipped through wine as a sacrament, and the lord of the dance; but as a nature-god, Dionysus was cast into Shadow. The nature-gods were associated with love, sexuality, and spiritual intoxication. They were wild and instinctual, embodying much of the mystery of the transformation of these forces that has now been lost to our culture. Gradually even Carnival, the period in the church calendar during which the wild side was allowed to be openly expressed, lost its meaning.

Throughout Christian history there has been a gradual loss of means to transform the Shadow, particularly its instinctual, primitive, archetypal roots. These forces are easily regarded as the workings of the devil, to be feared and rejected rather than transformed. The struggle of good and evil has become one of separation, and there is an ever-increasing rift between irreconcilable, absolute opposites. The medieval alchemists attempted to resolve this split of "absolute" good and evil. We must also try to resolve this split in the psyche and bring the archetypal Shadow back into a healthier relationship. If we do not, we will perpetually cast out the "devil" and project it onto those we fear as evil sinners, heretics, and witches. Throughout history we have scapegoated those who did not uphold the values of society. Once even the mentally ill were cast into Bedlam, their illnesses regarded as the products of evil ways. Today we have contemporary loathed figures who carry our cultural collective Shadow, figures like terrorists and pedophiles. However, our archetypal and collective Shadow needs to be integrated and elevated into a higher state and transformed.

## THE CHANNEL OF TRANSFORMATION

Today in the West we have largely lost the myths and archetypes that are vehicles for transforming the powerful forces of the archetypal Shadow. Jung knew that when these forces were unrecognized and not given their place in the psyche, they would become diabolic, demonic, and destructive. When repressed and denied, they can take us over and lead us to behave in ways that can be called evil. If these forces are given a vehicle for transformation, they have the potential to become like a *daimon*, a source of potent energy.[19]

According to Jung, archetypal energy requires a symbolic expression to constellate and transform its instinctual power. An archetypal pattern needs an archetypal image or metaphor to become conscious. Our raw, primitive emotions and instinctual forces must be magnetized, held, and enthralled by the symbolic metaphor. In order to be a suitable channel, this symbol must have fascination, charge, and numinosity. Indeed, when the energies themselves resonate with a particular symbol, it becomes imbued with tremendous charge.

For transformation to take place, a number of conditions must be fulfilled, foremost of which is providing a context that holds the forces to be transformed. When the instinct or emotion channeled is no longer acted out in the habitual, unconscious way, a natural gradient develops towards symbolic expression. Once the instinctual forces are held in a suitable container, a symbolic metaphor provides an expression for them and begins to transform the "god being released from the darkness."

Once contained, the instinctual energy of the archetype begins to be symbolically expressed. The symbolic image provides a channel or vehicle for the energy to be elevated to a higher level. It is necessary, however, that the symbolic channel—the most powerful gradient for transformation—is of the same nature as the forces being transformed. For example, if the energy to be transformed is sexual, it needs a sexual metaphor; if it is violent, it needs an active, violent metaphor.

The symbol of transformation must also hold the paradoxical polarities of good and evil, light and dark, because it can then hold the tension between the light of consciousness and Shadow's darkness. While we continue to view the archetypal Shadow images as evil in an absolute sense, we will fear them, and the only way they can be dealt with is by rejection. We drive them into the unconscious and cultivate different ways to maintain a threshold between ourselves and potential invasion by these powerful forces.

As already mentioned, our Western split is between absolute good and absolute evil. The Eastern duality is not between good and evil, but between ignorance and wisdom, or blindness and insight (Tib. *marigpa* and *rigpa*). While we remain ignorant and unconscious of the archetypal darkness of the Shadow, it has power to dominate us unconsciously. In Buddhism, possession by the Shadow is seen as a state of delusion rather than the workings of an ultimate evil force. With the growing light of awareness, the power of this side of our nature can be elevated into a higher state, healed and transformed.

Thus the symbolic deity that will lift the Shadow into consciousness must embody the wisdom that realizes the essential nature of the force to be transformed. It enables the light of consciousness to be brought into the Shadow, like going deeply into a dark cavern to shine a light on some wild creature dwelling there. The tantric deity that embodies the Shadow enables its forces to be experienced with an awareness that recognizes its essential nature as neither good nor evil, but as emptiness or nonduality. The true nature of the Shadow is dharmakaya, empty of the dualities of light and dark or good and evil.

While we remain bound up in the ego's limited conceptions of relative good and evil as absolutes, we stay trapped in their power, and—whether we are fixed upon light or upon darkness—we still cling to a relative stance that has no ultimate truth. The deity stands between these two worlds; it is both, and sustains the paradoxical middle ground where consciousness transforms the Shadow and enables it to be freed into its true nature. Rather than remaining demonic, the Shadow is returned to the temple as a powerful daimon.

*The Wrathful Deity* 15

❖ ❖ ───────────────────────────────

A NYONE ENCOUNTERING Tibetan art is often deeply affected by the extraordinary power of tantric deity images. These deities fall into two main groups; peaceful and wrathful. While the peaceful forms can be beautiful, Westerners can find the wrathful images bizarre and confusing. Early encounters with Tibetan culture, with its ferocious and erotic deities, led its religion to be viewed with great suspicion. Those of a missionary disposition even tried to convert the Tibetans to Christianity, presumably to save them from what they saw as demon worship. The Tibetans' use of wild demonic and erotic images of enlightened activity can indeed seem incongruous when they are supposed to embody principles of enlightened compassion, moral purity, and wisdom.

The Tibetan tradition has now emerged in the West, together with its iconography and deity practice. Many Westerners are fascinated to hear the chanting of tantric lamas and to see the elaborate rituals and costumes the lamas use as they perform their rites and practices. With our Western thirst for the exotic, these rituals appear mysterious and dramatic, but beneath this pageantry lies a profound meaning. It is difficult to comprehend at first, but in our search for a way to understand the transformation of the many facets of the Shadow, Tantra can be of great significance.

We have lost the symbols and rites of transformation that elevate the dark angel from an unconscious, potentially demonic state into a healthy conscious relationship. Our "civilized" culture is pervaded by an underworld of sick, perverse, violent, and corrupt life we would prefer to ignore and cover up. Despite our best efforts at curbing and containing aberrant human nature, the daily news is filled with its shadowy effects. The question still stands as to how we transform rather than suppress its forces.

When the tantric wrathful deity is understood and related to skillfully, it has the necessary qualities to be a catalyst of transformation. One deity that embodies the power to transform the destructive, aggressive aspect of the Shadow is Yamantaka (fig. 10). Vajrabhairava, as he is also called, is practiced to overcome emotional and karmic obstacles, in particular the violence of anger and hatred. Bhairava means "terrifier," and Vajrabhairava is said to be the destroyer of Yama, the Lord of Death. His domain is the underworld; he lives in charnel grounds and is lord over all fearsome protectors, demons, spirits, cannibals, and a host of underworld characters, which he brings under his power. We can see some parallel to Hades/Pluto as lord of the underworld.

Yamantaka is archetypally a horned god, bull-headed, like the Minotaur, and horned like the nature-gods Kernunos, Pan, and Dionysus. He is a wild beast, with his powerful sexuality potent yet contained, symbolized by his erect phallus. He bellows, roars, and stamps his feet, trampling on the forces he is bringing under his control. He is adorned with implements and animal skins that exemplify the qualities of his power to destroy and transform ignorance and ego-grasping as the basis of evil and the various emotions that arise from it.

Archetypally, Yamantaka is a personification of the dark angel. He is of the same order as the forces of the underworld, the Shadow that is to be transformed. He appears diabolical, demonic, wild, and terrifying, and yet upon the crown of his head is an image of his peaceful, compassionate essence, the head of Manjushri (fig. 2). As a manifestation of the wisdom of dharmakaya, he embodies the power of wisdom to overcome the Shadow's demonic side, not by repression, but by absorbing its forces into his nature. While the demonic Shadow is maintained by ignorance and darkness, Yamantaka is wisdom in its most forceful and wrathful aspect, directed to overcome unconsciousness. His nature is the wisdom of indestructible bliss and empti-ness—one of the meanings of the Sanskrit word *vajra*—and his aspect is Bhairava the Terrifier. For this reason, he is known as the Vajra Terrifier.

Like other wrathful deities, Yamantaka gives the forces of the Shadow a symbol that hooks their energy and provides a channel and direction for their expression and transformation. Indeed, in one of his left hands he holds a lasso to symbolize his power to bring the forces of darkness under his control. He is able to harness their energy and embody their power consciously. The archetypal forces of the instincts and emotions held in the Shadow are given a channel through Yamantaka so that they can be brought into consciousness, transformed, and integrated. Yamantaka's archetypal root is of the same nature as those forces that are to be transformed. If this were not so he would be ineffective.

To make this clear, we can look at a contemporary Western analogy. If we think of a gang of Hell's Angels that has become totally wild and anarchic, how might their energy be brought under control? If a man dressed in a pinstriped suit with good intentions said to them, "Now look, you fellows, this just won't do," we can imagine how predictably derisory their response would be. On the other hand, if they were addressed by a Schwartzenegger-like figure who looked powerful and tough, dressed like a wild man, disheveled and scarred, carrying chains, knives, and other weapons, the response would be different. They might develop respect or interest and be drawn into some kind of rela-tionship, even to the point where, becoming their leader, he could change the direction of their behavior. This could lead to a "might for the sake of right" attitude, and their aggression would be gradually channeled.

As the Shadow forces are transformed, their energy is not lost, but integrated into personal power. This is depicted symbolically by pas-sages in which the heroes in legends wear the skins or masks of the ani-mals they have overcome, or carry the implements and attributes of those they have conquered in battle. For example, Parzival wore the armor of the Red Knight, and Hercules wore the skin of a lion he slew. A similar phenomenon occurs with the tantric deities. We see Yamantaka wearing the skins of many animals, such as tigers and elephants, which represent the various instinctual forces he has subdued.

Yamantaka is one of a number of similar deities who embody wrathful characteristics. They all appear in demonic forms, brandishing frightening weapons and surrounded by wisdom fire. When a practitioner evokes the presence of these deities, their power can be almost tangible, though the feeling is certainly benign and not evil. The ego may nevertheless feel quite threatened, sensing unconsciously that all these forces are directed towards its subjugation.

In India I lived for a time very close to a lama called Ling Rinpoche, who was recognized as an embodiment of Yamantaka. On a number of occasions I had the opportunity to meet him for interviews and receive tantric empowerments. While the lama had a wonderful quality of gentleness and compassion, perhaps the most extraordinary sense I used to feel from him was his immense power. He had the capacity to suddenly "switch on" a terrifying quality that was awesome and quite tangible, particularly if he felt people were being frivolous in their practices. It was a great relief when the lama switched off and started laughing.

We have a confused and ambivalent relationship to power in the West, and, as a result, most of the time it is expressed in anger. The therapeutic world has increasingly tried to assert that anger must be voiced and not repressed, and that repressed anger is unhealthy and destructive, borne out in those who suffer its consequences. However, there is more to anger than we imagine, which we find out as we truly begin to discover its roots. Anger arises for most of us as a result of our inability to embody our power effectively. Often an inability to stand in our own strength and assert ourselves skillfully lies behind our angry reactions. We are equally unfamiliar with the expression of what the Tibetans call "wrathful compassion," which is the ability to assert a quality of power that gives a clear and unequivocal awareness of some truth or boundary.

When a deity like Yamantaka is practiced, it has the potential to turn our normal, egoistic, reactive anger into clarity and power. Anger contains a power that is caught up in some form of reactive clinging, turning our effectiveness into a defensive reaction. When we release the power contained in anger from defensive reaction, it can be expressed clearly. This clarity has the capacity to cut through nonsense in a way that is not caught by the ego's need to defend itself or to be nice and yet retains openness and compassion. However, it is rare that we have the courage or confidence to express truth clearly to others, and even with our friends we often collude and appease rather than being honest. The wrathful incisiveness of Yamantaka is not defensive, ego-centered, or reactive anger. It is the power to be ruthlessly straight, honest, clear, and compassionate when necessary. If we learn to stand in this power, there is little need for our normal emotionally reactive anger.

The deity appears in a wrathful form because it embodies this potent power, and the object of this force is not projected outside blaming outer enemies. Having recognized that the true enemy is the ignorance and ego-grasping that lies within us all, there is a change of direction. All the destructive demonic characteristics exemplified in the deity are directed at the ultimate destruction of stupidity, selfishness, and ego-grasping. (Remember, I am saying "ego-grasping," not "ego.") Defining Shadow as unconscious means ego-grasping—the unrecognized, ignorant, unconscious side of the normal functional ego—lies at the very heart, or root, of Shadow. Ego-grasping is the demon against which all the forces of the wrathful deity are directed.

The primary cause of all suffering in the world is ego-grasping. All cruelty, violence, maliciousness, and evil arise from this ignorance, which clings to the ego as inherently existent and then seeks its own selfish ends at any cost. The wrathful deity is intended to tame and transform this at its most primal level. Two verses from a Tibetan text in praise of Yamantaka called *The Wheel of Sharp Weapons* show this attack on ego-grasping as the source of all evils in the world:

> Frantically running through life's tangled jungle,
> We are chased by sharp weapons of wrongs we have do.

Returning upon us; we are out of control.
This sly deadly villain—the selfishness in us,
Deceiving ourselves and all others as well—

Capture him, capture him, fierce Yamantaka,
Summon the enemy, bring him forth now.

Trample him, trample him, dance on the head
Of this treacherous concept of selfish concern.
Tear out the heart of this self-centered butcher
Who slaughters our chance to gain final release.[20]

These verses clearly express total abhorrence of the selfishness that causes so much of the trouble in our world. It is this ignorance and stupidity that the forces of Yamantaka and other wrathful deities are directed against. We Westerners are seldom confronted with such a challenge to our ego-centeredness and, when we are, may find it hard to cope with the power of this threat. We are used to indulging our egoistic vulnerabilities and to seeking out lives that collude with them. These wrathful deities present us with quite a challenge, but their nature is nonetheless wisdom and compassion.

Most of the wrathful deity forms are manifestations of their peaceful counterparts: thus, Yamantaka (fig. 10) is the manifestation of Manjushri, the Buddha of wisdom; Mahakala (fig. 11), of Chenrezig, the Buddha of compassion; Hayagriva, of Amitabha; and Vajrakilaya, of Vajrasattva. They demonstrate an important balance of the light and dark faces of the same deity. This is perhaps reminiscent of the terrible, vengeful, jealous, and angry Old Testament God, the God who balances the benign New Testament God, the God who will cast down tempests and plagues upon those who do not respect him.

This is not the sweet, light, loving face of the Self. The dark face of the Self, our wrathful Buddha nature, manifests in the wrathful deity, which in Tibetan Buddhism is viewed as the embodiment of enlightened activity, just as much as the bright face is. But, like the dark face of the Self, it can put us through the tearing and rending that demands we change and grow when necessary. The wrathful side of our Buddha nature makes us face ourselves in powerful, often terrifying ways. It pushes us beyond our fearful limitations, even initiating a breakdown to break through to a deeper level of understanding.

So far we have considered principally male deities, but there are also female deities associated with the dark side of the feminine, such as Palden Lhamo (fig. 12), Ekajati, and various wrathful aspects of the goddess Tara. Ekajati is a wild demoness with one blind eye, one tooth, and one breast. Palden Lhamo, the female parallel to Yamantaka, is a manifestation of the peaceful goddess White Tara. She is a ferocious-looking crone, a wild and terrible demoness, riding a mule across an ocean of blood. She is the queen of witches and spirits, bringing them under her power. She scatters vile diseases on those who disregard her, or who act in ways that are malignant to the Dharma. She bestows psychic powers such as clairvoyance and a knowledge of healing.

Palden Lhamo reminds us of the Greek goddess Hecate, who is also queen of the underworld. As the old death crone, the dark, deep, mysterious, and fearful side of the feminine, lunar nature, Hecate has a similar connection to psychic powers. Palden Lhamo has a lunar link, with her hair adorned by a moon, as though she is—like Hecate and Eriskegal—the dark moon. Hecate also rides an ass, and she is said to spread disease. This dark side of the feminine can clearly be seen as a Shadow to the light lunar forms, which White Tara most closely embodies. Her lunar connection is depicted by her aura of the full moon.

Thus, in all deities, a dual nature is evident; light and dark, upper world and underworld, peaceful and wrathful. The forces of the Shadow are not inherently demonic and terrible. Light and dark, good and evil, creation and destruction are relative dualities that have no ultimate true nature. They are not absolutes. It is our ignorance and lack of insight that seeks out one and fears the other.

The forces of the Shadow become demonic because they are not given appropriate recognition, conscious understanding, or respect.

Does this mean they are evil, as the Christian Shadow, in the form of the Devil, is believed to be? But Lucifer is also the bringer of light, just as Pluto, lord of the underworld, is the bringer of riches. Because we fear these forces, we cast them out of the temple, so they become diabolical and demonic.

In the East, the dark side of reality, with its potency, wildness, and destructiveness, is given the due respect it requires and placed in the temple as the wrathful deity, the bringer of wisdom and light. In the West, we tend to accept as spiritual only what we view as light, positive, and life-giving, and deny the vital counterpoint of destruction, death, and descent. Yet these are the two sides of reality, creation and destruction, existent at all times in all things by their very nature. Destruction is not inherently bad or evil; only if we fear it or become possessed by it does it become diabolical and tear us apart.

It is important to distinguish between two different dimensions of the Shadow; one that has become sick and demonic because it is repressed, and the other, which is related to darkness, death and destruction. The former may contain many important positive qualities we are unable to embody, such as our power, creativity, or sexuality. The latter is archetypally dark, wild, chaotic, unknown, and includes forces of destruction, yet is still an aspect of Buddha nature, or the Self. We fear this side of the Shadow as antithetical to the ego's need for security and predictability, but it cannot be made light and beautiful; that is not its nature.

The former dimension relates to archetypal qualities that become shadowy because of denial, but this is not their innate nature. These are the gods that become our diseases when they are not acknowledged. The dark side of our nature is a subtle interweaving of what is archetypally dark, as well as what is repressed and sick. We fear the wild forces of archetypal darkness behind our personal Shadow, which becomes infused by the archetypal and can then become demonic and diabolical.

From a tantric perspective, there is no absolute archetypal evil. The term "archetypal Shadow" is not the archetype of evil, but of dark,

dreams —
Rich gentle
plant in

several different states to ban or restrict it from p

sustained three unrelated objections. The call for

libraries was indisputable.

In a pole taken of two-hundred adults in

on views of content censorship revealed a few i

that seventy-five percent of those surveyed beli

censored. To what extent could this censorship

ninety percent believed that it was also import

points in order for them to have a worldlier ot

obscene language should be permitted the pe

percent. The results of the survey most close

censorship is one that must be taken into ste

wild, chaotic, and powerful instinctual forces, the dark unknown, the potent and awesome dimension of the psyche. If someone's personal Shadow is dominated by a pathological thirst for power, sadistic cruelty and exploitation, this becomes the real source of evil.

When ego-grasping dominates the personal Shadow and becomes possessed by the archetypal forces of the psyche, it may manifest in evil that tries to use this power for its own ends. This inflation is not uncommon among corrupt and sinister figures throughout history. Once endowed with power, many political and spiritual leaders, kings and queens, became possessed by it and went mad. All the forces of the Self in the aspect of the wrathful deity are directed against this egoistic abuse of power, and Yamantaka is traditionally considered the most potent deity to overcome these obstacles.

Only when this egotistical disposition is tamed and transformed can the Shadow be integrated into the spiritual path rather than remaining a cause of suffering. Once this practice had been cultivated for some time, the meditator moves on to explore the next aspect of the tantric journey. This brings the practitioner into relationship with further archetypal forces of the psyche, this time encountering the masculine and feminine seen as the *daka* and *dakini*.

*Figure 12. Palden Lhamo*

IN THE SUTRA TEACHINGS, the Buddha taught that the path required two dimensions of practice and that these paths were like the two wings of a bird. These are described in a variety of ways and are considered essential for the awakening experience of buddhahood. On one level, they are seen as relative and ultimate truth. Relative truth is the practice of method and compassionate skillful means, while ultimate truth is the wisdom realizing the nature of reality. These two truths are exemplified in a Buddha's purified form body (rupakaya), and the perfection of the wisdom body (dharmakaya).

In the tantras, these two aspects of the path are viewed symbolically as masculine and feminine, and only the tantras characterize attributes of enlightened activity in these terms. Tantric deities that convey the masculine and feminine are numerous, but consistently the underlying or definitive meaning is the union of relative and absolute truth, or of form and emptiness. The deities that exemplify this have particular characteristics that need to be explored deeply to understand their meanings and psychological functions.

In Highest Yoga Tantra, the deities that embody the masculine and feminine are known as *dakas* (Tib. *khadro*) and *dakinis* (Tib. *khadroma*). They are understood to personify the male and female attributes of both men and women and their gradual awakening and transformation on three levels—outer, inner, and secret. According to Tantra, these qualities are present in us, but are undeveloped or unconscious. The path of awakening is the gradual cultivation of the deity that embodies the union of both daka and dakini within the psyche.

In order to understand the daka and dakini, we can look at the Western parallel found in Jung's view of the Animus and Anima and at their influence both individually and in relationships. Much is owed to Jung for his insight into the masculine and feminine dimensions of our nature and how they manifest through us in ordinary life. The most dramatic encounter with the archetypal power of these polarities for many people is when they fall in love. Romantic love in the West has not always been expressed as it currently is, and significantly it differs greatly from its counterpart in the East.

In the West, much of the power and magic of our inner archetypal masculine and feminine is projected into our relationships. The loved one becomes imbued with the awe and numinosity of the archetype that is activated from within and then projected outside. In the East, as Robert Johnson suggests in his book *We: Understanding the Psychology of Romantic Love*, the powerful numinosity of these archetypes has been held within religious traditions. The masculine and feminine deities in both Hinduism and Buddhism draw to them much of this need for a carrier of projections. In Hinduism, young men still project their romantic needs for the divine feminine onto goddesses such as Parvati, Saraswati, or Lakshmi, while women focus their projections onto gods such as Krishna or Shiva.

The erotic intensity in these projections has been contained within religious forms until recently. However, in India today, this need for erotic union with the divine is turning increasingly towards human relationship. The Indian film industry has contributed significantly to this process. Young Indian males idolize and idealize movie stars and then, inevitably, begin to fantasize about bringing these feelings into their own relationships. To some degree the movie star has become like a deva, a god, remaining outside of the normal individual's world. Indian marriages still tend to be arranged, and "love marriages," as they are euphemistically called, are less common.

When we have no spiritual context to carry the erotic enchantment of the archetype and the potential for inner union, it can be projected into many different places. Foremost of these in the West is within romantic relationships, where we fall into a kind of love enchantment. The power of this process can be felt in the intensity of how we see the partner as captivating and irresistible. We get drawn into an intoxication that makes us unable to separate from the partner and that only feels complete when we are in intimate union. We become enthralled in the power of our own projections. The fact that this process of projection is unconscious—and that, even when made conscious, can still enthrall us—is testament to the power of the archetype and its intent. As Jung suggested, what we are unconscious of within ourselves tends to be projected outside, and Animus and Anima are potent examples.

In Buddhism, the idea of attachment is relevant to this experience, but understanding projection throws a subtly different light on the meaning of attachment. Attachment is often defined as "the mind that exaggerates the positive attributes of an object and then seeks to grasp at it." Thus we see attachment at work in our relationship to many objects in our lives, whether it be attachment to food, clothing, places, possessions, values, or anything else. Our exaggeration and fantasies about the quality of an object and our consequent grasping at it takes us away from its reality. The degree to which we exaggerate is often reflected in the degree to which we suffer as a consequence when the actuality of the object becomes apparent to us.

When archetypal projection and the beguilement of Animus or Anima is present, it obscures our capacity to see the actuality of an individual. The power of projection is experienced most noticeably because, as with attachment, we cling to an idealized image and yearn for its concrete presence in the outside world. This attachment brings all manner of hopes and fears, the joy and pain of seemingly finding what we desire, along with the pain of finding ourselves deceived by its elusiveness. In time, the projection weakens so that the real person shows through, resulting in conflict with the ideal. This can bring disappointment and dissatisfaction—even anger and aversion—and the wish to find someone else to embody the divine so we can regain the sense of enchantment.

The potential lure of this experience is depicted time and again in mythological images, and entrancement occurs equally for men and women. The story of Odysseus contains some particularly vivid examples of encounters with the feminine as a powerful deity. On the island of the sorceress Circe, Odysseus needs the help of Hermes in order to foil Circe's power to beguile after the sorceress turns his sailors into pigs. She embodies the capacity of the feminine in men's psyche to totally enthrall and to cause them to regress to basic infantile, animal neediness. Circe, like the Sirens, represents the power of the archetype to draw us into an unconscious relationship. This is the kind of relationship in which we lose the ability to think straight; we become overwhelmed and lose hold of reality. We then fail to recognize that being absorbed in a projection blinds us to the reality of who someone really is.

In our projection of Anima or Animus, we may have been beguiled into a relationship—not in the outer world, but with an inner reality. In the myth of Tristan and Isolde, Tristan falls irretrievably in love with a female figure who is not a real woman. She is like a chimera or a muse. When he meets a real woman who is able to help him back to some semblance of normality, he cannot love and accept her for who she is, even though she loves him. He is pulled so strongly to the romantic image that he chooses to return to imaginal reality and, in so doing, meets his eventual doom.

This story depicts something each of us yearns for—an intimate union with the divine. This search for soul union promises us meaning and fulfillment and points to its spiritual significance. We sense the potential of totality that is only possible through this union, but fail to recognize that this is an inner experience, not an external one. When we seek this in relationships, we will at some point have to face a time when the beguilement fades and the real relationship begins. Those who fail to come to terms with this reality often suffer the endless torment of disappointment and sadness at the loss of the mythical dream soulmate. The myth of Tristan and Isolde is the tragedy of humans who becomes possessed or obsessed by seeking their imaginal idealized fantasies, resulting in the eventual death of conscious volition. This painful journey is a destructive and lonely path. The archetypal quality becomes consuming and ultimately overwhelming, like a *femme fatale*.

The power of romantic love is embedded in the nature of the awakened archetypal qualities. These archetypes are not humanized; they are powerful forces, like gods that have been awakened from the deepest level of the psyche. They have not been integrated into our lives in a way that makes them manageable and conscious. As a result, they have power over us and we are subject to their volition. We see this in the relatively amoral disposition of those enthralled by their power. It can make them willing to destroy relationships, break up marriages, and hurt others badly, all for the sake of their love.

To begin to come to terms with this side of our nature, we need to see the power of these archetypal qualities and relate to them consciously. When there is no religious form that offers a context for integration, the power of these daimons will dominate our relationships. If the Anima and Animus could be placed back in the temple, it would make possible a different way of integrating their power into our lives.

Animus and Anima are known as the *daka* and the *dakini* in Tantra. The only major difference from Jung's scheme is that they are equal components of men and women's psyches. The daka and dakini are the innate potential of the masculine and feminine potencies in us that are at the root of our present experience. Their gradual awakening evolves and transforms us both psychologically and sexually.

The deities that embody the daka and dakini are intended to give a symbolic channel for sexuality and eroticism such that their union becomes an inner experience for each individual. They bring the powerful energies of romantic love back into the experience of meditation as deities, rather than just projected into our relationships. Though Tantra emphasizes the experience of inner union as a means to attain enlightenment, this does not imply that the absence of projection will make our relationships bland or devoid of the excitement of the "in love" experience. The tantric approach honors and validates these archetypes for what they are and cultivates an awareness that sees the partner as the embodiment of daka or dakini. This consciously honors the divine within the sexuality of all men and women.

## THE DAKA

We have no present-day Western cultural rites or rituals associated with the transformation of the instinctual sexuality of the masculine. As a consequence our relationship to the masculine principle, with its raw sexuality, potency, and wildness, is confused and often shadowy. However, there is a growing movement to understand this deep aspect of the male psyche expressed in the form of the wild man, or the Green Man, which is beginning to offer a conscious symbolic acknowledgement of its archetypal significance in men's lives.

When we relate to the primal masculine with greater awareness and understanding, it begins to be harnessed and expressed creatively and healthily. But when there is little awareness of its innate potency, the instinctual masculine is suppressed and unavailable, or becomes brutish, rapacious, and destructive when uncontained. Those who fear these powerful impulses and try to contain or repress them drive masculine instinctuality into the Shadow, where it gains even more power to potentially become overwhelming and destructive. Neither wildly, uncontrollably acting out shadowy male sexuality nor repressing its potency can bring it into a healthy relationship.

A shift has taken place in men's lives, partly as a result of the women's movement, which is causing many men to rethink their relationships to the masculine. Many men now recognize that the old masculine modes need to change and that patriarchal authoritarianism and aggressive, macho, power-oriented behavior is no longer acceptable. Competitive ambition and the quest for status and power so prevalent through the "yuppie" mentality of the eighties did not address this crucial underlying malaise; it merely diverted the phallic masculine through the intellect and the business world. Both men and women have tended to become intellectually phallic, aggressive, and competitive. The deeper aspect of the masculine relating to potency, creativity, and strength in a more instinctual, earthy, embodied sense remains unaddressed. Yet it lives on in the underworld of our culture, emerging or erupting in acts of sexual violence, or brutish stupidity.

Some men have reacted by abandoning this macho behavior, considering it shameful or wrong, and many have become soft, caring, gentle men who have tried to develop their feeling and spiritual sides. However, this is often at the cost of their relationship to the raw instinctual nature of male potency, and tends to leave men weak, ineffectual, and even impotent on some level. Ironically, many women love this caring sensitivity, but yearn for a return of the raw potency and strength of the masculine. The result is confusion, a loss of male identity in many young men, and a lack of role models to show the way.

Our culture has long needed a suitable vehicle to awaken and healthily integrate the deep instinctual masculine. The Christian incompatibility between sexuality and spirituality that pushed instinctuality into the Shadow as the devil's work is partly responsible for its lack. The romantic notion of the noble savage prevalent during the colonial era may have validated some aspects of native life, but this still needed to be "civilized" by Christian dogma to suppress any instinctuality.

The pre-Christian culture that recognized and venerated the nature gods provided some kinds of initiatory experiences for young men. These would have offered rites and rituals to help integrate this instinctual quality, giving a context in which to understand its power and archetypal nature. In Christian culture these spiritual rites and mysteries were cast into the domain of the devil and therefore considered unacceptable. Today we need to return to some rite of transformation that can restore the health of this archetypal force and its vital energy.

The tantric practices associated with the daka offer something of the rites and initiatory processes we need. The deities Heruka Chakrasamvara (fig. 14), Hevajra, and Gyalwa Gyatso—a Higher Tantra aspect of Chenrezig—in particular embody the process of an inner integration of the masculine in union with the feminine. They act in a manner similar to the deities used for transforming the destructive Shadow, giving the power of masculine sexuality a suitable channel for its awakening and elevation to a higher level of consciousness without losing its essential potency.

Heruka Chakrasamvara has many characteristics in common with other nature gods such as Dionysus, Shiva, and Kernunos. His rites help cultivate what we could describe as spiritual intoxication through sexual union and the symbolic ritualistic use of intoxicants. For Shiva, the Hindu god closely associated with Heruka Chakrasamvara, the intoxicant was generally hashish, but also alcohol in certain rituals. Dionysus used wine. Heruka Chakrasamvara also uses alcohol, which is transmuted into a wisdom nectar called *amrita* (Tib. *dutsi*). Heruka Chakrasamvara's rites and rituals aim to generate sublime bliss and emptiness through intoxication. In traditions such as that of Dionysus, the use of wine led to a release of the wild god of madness, but in the rites of practice associated with Heruka Chakrasamvara this is principally symbolic.

Heruka Chakrasamvara as the daka is primarily a sexually potent and erotic aspect of the masculine. Like Shiva and Dionysus, he is associated with many female figures, being a male principle at home with the feminine, unlike the intellectual Apollonic dimension of the masculine world. He is known as a Heruka ("blood drinker") deity because he becomes intoxicated through drinking blood as a symbol of the wisdom of bliss and emptiness associated with the dakini. Heruka Chakrasamvara has tiny fangs that show a connection to the archetypal vampire, and this underworld symbol of sexual power and lust is here given a vehicle for transformation in the daka. As a nature god, his quality is fundamentally phallic. He is symbolized by the vajra (fig. 15), the Buddhist symbol of the phallus, like the Shaivite *lingam*, or the Greek *herm*.

As the foremost daka within the tantric tradition, Heruka Chakrasamvara has a close association with Shiva. Indeed, it is said in the Chakrasamvara Tantra that he was intended to subdue the forces of Shiva and bring them under control. In the Chakrasamvara Tantra,

Shiva represents the wild instinctual masculine in its primordial form, and Heruka Chakrasamvara its potential for transformation.

Buddha recognized it was time to subdue Shiva, whose cult had become increasingly degenerate and unwholesome. Shiva's powerful influence had led to sexual depravity and abuse, intoxicated destruction, and blood lust through human and animal sacrifice in his worship. We can all too often see this influence of the degenerate god, the archetype in its unhealthy aspect, in our Western culture. Heruka Chakrasamvara, as a manifestation of the Buddha, descended into Shiva's mandala to subjugate him. He took on Shiva's characteristics and attributes. His implements and weapons were blessed and purified, as were his ornaments and garments. Heruka Chakrasamvara took Shiva's consorts and awakened them to the wisdom of bliss and emptiness. His places of worship and his followers, the Hindu dakas and dakinis, were also blessed and transformed. The cult had used alcohol and meat sacrifices in ritual worship, and these were transformed and adopted in a ritual form.

Shiva represents the prima materia, the raw instinct to be transformed, and Heruka Chakrasamvara the Subduer is of a similar archetypal nature. However, in the act of subduing, the energies and attributes of the instinct are given a new channel to be transformed and brought onto a higher level of consciousness. Thus the power and qualities are not lost; they are taken into the deity on a higher level and integrated. Hindus would probably not share this view of Shiva. However, if we look at the process symbolically, the tantric Buddhists have created a myth that enables them to integrate what Shiva represents on a level that is more appropriate within Buddhist philosophy.

This is like Christianity adopting many of the attributes of Dionysus and using them in ritual, such as the wine as blood and the wafer as flesh. It is interesting to note that the Shaivite *sadhu*, or practitioner, often lives in charnel grounds. The Buddhist Heruka Chakrasamvara practitioner visualizes him or herself dwelling in charnel grounds. Indeed, many of the rituals performed literally by the earlier cult, such as creating offerings out of pieces of the body, are visualized in the

Buddhist tantras. The inner offering described in Chapter 17 shows how an actual sacrificed material is visualized as symbolically transformed.

In this way the practice of Heruka Chakrasamvara offers a return to the rites and rituals of the nature-god and the potency of the masculine principle. As a daka, we can see him on the three different levels—outer, inner, and secret. On an outer level, the daka is a man who has come to embody the qualities of Heruka Chakrasamvara. The Chakrasamvara Tantra gives masculine potency a channel for transformation, enabling a man to contain and harness this power in a healthy way. Someone who attains this ability has a subtle influence on the energy of the surrounding environment through the power of the deity. The daka's profound connection to the elements in the body opens up a subtle relationship to the natural world. Heruka Chakrasamvara personifies masculine potency in nature.

On an inner level, the daka is the potency of the masculine essences within the body of both men and women. It is described as "white bodhichitta," a subtle element of sperm (possibly testosterone) that abides primarily in the crown chakra, but also passes throughout the body. This essence is called the "spring drop," and is associated with the potency of bulls in spring. This connection to the bull is reminiscent of the many nature god religions both in the East and the West, particularly the brahma bull in Shaivite religion and the Minoan bull. Integrating this potency is a vital part of the daka's relationship to the dakini, in which inner union brings the experience of the deepest level of daka, the secret daka of great bliss. The daka is the bringer of great bliss in union with the wisdom of emptiness. The word *daka* in Sanskrit is "sky-walker" or "sky-goer," which conveys the subtle meaning of daka as one who enacts the dance of emptiness, symbolizing that all phenomena are the play of bliss and emptiness

Thus, the practice of the daka in Highest Yoga Tantra is the cultivation of a spiritual intoxication known as the Wisdom of Great Bliss as the masculine principle is awakened and integrated. This bliss is conjoined with the female principle of wisdom and is experienced pervading the body/mind continuum. Its awakening has a profoundly transformative effect on every aspect of the tantric practitioner's life, leading to a deepening experience of the innate nature of all reality as the wisdom of bliss and emptiness. This is the ecstatic inner union we try to find externally in sexual intimacy with the lover.

## THE DAKINI

The dakini is the tantric aspect of the many facets of Anima and is also understood on the three levels—outer, inner and secret. The outer dakini is a woman who embodies the development of the inner dakini and who has awakened, contained, and transformed the full power of her sexuality.

Western culture has offered little to support a woman's embodiment of the wild, raunchy, passionate side of her nature. It may be given some freedom in adolescence, but our social mores soon begin to demand its civilization, because a male-dominated culture usually fears its power, unpredictability, and wildness.

There has also been a fundamental conflict between Western Christian values and this quality, which has been cast out as unacceptable and antithetical to spirituality. Many women therefore yearn for the opportunity to let this side of themselves out, yet also fear it as dangerous. However, there must be a place in our lives to express this passion and energy, but our culture will continue to have an ambivalence towards the feminine in its entirety without a vehicle for its awakening and transformation. Spirituality will continue to split the feminine into that which is acceptable and pure and that which is wild and too dangerous to include. Patriarchal religions have always feared and condemned the powerful, sensual, and profoundly intuitive nature of the feminine. The Christian attitude towards Lilith, the first Eve, is symptomatic of this fear. She is too disruptive for the spiritual authority of the Christian doctrine to allow in any other role than the serpent that tempts Adam.

Feminine power, wildness, and passion need redemption, and the tantric dakini provides such a vehicle. As an archetypal symbol of the feminine, the dakini brings the fiery wildness and deep instinctuality of the feminine back into the temple. As an aspect of Anima, she is at the heart of our relationship life. The dakini is known as a messenger, the bringer of profound intuitions, wisdom, and insight into the deepest aspects of the psyche.

The dakini is particularly embodied in the deity Vajrayogini (fig. 13), who offers a potent validation of this quality. Her fiery red, dancing form reflects a quality similar to the flamenco dancer—proud, undaunted, powerful, and erotic. She carries a curved knife to cut through the ignorance and stupidity she encounters, and, holding a skullcup of blood, she drinks a blissful nectar of the essence of her feminine power. Across her shoulder is a staff, called a *khatvanga*, symbolizing her integration of the masculine. She is adorned with bone ornaments and a crown of skulls and around her neck she wears a necklace of skulls. She is standing on Shiva and Shakti, demonstrating that she is a transformation of their primordial power onto a higher level. Shakti, the raw power of the feminine, is elevated to the level of *prajna*, or wisdom. As a symbol of transformation, Vajrayogini offers a vital channel for the integration of this powerful female energy. Women who embody this become dakinis. Men who do so awaken to an inner relationship with their dakini energy.

The dakini as a woman living in the world is often described as a messenger because she helps others access particular inner qualities. She takes people across a threshold of awareness to experience a deeper reality and opens them to the richness of the psyche. In the mahasiddha stories of India, it was often an incarnate dakini who initiated the yogi into a tantric practice, as it is she who awakens the quality of inner vision and introduces the deity. Whoever begins to awaken the inner dakini, man or woman, enters the realm of subtle consciousness and the experience of sambhogakaya, the creative, visionary sphere of reality.

The messenger dakini parallels Jung's description of the Anima as the *psychopomp*, or mediator, to the unconscious and its mysteries. She is the bringer of intuitive wisdom, feminine lore, and the language of symbols. She brings the ability to live within the world of symbol and inner vision on an intuitive level that becomes increasingly psychic. The world of conventional appearances is pervaded by a symbolic visionary quality that brings what the Celts called "sight." Awakening the inner dakini has parallels with the Anima as the muse and as the bringer of creative vision and inspiration, the archetype of animation and of the vitality of life itself. A woman who has cultivated this inner vitality will manifest a quality the Celts called "glamour," a powerful presence. The term glamour has unfortunately become misused in modern times. The Celts used this term to describe a woman whose inner power could be felt around her. It was, in part, a protection, but could also be extremely attractive. Many such women would have been instantly viewed in the Christian world as witches and harlots in league with the devil because of their potential power.

Inner dakini also refers to elemental female essence within the body of both men and women. This is known as "red bodhichitta," possibly estrogen, inherited at conception as consciousness enters the conjunction of the sperm and egg. It is shared by women and men. In the Chakrasamvara Tantra, the female element is described as a subtle form of blood that abides primarily within the navel chakra and is able to flow throughout the body. This subtle blood at the navel is known as the *tummo,* or "wrathful female," and is responsible for a particular quality of heat, felt strongly most often at the time of sexual intercourse. It is symbolized as the deity Vajravarahi, or Vajrayogini, whose red body and fiery aura depict the psychic heat at the navel that is generated by her awakening.

Throughout the body, both the male and female elements localize in twenty-four particular places, which, according to the Chakrasamvara Tantra, have specific functions in maintaining our bodily organs. These inner elemental centers correspond to the surrounding land, which gives Tantra a particular significance in relation to nature. In India, and potentially in many places in the West, there are twenty-four corresponding sacred places found in the land that have a subtle elemental relationship to the energy centers in the body. The elemental forces in these outer locations connect with the dakas and dakinis who inhabit this environment, which are also locations associated with Shiva. When a tantric practitioner visits and meditates in these outer places, the energy present enhances the experience of deeper insight. We potentially stand upon a threshold to deeper experience of psychic reality in these locations, the reality of the Pure Land of the Dakinis, Khacho Shing.

Just as we see Anima as the vitalizing quality of life and nature, so too the inner dakini relates to nature. As the dakini, or daka, quality awakens, an inner relationship to the elemental energies of the natural world also awakens. There are dakinis with particular qualities of the earth, water, fire, and air elements.

The dakini inhabits a threshold world where the psyche and nature are inextricably interwoven and where inner and outer are permeable. This world is imbued with the animism Jung spoke of in his notion of *participation mystique*, the pre-conscious dreamtime world which fuses psyche and nature without separation. With the dakini, we consciously reenter Khacho Shing, the Pure Land of the Dakinis, and its richness of insight and imagery are intuitively understood. An intimate relationship with the elemental energies of the surrounding land is experienced through body feeling and intuitive sight.

Here we enter the realm of sambhogakaya as the expression of pure energy and creative vision. The dakinis or dakas who inhabit this realm are messengers of a different order. They may initiate meditators through inner vision, manifesting in bodies of pure light to introduce a new level of perception. The dakini here is able to guide those ready to pass through a gateway into a quality of awareness where the natural world and the psyche are no longer split apart or in duality. When considered in this way, the dakini is reminiscent of the Fairy in the Celtic world, a changeling who was able to cross from one level of reality to another.

Perhaps the most profound sense of the dakini as a messenger is in relation to the insight of emptiness. Here she becomes a threshold dweller between relative and absolute, form and emptiness. In his descriptions of Anima, Jung tried to convey her deceptive, ephemeral quality. When men try to pin her down or cling to her, she shape-shifts. She is often symbolized by the butterfly and is experienced that way by all men who try to possess the woman they have fallen in love with. She slips away and will not be held. Grasping at her ephemeral, elusive nature, as with a woman embodying her glamour, can be fatal. When a man continues to cling to and try to solidify and possess this quality, he is bound to suffer, because he fails to recognize that what he grasps is an illusion created by his own projection. If he can let go and, at the moment she slips out of his grasp, dance with her instead of grasping, he can experience her differently.

Many artists and photographers try to capture the beauty of an Anima image, whether it is the subtle shades and tones of nature, or a shimmer of light on water. However, few succeed in a way that does not freeze this ephemeral beauty into something static and dead. In his paintings of Giverny, I feel Monet has managed to create a sense of the elusive subtlety of light in nature. This draws the observer deeper without becoming caught in solidifying form. In this way, Anima can draw us deeper into her nature to the point where the form we saw as solid softens and dissolves until there is nothing to hold onto.

The dakini attracts us by her fascination and vitality. Men becoming aroused by the dakini's glamour may seek to grasp at and hold her to them. But in that moment she shifts; she will not be clung to as something inherently solid and static. This shift can bring the sudden recognition that there is nothing solid to grasp; she is empty of solid substantiality, fleeting, and elusive, which leads to a deeper awareness of her empty nature. She is the dance or play of emptiness, like the play of light rippling on the surface of water. Her appearance is manifest, yet illusory. When this is recognized, it causes the obsessive, passionate grasping to burst open. We are left in space; open, empty, and free to dance the same blissful dance.

Like the daka, the term "dakini" is often translated as "sky-dancer" to demonstrate that her nature is the dance of emptiness. This is the profound quality of both daka and dakini. They are personifications of the play of phenomena in the sphere of bliss and emptiness. They symbolize the threshold of awareness where appearance and emptiness are no longer separable. Phenomena are emptiness emerging momentarily into relative form and, in the same instant, being illusory and transient, like writing upon water. Thus the outer dakini is a messenger that leads to an experience of the "secret" or "suchness" dakini, which is the wisdom of emptiness itself.

When this understanding awakens through the practice of Tantra, our relationships take on a subtly different quality. They loosen and open, becoming freer and more vital, rather than fixing and solidifying our projections. In Tantra, the magic of the dakini is not withdrawn as mere projection, but is enacted consciously, with an awareness of its illusory nature. This frees our disposition to grasp. Rather than destroying the very vitality and beauty that is so intoxicating, it is allowed to live freely. Fear of losing the person who embodies this daka or dakini quality causes us to cling and crush the life out of them, like Madam Butterfly in Puccini's opera, trapped and sentenced to a slow death.

When we value openly the daka or dakini in our partners, they are free to express fully who they are and live their creative vitality to the full. If we can retain this recognition while at the same time seeing the human quality, we have brought together two worlds. We cultivate a deep honoring of the daka and dakini nature within our partner and ourselves, enabling it to emerge within the vessel of the human individual. Any time we grasp at this vitality and power, attempting to possess it or pin it down, we destroy it. But so long as we value its empty illusory nature, we dance freely in our relationships and do not bind each other.

Thus, in the dakini, we discover a channel for awakening and embodying the depth of the feminine in the psyche, her intuitive vision and wisdom, as well as her wild sexual vitality. As with the daka, placing this archetypal quality back into the temple provides a context in which to honor her rather than reject her, or banish her to the Shadow through fear. Romantic love has provided a place where she can live, but the difficulties this so often brings are extremely painful. In the practice of Highest Yoga Tantra, Anima as the dakini lives and stands in her full power as a deity in her own right. The feminine remains sacred and fully awakened in all her passion and wisdom without being overshadowed or denigrated by the masculine. Men must then learn to respond to her without fear or grasping.

*Figure 13. Vajrayogini*

# PART IV
## *The Fruit*

*Figure 14. Heruka Chakrasamvara*

# *The Completion Stage* 17

❖❖ ─────────────────────────────────────

.

THERE IS a powerful natural magnetism between masculine form and female emptiness that draws the two irresistibly into union. The spacious openness of the feminine yearns to receive the solid form of the masculine, which in turn longs to be embraced and received by the receptive spaciousness of the feminine. Emptiness yearns for form, form yearns for emptiness. Every artist or musician recognizes the subtle balance and interplay of form and space as crucial to the creative process. The universality of this move to union between masculine and feminine is seen in virtually every sphere of life, within nature, science, the creative arts, and in relationships. This instinctual urge is irresistibly experienced in relationships time and again, yet is often fraught with struggle and confusion. The feminine may wish to be held in form but not trapped and bound by its constraints. The masculine longs to hold the vitality and beauty of the feminine, but is threatened by its elusive unpredictability. Nevertheless, the union of masculine and feminine is central to much of life, both inwardly and outwardly.

The *conjunctio*, as Jung called this union, is equally central to the completion stage of Tantra, where the male and female aspects of the meditator are brought into union on an inner level.

In the generation stage, the union of male and female, daka and dakini, is energetically and psychologically developed through the symbolic power of the deity. Deities such as Heruka Chakrasamvara or Vajrayogini present a channel for the integration and transformation of these aspects of our nature. In the completion stage, this union is cultivated directly within the elements and energies of the body through specific yogic practices. The meditator then begins to awaken one of the most profound aspects of the alchemical process of Tantra. The union of the masculine and feminine elements in the body leads to a kind of psychological death, a process of cleansing and transformation that totally and radically changes the inner reality of the individual. The meditator as he or she was dies, and a new relationship to reality dawns. In this completion stage, there is no return to narrow, ego-centered reality.

The completion stage brings us into the greatest mystery of the tantric path. The term "mystery" has been applied to the esoteric aspect of most of the great religious traditions. Because of its esoteric nature, the completion stage has also been couched in language that is poetic and often obscure. The tantric practitioner enters the boundaries of secrecy in order to understand its deeper meaning. Explanation is part of an oral tradition passed from teacher to disciple. The poetic, metaphorical language of the completion stage is found in songs and chants that express the erotic nature of the relationship between the daka and dakini. These verses convey a very different sense of a process unfolding than the rather scientific, almost clinical descriptions given in tantric commentaries. Both languages are nevertheless equally significant in their description of the inner process.

Both the Hindu and Buddhist tantric traditions describe the erotic play and eventual union of the male and female deities. In Hinduism, the primary deities that express this erotic union are Shiva and Shakti, and in Buddhism they are Heruka Chakrasamvara and Vajravarahi (Vajrayogini). These are not the only deities in Buddhism to personify this quality, but they play a particularly important role.

The stirring of these inner forces is most beautifully described in the *Song of the Spring Queen*, verses said to have been composed by dakinis. Here the sexual play between the dakini Vajravarahi and the daka Heruka is described.

Through inspiring the mind of great bliss
And the moving dance of their bodies,
There arises the play of great bliss
Within the lotus of the consort.
This bliss we offer to you,
Multitudes of powerful Yoginis.

Great bliss, which is endowed
With countless liberating qualities,
Without which freedom cannot be gained,
Though one endures great austerity;
That sublime bliss so abides within
The center of the supreme lotus.

Just as a lotus born out of mud,
Great bliss, though evolving from desire,
Is unsullied by its defilements,
Arising immaculately pure.
May samsara's bonds be swiftly loosed
By your lotus bliss, great Yoginis.

Just as swarming bees will so draw forth
The purest nectar of fragrant flowers,
May we too be fully satisfied
By the captivating nectars of
The lotus in full maturity,
Possessing six refined qualities.[21]

These verses describe the beauty and power of the dakini and her
capacity to invoke the realization of the mind of great bliss. The lotus
as a metaphor for the vagina is seen as the most profound, wonderful,
and sacred mystery. The symbolism of the vajra (fig. 15) as the male
phallus placed within the lotus echoes the *lingam* and *yoni* of the Hindu
Shaivite tradition. This sacred union of vajra and lotus leads to the

awakening of the ecstatic quality of wisdom unified with bliss. The Seventh Dalai Lama describes this union in the *Songs of Spiritual Change*:

The tip of the vajra is placed firmly in the lotus
And mind as the letter HUM is brought into the central channel;
One drinks and drinks the essence of nectars
and goes mad with innate joy unmoving...

Mind fixed on the bliss and mudra of the consort,
A rain of innate joy pours down.
Again and again seducing the beautiful one,
Symbol of the mind embracing reality itself,
One melts into the sphere of spontaneous ecstasy.[22]

The arousal of the red dakini Vajravarahi as the tip of the vajra (the penis) is placed within the lotus (the vagina) is the awakening of the fire of tummo in the navel chakra. As the powerful heat of her passion rises, she reaches up towards the daka Heruka Chakrasamvara to draw him into her embrace. Heruka Chakrasamvara is the white element at the crown, who, like the bull of heaven, or the spring seed, melts and descends into the goddess. The union is aroused and consummated within the central channel. The meditator, man or woman, uses this blissful quality of awareness to open fully to the nature of emptiness. This transforms the play of the daka and dakini into the ecstatic union of bliss and emptiness experienced within the body in the central channel.

The language of erotic love and sexual play used in the completion stage is an expression of the most sacred part of the path. In Tantra, this erotic imagery is not an expression of an external sexual act, but an inner symbolism. However, to understand the inner meaning and the actual processes involved in the completion stage, we need a deeper explanation of the subtle energy body and the channel, or nerve, system. In the completion stage, the body is seen as the alchemical vessel within which a powerful transformation takes place through the generation of bliss.

## THE CULTIVATION OF BLISS

Westerners involved in Buddhism are often confused by the emphasis on cultivating bliss in tantric practice, though there is a profound basis for it. It can easily be misunderstood, which leads many people to dismiss Tantra as decadent and degenerate. Others are drawn to the exotic nature of the tantric approach to sexuality, perhaps with some justification. Our Western lack of understanding of sexual experience as a deep inner process leaves us little knowledge of its potential, and a Christian background often blocks us from seeing how our sexual energy is valid within the spiritual path.

We are often seeking an experience of union in our intimate relationships that can be expressed on many different levels, whether we are conscious of it or not. Some people are searching for an experience of wholeness or completion; others yearn for a union that will bring a loss of self, a dissolving and merging with another. For others it may be the quest for an opening to something ecstatic and transcendent. This searching may be clouded by all manner of psychological needs and expectations that surface over time and hinder the experience of union. When problems occur in our relationships, their roots often lie more in our childhood pathology relating to parental influences than in the innate qualities of the archetypal and elemental masculine and feminine. However, to uncover and free the innate potential of the daka and dakini within each of us, it may be necessary to address the layers that obscure their awakening.

Our relationships are not considered an obstacle to spiritual growth in Tantra, if they are lived with awareness and openness. There are Buddhist traditions and organizations that hold a relatively puritanical position, believing relationships to be a hindrance to spirituality. Segregating the sexes, celibacy, and the avoidance of any sexual contact may be suitable for some people at certain periods of their lives, but can lead to a deepening of the Shadow by repression and denial. No such abstinence is prescribed in Tantra, except for celibate monks and nuns. It is understood that the energy of sexuality is an intrinsic part of us and must be acknowledged and transformed if it is not to become unhealthy. This is not to imply it must always be transformed through the sexual act itself; indeed, one of the most significant aspects of Tantra is its capacity to transform sexuality through meditation practice.

Nevertheless, the experience of sexual union between lovers bears much of the innate quality for union that is taken to its most refined level in the completion stage. We can begin to recognize the nature of the qualities of the daka and dakini through our relationships. Sexual experience can deepen as these qualities are allowed to awaken and live together more consciously, while the fear and grasping that limits and blocks sexual energy will diminish.

The disposition to grasp is the main reason for views on sexual abstinence. However, it is not our sexuality that is the problem, but the habit of grasping which leads to suffering. While teaching on the Vajrayogini Tantra, Lama Thubten Yeshe once said, "How much bliss can we take without turning it into suffering?" He was trying to convey how hard it is for us to experience pleasure in a way that does not turn it into an obsessive, narrow grasping, leading to endless pain and dissatisfaction. It is not easy to learn how to enjoy pleasure in a genuine, open, and nongrasping way. A dogmatic emphasis on abandoning craving and grasping can often lead to a fear of enjoyment for many people who become involved in Buddhist practice. This puritanical tightness then becomes just another form of attachment and suffering.

This is not the tantric approach, which sees the value and power of pleasurable sensory and sexual experience as a vehicle for the development of bliss. When we are unable to experience bliss without grasping, it becomes limited, ordinary excitement leading to eventual disappointment and suffering. When the blissful energy of our sensuality and sexuality is allowed to arise without grasping, its nature is able to transform. Learning to enjoy ourselves requires great skill and awareness from a tantric perspective, and the capacity to be truly open comes particularly through the awareness of emptiness gained through Mahamudra.

There is great emphasis in tantric practice on sensory experience in general, not just on the bliss generated through sexual energy. The five senses are the doorway through which we experience bliss, and these are used in a very subtle and sophisticated way in Tantra. Much of the visualized offering and the actual ritualized material offering and feasting is partly a recognition of the potentially blissful nature of our sensory experience. The idea is to enjoy the richness and beauty of the sensory world as an offering that gives rise to bliss, not to fear it. Indeed, all appearances are seen as having the nature of bliss and emptiness and thus are able to arouse great bliss.

The name of the deity Chakrasamvara means "the wheel (*chakra*) of all phenomena are in the nature of bliss (*samvara*)." Similarly, the most common symbol in Tantra, the *vajra*, means the inseparability of bliss and emptiness that is the essential nature of all reality. Once we recognize this, there is no obstruction to our potential to experience bliss with every sensory experience.

In some Buddhist views the world around is seen as samsara, the cause of suffering, and is therefore to be renounced. In Tantra, no such literal rejection is intended. The key is to recognize that once we are able to live with a more spacious, open view of reality, understanding its empty nature, we can see all phenomena in a new way. The world then becomes the play of bliss and emptiness.

In tantric deity practices, great emphasis is given to the generation of bliss within the nervous system through extensive visualized offerings, as well as the experience of our innate sexual energy. The intention is to recognize the empty, illusory, yet blissful nature of these experiences, remaining open and free of grasping.

Gradual control of sexual energy in the body is possible through meditation. By developing tummo practice, our sexual energy can be used in a profound way that does not dissipate through conventional orgasm, nor does it become a cause of suffering. Contrary, however, to some misconceptions, the practice of Tantra does not entail an external sexual act to attain the control and transformation of sexual energy. Once sexual energy is contained in this way, however, our normal sexual experience need not be seen as an obstacle on our spiritual path, as it is often feared to be.

It is important not to be under any misconceptions about the potential of mastering the energy in the body. From a Buddhist point of view, those who become interested in the yogic practices of Tantra because they wish for an exotic sexual experience are missing the point. A clear motivation for developing these practices is essential. The completion stage processes that cultivate and refine sexual energy have only one purpose; to generate a subtle awareness known as "the clear light mind of great bliss" in order to attain the wisdom of dharmakaya for the welfare of all sentient beings.

The practices that centralize and dissolve the energy into the central channel and that lead to the clear light of bliss are by no means easy. Only with skillful meditation will the depth of subtlety of this clear light mind be awakened. This pure, inseparably united bliss and emptiness is the ultimate aim of the completion stage practice of union, where bliss is symbolized by the daka Heruka Chakrasamvara and emptiness by the dakini Vajrayogini.

## THE SUBTLE NERVOUS SYSTEM

The actual practice of the completion stage requires a detailed understanding of the workings of a subtle energy system that pervades the body. Detailed instruction on this complex aspect of practice depends upon a particular tantra and is usually given by the teacher as secret oral teachings. We have already examined the nature of subtle energy-winds and the existence of elemental essences, or bodhichittas. To bring these together we need to consider a map of the body, which includes the channels (Skt. *nadi*) and chakras through which these energy-winds and elements flow.

I am conscious that within the world of Western empirical thinking there is as yet little proof of the reality of a subtle nervous system. Although it is possible to experience this nervous system subjectively, there is no existing empirical method of measurement. Even so, for many hundreds of years the East has been able to use the knowledge of this subtle nervous system powerfully and effectively in healing and spiritual practice. It is important to remember that this is the map used in Buddhist Tantra, not Hindu Tantra.

The heart chakra is said to be the first chakra that emerges in the fertilized egg. From here the *shushuma,* or central channel, develops, followed gradually by all the other chakras that exist along its length. The shushuma begins at the point of the brow, curves up towards the crown and then passes down a little in front of the length of the spine. It splits in two at a point about four or five finger-widths below the navel; part goes to the anus and part to the sexual organ—the clitoris, or the tip of the penis.

The chakras, or "channel wheels," as they are sometimes called, are like conjunctions of channels that flow out into the rest of the body and carry the energy-winds. The central channel is the carrier of the wisdom energy, the subtlest level of energy-wind, and the extremely subtle mind associated with it. The relationship between the central channel and the outer channels is such that, for most of us, access to the subtle energy-winds is largely obstructed or closed. This is usually experienced as an emotional block or a region of pain that has created a disjuncture between the outer channels and the shushuma. When this blockage is addressed it is then often experienced as some level of pain or distress located in the region of the chakra.

There is an increasing interest in working with the energetic system of the chakras in a therapeutic context. When we do so it becomes immediately evident that we can each experience them in totally different ways. Some chakras are more open than others, some are more or less painful or healthy.

The presence of two lateral or side channels that pass in close proximity to the central channel is partly why the chakras are closed. They are called the *ida* and *pingala,* and they carry more gross energy-winds. These channels begin at the nostrils and also curve up to the crown, then descend either side of the shushuma to the lower chakra. The energy-winds that pass through these lateral channels are often disturbed by sufficiently powerful emotions to cause constrictions at the chakras, which obstruct energy-wind flow into the central channel. This obstruction is often visualized as the side channels twisting around the central channel, thereby creating constricting knots. This is, however, a somewhat literal way of considering this constriction.

There are five primary types of energy-wind considered in Buddhist Tantra that are located specifically in the chakras. Therefore, there are also five primary chakras; they are located at the crown, throat, heart, navel, and what is called "the secret place," about five finger-widths below the navel. This latter is seen as the base chakra. The solar plexus is not considered in this system. The only other chakra significant in certain practices is located at the brow, which some people call the "third eye."

In the lower chakra, the energy-wind is associated with the release of feces, sperm, urine, and gas. It is called the "downward-voiding wind," and is connected to the earth element. The navel is the seat of the "equal-place wind" associated with the air element, and this wind is closely associated with the heat generated in the process of digestion. It is also associated with the generation of *tummo*, or psychic heat.

At the heart is the "life-supporting wind," which is connected to the water element and carries the extremely subtle quality of the mind, the mind of clear light. This wind enters simultaneously as consciousness enters the fertilized egg at conception. At the throat is the "upward-moving" or "voiding wind" associated with expression through the throat and mouth, related to the fire element. Although the crown is seen as the seat of the "pervasive wind," in actuality this energy-wind pervades the entire body and affects motility.

Channels radiate out throughout the entire body from these chakras, carrying the energy-winds to the rest of the body. It is often said there are eighty-four thousand channels in the body, although this is a euphemism for a vast number.

There are two other important aspects of this subtle nervous system to take into account. When we are born into this body we inherit an elemental essence called a *tigle*, or "drop," part of which is male and part female. This is usually described as a subtle quality of blood known as "red bodhichitta" forming the female element and a subtle quality of sperm known as "white bodhichitta" forming the male element. While this flows through the body and becomes localized in specific parts of the body, it originates from the heart chakra. In the fully formed human body, the red drop then abides primarily in the navel and the white drop in the crown.

It is interesting to note that, according to Tantra, it is only the human form with its particular nervous system that can practice Tantra. The tantric worldview considers there are many other realms of existence into which we could be born, but in which we would not have such a nervous system and therefore would not be able to make use of such practices.

## THE COMPLETION STAGE ALCHEMY

Practice in the completion stage is oriented primarily towards the purification and transformation of the energy body. In the generation stage we explore an alchemical process that channels energy through symbolic expression. In the completion stage, a deeper level of transformation occurs when the energy is related to directly through yogic techniques. The physical body now acts as a vessel within which this takes place.

The actual process of transformation that occurs in the completion stage is symbolized within a generation stage practice called the "inner offering" (fig. 5). In the generation stage, the inner offering is performed as a symbolic ritual for the creation of an elixir to bless and heal the nervous system. However, the actual meaning of the inner offering relates directly to the body as a vessel within which a transformation takes place during the completion stage. As a symbolic visualization it embodies the essence of Buddhist alchemy. Although the details of this offering are somewhat obscure and require much interpretation, it is interesting to look at this ritual to see the significance of the completion stage as an alchemical process.

The visualization begins by imagining a skullcup supported by a tripod of three human heads. Beneath them arises a triangular, red fire mandala, and beneath this arises a blue, bow-shaped wind mandala. Within the skullcup arise five kinds of meat, visualized as five animals, and five liquids, or nectars.

The wind element is then imagined to blow, and the fire element blazes and boils the substances within the skullcup. The substances melt and merge, transforming at first into a liquid the color of mercury. In space above the skullcup arise the three seed syllables OM, AH, and HUM, symbolizing the purified aspect of body, speech, and mind of the Buddhas. One after the other they descend and dissolve into the liquid, which becomes golden nectar, with the properties of an inexhaustible healing elixir.

This visualization can be viewed as a symbolic, sacrificial offering of the meditator's own body together with psychological attributes symbolized by the various substances. In India, Shaivite yogis practice a similar ritual performed in a cremation ground during which they actually use pieces of human corpses to represent these substances. They perform this as a ritual fire offering, where the external fire represents inner processes. It is considered one of the most sacred aspects of the Shaivite path to perform this ritual using external substances as a vehicle to transform the inner energies by the power of meditation. Buddhist tantric practice may have had similar origins, but has been developed into a principally visualized ritual. The practitioner even visualizes him or herself meditating within a cremation ground.

The wind and fire that heat the vessel and begin the alchemical process represent the ignition of the psychic heat, or tummo, that abides in the navel chakra. This visualization is therefore symbolic of a process that actually takes place within the body. The substances symbolize the physical and mental energies being transformed into their enlightened natures. The five meats symbolize the female aspect of the five elements, and the nectars symbolize the five male attributes of the five aggregates. These are transformed into their purified aspect as the five Buddha attributes, called the Five Dhyani Buddhas, and their five elemental wisdom consorts.

In the generation stage, a meditator performs the inner offering by creating this visualization each day. This is done using an actual liquid containing special herbal substances that represent the five meats and nectars. The meditator then takes a very small amount of this nectar each day, visualizing that it is healing and blessing the nervous system in preparation for the completion stage.

## COMPLETION STAGE MAHAMUDRA

The visualization of the inner offering is a metaphor for an alchemical process in the completion stage that gradually unfolds in the body during meditation. As the name "completion" or "fruition stage" implies, this is the final process a practitioner goes through to accomplish the state of buddhahood. Some Tibetan teachers consider any exploration of the completion stage to be both impossible and inappropriate until a meditator has achieved the generation stage. However, teachers such as the Dalai Lama say that to have even a small intellectual comprehension of this process is like discovering a priceless jewel. Even if we are unable to make use of it at this time, it strengthens our faith in the value and potential of our human condition. Many teachers also consider certain aspects of the completion stage extremely helpful if practiced earlier in the tantric path to help meditation to develop. Mahamudra is an example of this.

Understanding the completion stage can also be important because practitioners often find things happening in their meditation practices that can only be made sense of when placed in the context of the processes of the completion stage.

A completion stage meditator spends considerable time purifying and cleansing the flow of energy-winds in the body. This facilitates the entry of energy-winds through the navel chakra and into the central channel by means of tummo, or inner fire practice. This purification also ensures that the processes that follow will be less problematic. For some people, the evolution of the completion stage is spontaneous because the energy-winds naturally draw into the central channel. Most, however, need to follow specific yogic practices skillfully. Many physical exercises similar to yoga are used in the completion stage to help free the flow of energy through the body. Some of these exercises can be found in the Six Yogas of Naropa teachings and in the practice of *kum nye*.

The completion stage refinements of the energy-winds naturally evolve from what was begun within the generation stage. The specific purification and accumulation processes of the generation stage are therefore a necessary preliminary to prepare the ground for what happens later. If a practitioner fails to prepare the nervous system, or if the practitioner's general psychological maturity is in question, there is a danger that the effects of the completion stage will be too dramatic or bewildering to integrate. It can be devastating when practitioners of basic meditations such as Mahamudra or Vipashyana experience sudden awakenings of the nervous system. If the kundalini rises, to use a Hindu expression, the effect can be overwhelming, possibly leading to a period of psychosis that is extremely hard to heal.

The generation stage processes are intended to prepare the meditator psychologically and energetically for what develops in the completion stage. The transformation that occurs through the deity practice of the generation stage blesses and enriches the vitality of the nervous system and aids purification. In particular, it prepares the meditator for the energy-winds to enter the central channel, usually through the navel chakra. This, then, facilitates ignition of tummo. Tummo practice is intended to awaken a quality of bliss in the elements in the central channel, similar to the awakening of kundalini. Essentially, this is arousal of the sexual energy in the body, but within the central channel as an inner union of elements. This sexual energy does not require an actual sexual act, even though the inner experience is very similar. Nonetheless, it is this aspect of Tantra that has been accentuated and popularized as a means of heightened sexual experience.

An experience similar to orgasm is felt through the arousal of tummo, or red bodhichitta, at the navel and the melting of the white drop, or white bodhichitta, at the crown. The principal difference is that no fluids leave the body; they are retained and held in the central channel. Learning to retain these elements so that they dissolve within the central channel requires much practice and control on a subtle level. Tibetans often joke about so-called high yogis who engage in sexual practices with consorts, yet are surrounded by children because they could not hold their semen.

There is a point in the completion stage where the sexual act can be helpful in order to bring certain energy-winds into the central channel. At such time, some meditators, men or women, may take a consort to develop this experience. Traditionally this was seldom made public and, within monasteries, was out of the question because of celibacy vows. Lamas not living within monastic vows who live with partners as wives have no obstacles to engaging in this aspect of practice.

Cultivating the heat of tummo is achieved through a specific meditation practice that does not require the sexual act. A small red syllable, or symbol, is visualized in the navel chakra, and, by a process known as "vase breathing," this syllable is "ignited." In vase breathing, the breath is held and slightly compressed by gently tightening and lifting the perineum and gently pressing down from the abdomen. This brings energy-winds into the central channel through the navel chakra to ignite the tummo. The heat this generates is at first held and then allowed to rise through the central channel to the crown. The white drop at the crown begins to melt and flow down through the central channel, awakening a powerful experience of bliss as it descends.

With practice the energy-winds are increasingly drawn into the central channel and eventually the heart chakra. As this happens, the mind in meditation becomes more and more subtle and the quality of bliss more stable. Eventually these energy-winds abide and dissolve in the heart chakra, giving rise to a quality of mind that is considered its most refined and subtle state, the mind known as "the clear of bliss."

This clear light of bliss arises following a series of inner signs as the energy-winds dissolve. These signs are similar to those that occur at the time of death, when the energy-winds absorb into the heart chakra prior to consciousness leaving the body. When this mind of clear light dawns as an extremely subtle quality of awareness, the practitioner meditates upon emptiness in the manner of Mahamudra, recognizing the innate clarity and emptiness of the mind. The duality that distinguishes mind from appearances, discriminating subjective mind and objective forms, disappears. This mind is known in Tantra as the "causal mind" and is considered to be the ground of being, the basis of all relative appearances within the individual's reality. All appearances arise from this causal clear light mind and are empty of independent, inherent substantiality. This mind is described as primordially pure, devoid of any inherent existence and free of duality.

In completion stage Mahamudra, therefore, the practitioner finally brings together the experience of the clear light of bliss generated by the tummo practice with the wisdom of emptiness or nonduality. He or she remains in a quality of pure nondual presence, without involvement in appearances that cause the mind to discriminate form and hold it to be inherently existent. The meditator experiences the first taste of dharmakaya as clear light awareness dissolves into nonduality like a clear sky, or a drop of water dissolving into the ocean. Once this experience arises, buddhahood, it is said, is possible within this lifetime, and practitioners with this quality of awareness can, within their present bodies, complete the final stages of unification.

Having awakened dharmakaya through the experience of clear light, a meditator has shifted awareness to the quality of nondual presence from which all relative appearances arise. For a tantric practitioner, this is the empty ground from which the purified energy-wind is able to manifest in the aspect of countless symbolic forms. These are the deities that embody the archetypal activities of a Buddha. The subtle energy-wind body emerging from dharmakaya then takes on the aspect of a deity. Although only perceptible by those who have the capacity to witness such forms, this play of emptiness nevertheless carries with it great power and dynamism for creative activity. The energy body and the deity are now identical. In passing through clear light dharmakaya, this subtle energy-wind body has been cleansed of all impurities and subtle defilements so that it becomes the indestructible "vajra body," or sambhogakaya, of a Buddha.

According to biographies of great yogis and yoginis in India and Tibet, the final stages of this journey are accompanied by all manner of miraculous and auspicious signs. Many stories tell of colored clouds, rainbows, storms, visions of symbols and deities in space, and the sounds of music and mantra filling the atmosphere. These stories suggest the extraordinary effect of a Buddha's power on the surrounding environment. As Westerners it may be difficult to conceive of the qualities and capacities of a Buddha's eventual enlightened state.

## THE NATURE OF ENLIGHTENMENT

The term "enlightenment" has become somewhat overused and can lead to much misunderstanding. Enlightenment in Buddhism has a very specific meaning, which can be seen in two different ways that are often confused—even in Buddhist circles. One definition of enlightenment is an *enlightened experience*, the experience of someone who gains a sudden realization of shunyata, the experience of emptiness within meditation. The veil of ignorance has been cleared; the wisdom eye has been opened. From one perspective, this person may be seen as enlightened. The difficulty is that this experience may or may not be retained over time. One of my retreat teachers, Gen Jampa Wangdu, once said, "Realizing emptiness is not difficult; the difficulty is maintaining this awareness." Once this awareness is attained it profoundly shifts our experience of reality, but it requires the development of samadhi, or tranquil abiding, to stabilize its presence. This experience is what could be called "the truth of the path," but it is not a final stage, as some may think. It is nevertheless a radically altered state of awareness.

Gradually developing an awareness of emptiness and nonduality frees the meditator from the influence of dualistic habits born out of grasping at identity. This cleansing of dualistic habits eventually leads to a point of cessation or completion, which in some Buddhist schools is the state of an *arhat*, one who has become liberated from the cycle of existence through purifying all potential for rebirth that arises from ego grasping and karma.

In the Mahayana and Vajrayana, or tantric, traditions, the state of completion is different. Buddhahood is considered a state in which all obstructions to omniscience are eradicated, and relative and absolute truths are unified. Buddhahood as a state of enlightenment is considerably more than a realization on the path. The Tibetan term *sangye* (Skt. *buddha*) refers to two qualities. The first is a state of awareness that is totally cleansed of all dualistic imperfection. The second is an awareness that has totally opened to all reality.

A Buddha, by virtue of the extraordinary capacity to unify two states of awareness—one of relative truth and one of ultimate nature—stands in a unique position. While retaining the innate awareness of dharmakaya, a Buddha's sambhogakaya can constantly incarnate in the world for the welfare of sentient beings. Thus, a Buddha, out of compassion for the welfare of sentient beings, will constantly return to embodied forms called *nirmanakaya* (Tib. *tulku*). When we are open to this capacity to manifest, we will, if we have faith and devotion, receive the blessings of the Buddhas. Like the sun always ready to radiate warmth and light whenever the clouds part, so, too, when our hearts and minds are clear and open, the inspiration of the Buddhas will manifest in our lives.

One of the ways it is said the Buddhas manifest is in the presence of the guru, where "guru" can mean any situation that acts to awaken us. In particular, this refers to spiritual guides who can lead us on our journey. We may not find this easy to consider; however, of all the times when a guide is necessary, the completion stage is one of the most critical. Working with the energy-wind body is subtle and tricky and needs the presence of someone who can recognize what is happening and knows where next to move. Particularly important is recognizing whether the meditator is ready to embark upon this process; if problems arise, it is because the preparations were not properly laid down earlier.

*Figure 15. The Vajra*

✦✦ _____

HAVING TAKEN the exploration of Tantra into rarefied and esoteric regions, we will now shift direction and return to its relevance in daily life. To begin with, we can consider ourselves as living
within the mandala, but understanding the significance of this is not
easy. The most familiar expression of the mandala is the highly deco-
rative, symbolic, symmetrical landscape, either painted or created in
sand, in which the deity abides (fig. 16). However, the psychological
meaning of the mandala is somewhat disguised by these elaborate
visual forms, and even the two-dimensional images in thangkas remain
obscure to the uninitiated.

Jung recognized the mandala as a universal image of wholeness and
a fundamental image of the Self that appears in most cultures in many
different forms. He became increasingly interested in the appearance
of mandalas as expressions of psychological wholeness as he observed
them in the artwork and dreams of his patients. He felt that there was
much to be discovered about their significance. Perhaps one of his
gifts to the West was to introduce this important principle, which has
had a significant effect on the Western understanding of the psyche.

The tantric tradition has taken the mandala form to probably its
most intricate level of complexity. Mandala, or, in Tibetan, *kyilkhor*,
means "center-surround," which implies a self-contained environment
with a focus or pivot which acts as its central axis. The realm within the
circle has the nature of a whole or complete system without interference from outside. The circle defines a clear boundary between what
is within and anything outside.

During an initiation into Higher Tantra, a vajra master, the presiding lama, leads the disciple into a mandala and opens the eye of insight into its details and meaning. This is performed ritually by removing a blindfold that has been worn over the third eye, so to speak, while the disciple has been prepared for entry. On entering the mandala, the vajra master describes and explains the symbolic world like a tour guide leading a group around a palace. But to understand the principle of the mandala requires more than simply being told the meanings of the various aspects of the visualized form.

The mandala has important psychological implications as a symbol of transformation and, from a Buddhist viewpoint, encompasses the totality of an individual's reality. This includes the entire phenomenal world experienced through the five senses and mental consciousness. Each of us lives within—or, we could say, *as*—a mandala, which encompasses our entire worldview. From a tantric viewpoint, this mandala of appearances arises or manifests from the causal mind or the clear light mind. When we are unaware that our relative world arises in this way, we believe it to be solid and inherently existent, but when we recognize its momentary, fleeting nature, its lack of inherent existence begins to be understood. This does not imply the relative world does not exist—merely that it is fluid, transitory, and illusory, like a dream, a mirage, or a rainbow.

It is therefore crucial to recognize that the mandala is a process unfolding, not just a structure of the psyche. Quoting Goethe's *Faust*, Jung wrote, "Only gradually did I discover what the mandala really is: 'Formation, Transformation, Eternal Mind's eternal recreation.'"

When we recognize that the mandala represents our entire experience arising moment by moment, we can develop the capacity to find a state of wholeness within each moment. We center ourselves, yet are constantly in a process of transformation and recreation. In this sense the mandala is not static, but is in constant flux. When we allow this flux and are in tune with it, whatever arises in our reality is experienced fully and allowed to take its natural course. If we experience trauma or pain, we can live with the experience, constantly adjusting and re-centering. However, if we get caught in our conceptions about our experiences, grasping at them as inherently existent, we freeze our reality and create suffering.

Psychologically, the principle of homeostasis is that our psyche/body whole always adjusts to find its healthiest state in any given situation. When the environment is unhealthy, our psyche/body whole finds the healthiest state it can, which often requires the manifestation of illness as an expression of wholeness. For example, when we experience trauma, the psyche's way of integrating the experience is often depression. Depression is not ill health unless it becomes stuck; rather, it is a natural expression of the process of integration and transformation.

The nature of the mandala is fundamentally homeostatic, as it also always finds the point of wholeness under each circumstance. However, our disposition to contract around or fight and reject our experiences blocks this innate potential and results in suffering and ill health. This suffering is an indicator that we need to allow ourselves to shift and let go of what we are holding on to. From this perspective, health is not about feeling wonderful and having no pain or problems. It is the capacity to allow what is unfolding, whether this is pleasurable or painful, to move and change into its natural condition. Essential to this process is the ability to maintain unconditional presence and clarity within our experience derived from the practice of Mahamudra.

When we are attuned to the significance of the mandala in our lives, it places us in a different relationship to the events that would otherwise cause us trouble. Above all, the mandala implies allowing an unfolding process of life to take its course with openness and trust. When we give space to what is arising without fear and clinging, all things settle into their natural condition, but if we block this, we experience suffering. I was reminded of this when a woman friend, a devoted and determined Buddhist practitioner, became pregnant. I wondered how she would come to terms with the radical changes this would lead to in her life, and whether her fixed notions of spiritual practice would block her capacity to open to this experience in a new and healthy way. Gradually she came to recognize that having children was, actually, her practice and would demand that she truly applied what she had learned. As I have discovered myself, children challenge us to let go of self-grasping in a way that sitting in retreat does not always do.

We are being changed by the innate homeostatic presence of the mandala as an unconscious process beyond the control of the ego. It is as though the mandala is changing us, and we can most usefully be open to it and trust it. When we do, we can re-center and integrate most of the traumas of our lives.

We can see this process at work in the way different people cope with a life-threatening experience, such as being diagnosed with cancer. The immediate shock of such a diagnosis has an understandably dramatic effect on patients' lives that requires considerable time to digest. At first it seems unacceptable and unbelievable. There may be strong and natural feelings of anger, despair, and terror in reaction to the devastating effect cancer will have on their lives. It can throw people totally off-center and out of relationship with the ability to re-center. However, other aspects of life need to readjust and be changed gradually as the old life is let go of to let in a new one. This new life and new mandala needs to include the trauma and to integrate what it brings to awareness so that a new point of equilibrium can be reached.

When people who have gone through this experience describe the effect cancer has had on their lives, it is often evident that they have awoken to a new depth of awareness and meaning. Many such people genuinely come to a place of acceptance and peace with what they are experiencing. They have allowed themselves to be reshaped and re-centered in a remarkable way.

The mandala, therefore, is the extraordinary power of homeostasis within each of us. It enables us to remain sane and relatively healthy in the most intolerable circumstances. As an expression of wholeness, we can see the mandala reflected in our ordinary human condition and also in the state of buddhahood. These two levels differ by virtue of the insight into the nature of reality present in the latter and not in the former. Both the ordinary person and a Buddha live in a world that arises as the momentary play of emptiness. However, the normal person is barely aware of this illusory flux and will tend to solidify its natural evolution into a fixed reality.

For a Buddha, the mandala is a process of constant creative manifestation, symbolized in its most refined aspect in the complex deity practices. We all create our reality moment by moment, but the mind, bound by confusion and ignorance, creates a chaotic and disturbed mandala. For someone whose mind is clear and free of confusion about the nature of reality, the mandala is an expression of that clarity. We can see this in people's lives; when we have a mess inside, for example, we create a mess outside. Each of us must take personal responsibility for the reality we create.

Our lives will change as clarity into our nature deepens and we become increasingly aware of the process of the mandala as it unfolds. Rather than staying caught in our narrow, limited reactions to life, we open up and allow life to unfold. This brings an increasing trust, not based on a divine intervention, or a caring God who keeps us safe, but on a profound understanding of the homeostatic principle of the mandala. We are personally responsible for our individual awareness and openness to whatever happens.

In tantric practice, the deity is considered central to the symbolic and sacred nature of the mandala. When a meditator shifts the focus of identification to the deity, it re-centers awareness in the very heart of the mandala's creative vitality. Lama Thubten Yeshe once said about this identification, "If we identify with a low-quality, confused sense of self, that is the mandala we create." When we identify with our essential nature, the mandala we then emanate is altogether different.

The heart of generation stage practice is the cultivation of a visualized mandala in which the meditator's consciousness arises in the aspect of the central deity. This repeated "self-generation," as it is called, activates the seed of the mandala within the psyche of the meditator. As a symbol of our innate potential for complete transformation, this mandala acts as a seed or catalyst for wholeness that begins to awaken and purify the practitioner's psyche into a more mature state. This is similar to a constitutional remedy in homoeopathy, where the remedy activates the inner move towards health and wholeness.

I experienced this process in a very ordinary way when I was at university. I went through a period of a breakdown, an identity crisis, which caused me to feel confused and disoriented. I found myself drawn to objects and images that were symmetrical and mandala-like. Objects such as flower heads, seed cases, pinecones; anything circular with concentric patterns became fascinating for me. I spent many hours exploring and painting these forms. This had a gradual healing effect, which I only later recognized was like having the seed of a mandala activated from within. In time this gave me a stronger, more cohesive sense of self, which brought me through the crisis.

The images we normally associate with the mandala are significant psychological symbols of what Jung called the Self, the center of our psychic totality. In the tantric mandala, these symbols represent a complete re-creation of the totality of the psyche on a symbolic level. Attributes of the mind are symbolized as deities, as are the elements in the body. The body itself is symbolized by a celestial mansion within which the deity stands. The mandala thus represents a psychic whole that gradually awakens and matures.

The tantric teachings say that all relative phenomena are the "mandala of pure appearance." When I was first taught this I was under the misapprehension that I had to see the world differently, that appearances would change, and I would begin to see an exotic mandala superimposed on the world around me. The implication of this phrase, however, is not that the world appears differently, but that we recognize that all appearances are the play of emptiness, the play of dharmakaya.

The world each of us inhabits is a reflection of individual karma. While we may share similar karma, and, therefore, similar worlds, they are nevertheless individually determined. Furthermore, it is considered in Tantra that our reality is the creation of our own mind, in contrast to the materialistic view that sees mind as an emergent characteristic of the brain. When we recognize that phenomena arise from the mind and lack inherent substantiality, we will begin to see the world as a creative play of illusion. The nature of this causal mind is clear, luminous, and empty, and becomes the basis of our individual experience of dharmakaya, the ground of being from which all appearances emerge and dissolve moment by moment, Goethe's "Eternal Mind's eternal re-creation."

The phenomenal world and the body/mind continuum is the play of dharmakaya as the mandala of pure appearance. Living in this mandala means being constantly aware of a threshold between form and emptiness, a dynamic place in which creation is constant as form comes into being as a fleeting expression of emptiness. The world then becomes vibrant and vital, filled with magical numinosity and meaning. When we are open to this awareness, there is no distinction between samsara and nirvana. Those who see the material outer world as samsara and the nature of suffering are still caught in a duality that is confused about its ultimate nature. When we understand the outer material world as the play of emptiness, the mandala of appearances is nirvana.

This understanding also affects how we experience the natural world as an expression of the mandala of pure appearance, where inner and outer realities are not distinct and separate. This important consideration, often overlooked by Westerners practicing Tantra, is that our relationship to and awareness of nature is also the mandala.

*Figure 16. A Simple Mandala*

IN TANTRA, we enter a relationship with the natural world that is easily misunderstood when approached from a Western viewpoint. Jung attempted to explain the animism of cultures that inhabit a world in which psychic reality is alive by calling it *participation mystique*. He meant that individual consciousness was still embedded in the collective world of nature animated by archetypal forces that govern life. In this dreamtime world, the collective psyche is all around, in the land, rivers, plants, and animals. The native Amazon Indians, for example, revere the rain forest as a spirit deity who is the sustainer of their lives. Hindus in India venerate the Ganga as a goddess, and the Tibetans make offerings to local guardians that dwell in the land around.

When Westerners engage in the practice of Tantra, they often overlook the deeply rooted, animistic relationship with nature that is so much a part of its worldview. One can see that the heart of tantric practice does not explicitly require such a relationship. It is, however, implicit in many of the practices a tantric practitioner will perform, such as the offering of food (Tib. *torma*) to local guardians and spirits.

It is perhaps expedient to ignore this animism to make Tantra more accessible to our need for psychological understanding. It then becomes a sophisticated cosmology of deity visualizations practiced in the clean and peaceful environment of the local Buddhist center or personal meditation room. This may be appropriate for an introduction to the processes involved, particularly when our own cultural views of nature are so different, but this is not how tantric adepts, particularly the mahasiddhas of India, would have practiced. It would, however, be

difficult for Westerners to live the kind of lifestyle these yogis and yoginis did. Meditators in India and Tibet would specifically go to remote
wild and potentially dangerous places where natural forces were present. They would then practice in such a way as to utilize these energies
to enhance their experiences. This would often involve invoking local
spirits, guardians, dakas and dakinis, and making special offerings to ask
for their help.

Tibetan lamas do not take lightly this relationship with nature, as we
might do in the West. They take seriously the need to maintain a clear
and healthy interaction with the environment, and they make offerings to local spirits and guardians before building houses, temples or
stupas. They recognize the presence of elemental spirits in rocks, rivers,
trees, and special places in the environment. They are careful to maintain the relationship to the local dakas and dakinis that inhabit the
realm of reality close to our own, which is intimately associated to
nature. They perform rituals to cleanse and protect the environment
they will meditate in from any kind of psychic or spirit interferences.
They also take seriously the potential harm that spirits can do to our
health, mentally and physically, and there are many sophisticated practices they use to guard and protect.

Over many generations in the West, we have slowly elevated consciousness out of its origins in nature. Consciousness has been extri-
cated from the preconscious world of nature like a lotus rising from the
mud of a riverbed, and we have gradually cultivated a sense of independent self-identity. This is an awareness that gives us the illusion of
separation and autonomy, as well as the insecurity and alienation that
accompanies it. According to Jung, as this separation from nature has
evolved, archetypal forces once experienced in the world around have
been drawn back and buried within the collective unconscious.

Seeing these archetypal forces as manifestations or projections of
the unconscious gives us a psychological understanding of why we see
the earth as a goddess, a forest as a deity, and the forces of nature as
dragons and spirits. They become symbolic projections rather than
real outer entities. This may give us autonomy and independence from

the power of these elemental forces and may make these natural forces more understandable psychologically, but it also strips the land of its numinosity. Our experience of nature then becomes spiritually arid. We may cease to respect and value it as a living process and will certainly ridicule those who still believe dragons exist, or that fairies live in the springs and spirits, in trees.

It is not easy for someone with this cultural heritage to then grasp the subtleties and peculiarities of the relationship to nature found in Tantra, as it is necessary to reenter the worldview in which it was born. Our beliefs as to the nature of reality, the split we have between mind and matter, and the power of our separate sense of self, make it very hard to shift from the dominance of these conceptions. It requires a leap of understanding that is not just an intellectual process. We may feel unhealthily disconnected from nature, and yet the road back into relationship is not simple. Our poor relationship to the body and its vitality exacerbates this separation, but is also a key to the potential for a return.

The tantric world is still animated, and the separation between psyche and the natural environment is still indistinct. What makes Tantra powerful is the potential for retaining this relationship to the collective nature psyche while developing a conscious creative participation. The tantric practitioner attempts to stand between these two worlds in order to bring about a dialogue between the archetypal forces that pervade our reality and the individual psyche. This helps to restore the natural world as something sacred. The nature gods and goddesses have their places within the temple as an expression of the sacredness of our relationship to the land. We then do not dismiss them as a romantic mythological superstition or sanitize them into mere psychological phenomena.

Tantra cultivates a return to the world where psyche and soma, consciousness and matter, are in an intimate inter-relationship. The understanding of subtle energy, both within the body and in the natural environment, makes this profound reconnection possible, principally through the body.

As a tantric practitioner begins to open up a relationship to the inner forces of the energy body, it gradually awakens this relationship to the forces in nature. As the practice of Tantra deepens, our natural felt experience of the world around becomes more sensitive. As it does so we begin to be more aware of the energies in the environment, whether we like it or not. This would be particularly so for anyone who begins to awaken the energy of the tummo or kundalini spoken of earlier. At these times it helps to have an understanding of what is happening.

The tantric world recognizes that the psyche is not just something inner, but that it pervades the world around and contains powerful forces that can be evoked and dialogued with. This is not superstitious thinking, but an understanding of the subtle workings of our energetic reality; how we interact with it, and it with us. Distinctions of outer and inner cease to be useful, and modern science cannot measure, nor rational thinking easily comprehend, its reality. Awakening the subtle interdependence of our mind and energy with nature is to some degree reversing the process that brought consciousness out of nature, returning to a sense of participation, yet with awareness.

During several years in retreat in the Indian Himalayas I was living on the threshold of an awesome wilderness. My retreat hermitage was high in the foothills of wild mountains, which were both spectacularly beautiful and ruthlessly hostile. Life at such an altitude gave an often overwhelming sense of the power of the elements; intense static storms, torrential monsoon rain, ferocious sunlight, and massive sculptured rock formations. The time I spent exploring the wild crags and gnarled trees, the ravines and waterfalls around me was slowly waking me up to the presence of forces and entities I was barely able to comprehend. It was only when I had returned to live in England that the significance of this experience of nature dawned upon me. I became aware I was losing contact with something I had intuitively felt while I was in the mountains. I was losing my land sense. I now recognize this was a significant part of the tantric practice I was engaged in.

Recently, while visiting Java, I met a Javanese man who would be considered a shaman. While talking about our relationship to nature, he said he felt like nature waking up to consciousness. In response I felt I was going the other way. I was like consciousness trying to restore my immersion in land sense. This man was acutely aware of the force and energies at work in the natural environment and was attempting to help Westerners reconnect with them, particularly through body sense.

In Highest Yoga Tantra, the relationship to the natural world is developed in a particular way known as "the body mandala." Especially in the Chakrasamvara Tantra, while the intention of the practice is to attain a quality of buddhahood, the medium within which this is achieved is intimately connected to the forces of nature. The name "Chakrasamvara" means "the circle of all phenomena in the nature of great bliss." Heruka Chakrasamvara and Vajravarahi as a union of the masculine and feminine represent the essence of the regenerative potencies of nature expressed in everything that lives. This is the fertility and potency of nature. Known as the creator and destroyer, like Shiva, the deity Heruka Chakrasamvara represents the ruthless creative vitality of nature that brings all things into being and then returns them whence they came.

The Chakrasamvara Tantra describes how specific energy centers within the body enhance the natural healthy functioning of the organs. These body centers form the body mandala as a complete homeostatic system, which also has corresponding centers within the surrounding land. In India and Tibet these land-based centers are clearly distinguished and are listed in the tantric texts.

The relationship between the inner body centers and the outer land locations is very subtle. In the Chakrasamvara Tantra, the forces that inhabit these centers take the aspect of dakas and dakinis. When a tantric practitioner meditates, he or she aims to tune into the relationship of these inner and outer forces and allow a process of healing to take place. In this way the outer land health manifests through the dakas and dakinis and blesses and heals the inner energies. The land is then experienced as if it were a complete mandala with specific locations for different functions, just as the centers in the body serve different functions.

In Britain many people are interested in ley lines and ancient sacred places. On several occasions Tibetan lamas visiting England have spoken of equivalent land centers described in the Chakrasamvara Tantra. The dakas and dakinis who inhabit these centers live in a dimension of reality known as Khacho Shing, a realm closely related to our own, yet more subtle and more intimately connected to the elemental forces of nature. Meditators in Tibet and India who developed the practice of Heruka Chakrasamvara were often visited by these dakas and dakinis, who led them into Khacho Shing, never to return. In the Chakrasamvara Tantra, the deity Heruka Chakrasamvara is described as "Lord of the Fairies," an interesting parallel to the Celtic realm of Avalon.

How do we make sense of this as Westerners with our skeptical, rationalist attitude? It would be easy to simply dismiss this aspect of Buddhist practice as meaningless nonsense, or to psychologize it as merely symbolic. But unless we try to enter at least part of the world within which Tantra lives, it will be extremely hard to discover any meaning in it. If Tantra is to be brought into a Western context, this relationship to the energy of the land may be very significant. Tantra can bring us back into relationship with the elemental forces around us in nature if we understand how it works.

When we are unable to relate to our land in this elemental way, we remain unaware of its health or sickness. Regenerating a relationship with this energy can have a profound effect on how we inhabit our environment. The beginning of this dialogue is a significant journey for many people. In developing consciousness we have come so far from our origins that a return to an awareness of nature on more subtle levels can provide a necessary healing.

In order to develop tantric practice, it is increasingly important to place it back in its original relationship to the land. This means reconnecting with the land sense that is so diluted in city life. Recently I moved to South Devon, on the edge of Dartmoor, for the particular reason that Dartmoor is one place where the "centers" referred to by the lamas feel present, still alive and accessible. Rather than practicing in the confines of the meditation room, it is perhaps appropriate to take meditation back to the wild places, upon rocky tors, by streams, and in deep forest valleys.

According to the tantric texts, this is where the ancient mahasiddhas of India meditated. It is possible to reawaken the sense of the elemental forces around these wild, natural locations and the dakas and dakinis that inhabit them. The dialogue that then begins is a mutual healing process for both meditator and the land.

Much of the land around us needs healing, as we have spent many years wantonly damaging it. There is little natural, unspoilt land left in England, for example, and yet it continues to survive. The Chakrasamvara Tantra states that the environment in which a meditator practices begins to be healed by constant generation of the energy of the deity. For me this means beginning to relate to Dartmoor as though it were a living entity, with its special centers of energy scattered throughout.

These places can be found if we are sensitive and aware. Our bodies will tell us because these are the places of communion. If we listen to our bodies when we enter the natural environment, we will learn to sense what is around us. Most of us intuitively find places in the environment where we feel good, refreshed and alive. We each have the capacity to open to the land around us and receive its vitality.

When we live the process of Tantra in this way, it becomes alive and vital. We are naturally drawn to special places in the environment where we can feel the energy and use it in our practice. As we begin to dialogue creatively with the natural environment, our sense relationship to the elemental forces around will grow. This can only enhance the restoration of a healthy interdependence in nature at a time when it is crucial. We live in the land, and its sickness is our sickness, its health is our health. The practice of Tantra is not separate from nature; nature provides the vitality that is its essence.

W HILE I HAVE described a sophisticated system of practice, the essence of Tantra can be present in many aspects of our lives in a simple way. The central principle of Tantra is that the energy of the instincts and emotions need not be repressed; it can be transformed. Once held in a suitable context, it requires a channel of symbolic expression as a vehicle for its transformation. The key is to find a channel that truly holds, interests, and engages the emotional energy and instinctual forces in order that they are transformed. If it does not do so, little is gained.

As these forces become symbolically or metaphorically expressed, they are brought onto a higher energy level of consciousness and integration, facilitated through the creative process. This means a creative activity in its broadest sense, not just artistic activity; forces can be focused through visualization, art, physical activity, or ritual. Even something destructive can be a suitable vehicle, as we cannot truly separate creativity from destruction; for example, in order to build a fire, we must cut wood. Jung felt that the symbolic metaphor that transforms must be of a similar order to the forces to be transformed. If the instinctual force to be transformed is aggression, for example, the metaphorical channel must have characteristics that are of a similar nature.

A contemporary problem of our culture is that we have lost many of the natural ways in which the energies bound up in our instinctual lives can be transformed, and, as a result, they become shadowy and often destructive. Young men are particularly vulnerable, as the opportunities to skillfully and creatively focus instinctual forces have become very limited. Nothing is gained by denying our instincts, whether sexual or aggressive. When these forces are understood, respected, and channeled, there is no reason why they should become sick and perverse.

If there is no appropriate outlet for sexual and creative energy, it becomes violent and destructive. Our culture has all these symptoms. Rape, violence, drunkenness, and abuse are apparently statistically higher today than during previous decades, and there seems to be little awareness in our society of how to resolve them. Punitive measures are limited if they fail to touch the heart of the problem, which is that these forces need something to channel them creatively. Indeed, punitive methods of control tend to build up barriers of contempt and resentment in those punished. This only exacerbates the problem, leading to even greater antisocial tendencies.

These extremes need not be reached if an appropriate solution is applied. Much preventative work is possible if those in power can understand what is happening and not simply react from authoritarian rigidity. Sometimes solutions are found. I was astonished at the stroke of genius that solved one such problem of young adolescents stealing powerful cars and driving them at reckless speeds.

The response of one police force to this upsurge of dangerous and often fatal joyriding was to introduce a scheme of controlled car racing for young adolescents. They found a racetrack, some beat-up old cars, and a number of driving instructors and mechanics. The young adolescent males were given the chance to learn to race under instruction and then to repair the cars they smashed afterwards—a perfect example of Tantra in daily life. The energy was given a vehicle (no pun intended) for transformation of a similar order to that which was being transformed. These young men became very involved in building their cars and learning to drive them under skilled instruction. This provided a creative outlet for their energy that harnessed their potential destructiveness in a far more constructive way.

Although the example above is of an antisocial extreme of behavior, each one of us has the need to find a vehicle of transformation. Everyone has these instinctual and shadowy forces within them on some level. Fortunately, many of us have found something in our life that fulfills us and channels our energy constructively. This helps us recognize how important it is to be fulfilled in this way and also have compassion for those who have no means of expression other than destructively. Even so, there are still times when our Shadow will need to be worked with, and then we all need to enter the alchemical vessel.

Modern society has a crucial need for a means of creative transformation on both an individual and collective level. There are few collective rituals that enable the expression and transformation of social malaise. At the same time, we need to recognize the value individually of a modern equivalent to the alchemical opus.

In the early 1970s I was in Bali, Indonesia, living in a beautiful village called Ubud, in the center of the island. I was fascinated by the richness of music, art, craft, dance, and theatre that pervaded every aspect of Balinese life. Creativity as an expression of their deep spirituality colors everything the Balinese do. Their culture, rooted in a mix of Hinduism and animism, also has an intimate relationship to the natural environment. A vast reservoir of ceremonial rituals, initiations, and rites of passage exist that gather the villagers together and enable both individual and collective transformation. In Bali, the living tradition of collective ritual survives. It is used specifically to propitiate the gods, educate the children through storytelling, and initiate them into the values of the society. There are also rituals to exorcise the collective neurosis of the village.

One dance I saw a number of times was the now-famous *ketchak*, which has a special significance if a village suffers from some communal neurosis, as I guess all villages must from time to time. On one particular occasion, there was a distressed period in Ubud, which started with a dispute between families and ended with a village depression, everyone bickering and unhappy. They arranged a *ketchak* dance in the village temple. In those days there were not many tourists around and I was allowed to take part.

The dance began with the men of the village in concentric circles chanting like monkeys and waving their arms rhythmically towards the center, where a tree stood with a buffalo tied to it. The chanting and music was powerfully evocative and generated tremendous energy with its staccato pulsing; great anger was being released. After a while a demon dressed in brightly colored strips of cloth, grass hair, and a ferocious mask leaped into the center, his long claws clutching at the chanting men. The chanting became wild and frenetic as the entire village felt the tension of this moment.

The communal village demon had been brought to the center. Suddenly the heroic warrior who was to overthrow this monstrous force and cast it out appeared in the circle. In a frenzied climax, the demon was defeated and banished, never to return. Gradually the energy began to subside and the atmosphere shifted to one of relief and ease that had not been present before. The hero had done his work, offerings were made to the gods, and the village was healed of its malaise.

We have a problem when our culture fails to offer such a vehicle of transformation for the shadowy side of our society. I cannot, however, imagine sophisticated Westerners wishing to gather together and do a *ketchak* dance.

Regrettably, the collective Shadow of many societies becomes constellated and expressed, most commonly in times of war. It often provides the vehicle for a collective projection of all that we fear and hate onto the loathed and feared enemy. This may vent temporarily all the underlying social hostilities and frustrations that cause disruption and disharmony by giving them a common focus. Ultimately, however, its destructive effect on the individual and the community is appalling.

Wars are obviously not a solution to heal our cultural malaise, even though some people believe the most constructive way to channel young men's aggressive instincts is to send them into the army. However, our culture needs some rite of passage that enables young people to pass through adolescence in a more creative and empowering way. Possibly the most valuable source of transformation and rite of passage—one which has almost completely died out—is apprenticeship.

In the days of crafts guilds, tradesmen, and engineering craftsmen, apprenticeship was a vital process in which young men were trained by older master-craftsmen. Whether it was as a carpenter, blacksmith, wheelwright, or silversmith, the process was similar. Apprentices taken in to train and study were required to work alongside the craftsman and follow his instructions to the letter. This was demanding and challenging, but over time had a profound effect on the apprentices as they began to refine and develop their own skills and disciplines.

When I left school I was fortunate enough to be one of the last people able to join an apprenticeship scheme. This was before subsequent governments eroded the entire principle and turned it into a pathetic facsimile, clearly not understanding the significant effect they had once had on many young people's futures. My apprenticeship days as an electronics engineer were not easy, but I look back on them with a certain gratitude.

The apprentice training officers were demanding and rigorous about the training we were put through. In machine-shop practice this was painfully clear as time and again we were expected to perfect skills that were far from easy. To finish a job only to be told it was rubbish and instructed to start again had a very powerful effect. Sometimes I wanted to do horrible things to "Old Doug," as my training officer was called, but actually I knew that he really liked us and wanted us to master what he had to teach.

I feel the principle of the apprenticeship process, perhaps without the authoritarian harshness, is potentially an excellent model for tantric transformation. Even though it may not specifically involve placing ourselves in the position of a craftsman's trainee, the principle of crafting ourselves is nevertheless an important one. It is perhaps even more important today that we each individually find our personal opus, our personal sadhana, or method of transformation.

We can still experience something of this alchemical process that provides a channel for our energy in our work and creative projects. Work is crucial for those whose dispositions tend to be spiritually ungrounded and idealistic and also for those who have difficulty bringing their countless wonderful ideas and visions down to earth. Similarly, work is essential for those with a lot of frustrated and potentially destructive energy, particularly in adolescence.

The process of mastering skills through work embodies what is important in creative alchemy from a tantric perspective. Whatever the task, however, it must challenge the creative forces within us so that we begin to master them. Whether it is learning to play the violin or becoming a carpenter, in principle, the process is the same. When we engage in the learning process, it makes us confront our weaknesses, and challenges us to overcome them. We can back down when it gets tough and go to something else, but no benefit is gained. When we overcome our infantile emotional reactions to the challenges a task sets us, mastery becomes a possibility. We can then gradually channel the unruly creative forces that are released from the darkness. With self-discipline and perseverance, we gain strength and refinement in whatever task we undertake.

If the creative process of the vehicle of transformation is to be effective, it must be able to attract and absorb the energy we wish to transform. This gives the task its vitality and interest. When our interest and enthusiasm is held, it absorbs us and concentrates our attention, focusing our emotions and instincts into the process. When the task is inappropriate it soon loses its numinosity for us and little happens, but when it is appropriate, the effect can be dramatic.

The example of the police setting up car racing schemes for young adolescent joy riders is potentially very effective. If we are dealing with powerful physical aggression, we need a channel that is of a similar nature. When we are transforming destructive impulses, destruction must be part of the process. If we want to transform sexual, sensual, and erotic energy, this must also be part of our channel. Someone who needs to embody their power in a creative way may require a cause to fight, while someone else with intense, spiritual, visionary experiences may need to express them creatively through some material art. If we need to express intense emotion through our bodies, then something physical is appropriate.

When we find the channels that inspire us creatively, there is something quite magical and almost compulsive in our relationship to them. If we discover or begin a new creative project, suddenly energy is released that can be quite overwhelming. We have opened up a channel to the source of our creative potential.

When our energy has been drawn by a task, we need a combination of commitment and willingness to engage in the process. We are truly entering the vessel at this point. This must be done willingly, because if we are not acting from our will, our energy will not be engaged. This is difficult for those who are fearful of commitment, and all manner of resistances, doubts, and ploys to sabotage and avoid engaging in the task may arise.

Many people become paralyzed by the fear that maybe this is not the right thing, the real thing, or the special thing. Others, in order to compensate for fears of failing or inadequacy, make what they want to do so grand and inflated that they are unable to engage with the task of making it real. A Tibetan once said to me, "Don't forsake the little horse because you only want a big one"—very practical advice that enabled me to see that the process was organic and would evolve over time, growing from small beginnings. Often we may not be able to see fully the result of our creative evolution; it may only become apparent as it goes forward. I am often surprised at the result of prolonged persistence in a project that began in one form and eventually becomes something quite different.

Once we commit to and engage in a task, we need disciplined perseverance and constancy. The Tibetans call it "enthusiastic perseverance." When things get hard we may want to run away and find something easier. Fear, anger, frustration, and doubt sabotage our efforts and steal away our resolve to remain in the vessel. Feelings of inadequacy, incompetence, and doubt inevitably arise and are part of the process we are going through. If the task engages us and really means something to us, at some point such feelings are bound to be released. Then the process of refinement and mastery can really begin.

The term "mastery" would appear to describe a phenomenon that is essentially masculine. Whether mastery is necessarily a masculine quality may be debatable. It is, however, equally significant in the creative life of both men and women. Jung certainly believed that when the masculine side of a woman was not being given a direction or channel, it could become destructive, but often self-destructive rather than outwardly aggressive.

Every artist, craftsman and craftswoman, musician, writer, and athlete knows the significance of gradual mastery and how it feels when the creative energy begins to flow more freely; likewise every healer, therapist, teacher, and gardener. Transformation takes place slowly within the vessel, and we gradually master our own creative vitality as it is expressed in the task. We also discover love and joy when we genuinely devote ourselves to the process.

As we deepen our experience we open to something almost divine. I have often marveled at the craftsmanship found in the cathedrals of Britain. There is a strong sense of the love and devotion of the craftsmen who carved such beautiful, intricate foliage, animals, and figures. Many of these craftsmen saw the symbol of the Green Man as their craft's daimon, and there is a powerful sense of this deity manifesting through their work. It is a wonderful expression of the richness and beauty that can be experienced through the mastery of carving.

As a painter of Tibetan Buddhist thangkas, I have spent many years trying to develop and master this devotional art. As time passes I have begun to see the changes that have taken place in my work. There have been periods of great struggle, trying again and again to create the effect I wanted of conveying the quality of light and inspirational power of the deity. It has demanded hours of disciplined work with tiny brushes and endless patience to refine and perfect the images, constantly learning new symbols and new details.

While I see my limitations, I have also felt the intense joy of seeing these wonderful forms take shape. I always have the sense that the more I open myself to the deities I am painting, the more I become a vehicle for them to manifest. I consider this art form a great devotion to the deity, which allows it to express itself in the world. By trying to give myself totally to its expression the effect is sometimes indescribable. Once gold has been applied to the detailed ornaments and robes, the tradition is to "open the eyes" of the deity, meaning to paint the iris and pupils of the eyes. At this moment something quite extraordinary happens. The deity is said to enter the painting and bring it to life, and from this moment the painting becomes a sacred object.

Probably each of us will find an image of mastery that is poignant for us personally. For me, the image of the gardener or master craftsman, such as the silversmith, carpenter, or shoemaker, embodies qualities of love, strength, and devotion in their crafts in a very down-to-earth fashion.

In the East there are samurai warriors, shakuhachi flute players, and Indian mahasiddhas, all spiritual practitioners who take the idea of mastery onto very subtle levels. They work with the subtle forces in the body in such a way as to develop special powers exemplifying their mastery. By controlling the elemental forces in their own bodies, they are able to change and control the forces outside, like the rainmaker, who, by balancing the elements within, can change and bring balance to the outside climate.

When we willingly place ourselves into the vessel of personal transformation, we contact our creative forces in a different way. During this process we can liberate the forces of the unconscious and gradually lead them out of the dark into the light of our creative life. The power and vitality of our instincts then become our greatest strength, rather than dominating us and being our weakness. The tantric yogis and yoginis in India who cultivated these forces in themselves were known as mahasiddhas, and there are many wonderful stories of their powers and abilities.

One such story is of the mahasiddha Vinapa, the musician son of a king. He learned to play the *vina*, and became so entranced by its feminine qualities and tone that he could not be parted from it. Because he was heir to the throne, his family were concerned that his obsession for the instrument would distract him and that he would make a bad ruler. So his parents sought the aid of a spiritual master called Buddhapa to help him.

When Vinapa saw this great master, he recognized his teacher and devoted himself to his instructions. Recognizing the prince's spiritual potential, the master gave him instructions in how he should use his music as the vehicle for his awakening. He was instructed to meditate constantly upon the sound of his instrument and free himself of all distinction between the sound and the mind that perceived it. Practicing assiduously for nine years, the prince gradually ceased all conceptions and contemplated pure sound, finally attaining the state of Mahamudra. The energy in his body became transformed and he was able to perform remarkable feats as a great mahasiddha.

Another mahasiddha, Chamaripa, the Divine Cobbler, was a humble shoemaker who worked constantly making and repairing shoes. He suffered great dissatisfaction because he felt he was not meant to be a cobbler all his life. One day, walking through the streets utterly sick of his work and in great despair, he met a Buddhist monk. Prostrating himself at the monk's feet, Chamaripa begged for assistance to free himself from his pain. The monk gladly responded and asked if he was ready to truly practice his sadhana (the means to attain full awakening, akin to the alchemical opus). On hearing he was, the monk instructed him to visualize his shoemaking as his meditation. After years of practice, Chamaripa attained Mahamudra and full awakening. Having completed his path, Chamaripa sang:

> Mold the leather of passion and conceptual thought
> Around the last of loving-kindness and compassion.
> Then, taking the guru's precepts as your awl,
> Stitching carefully with the thread
> Of freedom from the eight obsessions.
> Miraculously, you will create those slippers
> That cannot be seen by those with clouded vision—
> The marvelous slippers of *dharmakaya*.[23]

Once we are prepared to enter the vessel of transformation and engage in this path with all our heart, transformation will naturally take place. If we open ourselves to this process and persevere through times when we become disheartened and wish to run away, we will discover something in our lives we never imagined possible. As we see the effect of the process of transformation, we feel the love, joy, and bliss that lie at the essence of our being. Our innate potential to fully realize our creative Buddha potential is present right now, if we will only enter the vessel and allow ourselves to awaken to it. The mahasiddhas of India recognized that every aspect of our life can be seen as a vehicle for attaining wholeness once we wake up to its potential. In this way each of us can learn to create our life as a living alchemy.

# Dedication

*May all those who read this book, as well as those who enabled it to be written,
come to experience the everlasting peace and happiness of full awakening
and bring benefit to every living being.*

# Glossary of Tibetan, Sanskrit, and Jungian Terms

| | |
|---|---|
| Akanishta (Skt.) | A pure land inhabited by the Buddha prior to his incarnation. |
| alchemy | Historically, the process of transformation of gross substances into a refined material; metaphorically, a system for personal transformation theorized by the psychoanalyst Carl Jung. |
| Amitabha (Skt.) | The Dhyani Buddha of the Padma family. |
| Amitayus (Skt.) | The Buddha of long life; aspect of Amitabha. |
| Amoghasiddhi (Skt.) | The Dhyani Buddha of the Karma family. |
| amrita (Skt.) | Elixir of life; intoxicant used in rituals associated with Heruka Chakrasamvara (Tib. *dutsi*). |
| Anima | The archetypal feminine image. |
| Animus | The archetypal masculine image. |
| Anuttarayoga-tantra (Skt.) | Highest Yoga Tantra; the highest level of Tantra. |
| archetype | A primordial patterning for psychological life that emerges through the psyche of an individual in symbolic form. |
| arhat (Skt.) | Literally, "foe destroyer"; one who has attained nirvana. |
| bardo (Tib.) | Intermediate state between death in one life and rebirth in the next. |
| bodhichitta (Skt.) | The intention to attain buddhahood. |
| bodhisattva (Skt.) | One who aspires to buddhahood. |
| Charyatantra (Skt.) | Performance Tantra; the second level of Tantra. |

chakra (Skt.) — Literally, "wheel"; conjunction in the central channel.

Chakrasamvara (Skt.) — The deity of transformation through bliss; called Heruka Chakrasamvara.

Chenrezig (Tib.) — The Buddha of compassion (Skt. *Avalokiteshvara*).

collective unconscious — The level of the unconscious that lies deeper than personal unconscious and is considered to contain the archetypes shared by us all.

complex — A semi-autonomous, emotionally charged aspect of the unconscious.

conjunctio — The union of masculine and feminine.

dagdzin (Tib.) — Ego-grasping.

daimon — A powerful archetypal figure within the unconscious, particularly significant to an individual as a guide or protector.

daka (Skt.) — Literally, "sky-goer" (Tib. *khadro*); male tantric deity or practitioner.

dakini (Skt.) — Literally, "sky-goer" (Tib. *khadroma*); female deity or practitioner.

deva (Skt.) — A god.

De chen (Tib.) — The Pure Land of Amitabha Buddha (Skt. *Sukhavati*).

Dharma (Skt.) — The Buddha's teachings.

dharmakaya (Skt.) — The wisdom truth body of a Buddha; the ultimate nature of the fully enlightened mind.

Dhyani Buddha (Skt.) — A male Buddha representing the purified, perfected state of one of the five aggregates: a Buddha quality resulting from meditation.

disidentify; disidentification — The capacity to create an objective relationship between one's sense of identity and one's emotional state; being able to witness emotional states rather than be them.

| | |
|---|---|
| Gelugpa (Tib.) | One of the four principal schools of Tibetan Buddhism. |
| guru yoga (Skt.) | Practice of devotion to one's teacher. |
| guru (Skt.) | Teacher (Tib. *lama*). |
| gyu (Tib.) | Literally, "continuity" (Skt. *tantra*). |
| Heruka (Skt.) | "Blood-drinker"; used in reference to all wrathful meditational deities and in particular to Chakrasamvara. |
| ida (Tib.) | In tantric physiology, one of the two energy channels that run around the *shushuma*, or central channel; the white, left, or moon channel. |
| individuation | The process of unfolding of the individual toward the innate potential for wholeness. |
| jinlab (Tib.) | Blessing of the deity. |
| khadro (Tib.) | Male "sky-goer" (Skt. *daka*) |
| khadroma (Tib.) | Female "sky-goer" (Skt. *dakini*) |
| khatvanga (Tib.) | A skull-topped staff; one of the symbolic implements of tantric adepts. |
| Kriyatantra (Skt.) | Action Tantra; the first level of tantric practice. |
| kum nye (Tib.) | System of physical exercise. |
| kundalini (Skt.) | Psychic energy in the central channel. |
| kyerim (Tib.) | Development or generation stage of tantric practice. |
| kylkhor (Tib.) | Sacred circular surround (Skt. *mandala*). |
| lama (Tib.) | Teacher (Skt. *guru*). |
| lapis lazuli | A precious stone; also, a metaphor for the completion of the alchemical process. |
| libido | The intrinsic vitality or energy of the psyche/body. |
| lung (Tib.) | Energy-wind (Skt. *prana*). |

| | |
|---|---|
| lungta (Tib.) | Wind horse. |
| Mahamudra (Skt.) | Literally, "Great Seal"; meditation on the mind's innate clarity. |
| mahasiddha (Skt.) | Highly realized yogi. |
| Mahayana (Skt.) | Literally, "Great Vehicle"; the northern Buddhist school. |
| Maitreya (Skt.) | Embodiment of the great loving-kindness of all Buddhas. |
| mala (Skt.) | A rosary. |
| mandala (Skt.) | Representation of the celestial abode of a deity, or a representation of the wisdom emanation of that deity (Tib. *kylkhor*). |
| mani (Skt.) | Jewel. |
| Manjushri (Skt.) | The Buddha of wisdom (Tib. *Jempelyang*). |
| mantra (Skt.) | Literally, "mind protection"; Sanskrit syllables recited as part of tantric deity practice. |
| Mantrayana (Skt.) | "The path of mantra"; a name for Tantra. |
| Mara (Skt.) | Figure symbolizing hindrances to practice. |
| marigpa (Tib.) | Literally, "not-seeing"; ignorance. |
| massa confusa | Original state prior to alchemical transformation; the primordial substance to be transformed. |
| Meru (Skt.) | A metaphysical mountain; center of the universe. |
| Milarepa (Tib.) | Poet-saint of Tibet (1040–1123). |
| mudra (Skt.) | Symbolic gesture or posture. |
| namtok (Tib.) | The mind's discursive chatter. |
| ngejung (Tib.) | Renunciation; definite emergence; "a determination to wake up." |
| ngondro (Tib.) | Preliminary practices for Higher Tantra. |

| | |
|---|---|
| nigredo | The first stage of the alchemical process in which the Shadow and dark elements come to the surface. |
| nirmanakaya (Skt.) | The manifestation body; the physical manifestation of enlightened beings. |
| Nyingma (Tib.) | The oldest of the four schools of Tibetan Buddhism. |
| opus | The creative work of transformation. |
| osel (Tib.) | Clear light; extremely subtle nature of mind. |
| Padmasambhava (Skt.) | A mahasiddha from Oddiyana, brought to Tibet in the eighth century by King Trison Detsen; revered as the founder of Tibetan Buddhism and in particular of the Nyingma lineage. |
| participation mystique | A condition of the evolution of consciousness in which the individual is immersed in the natural world and has no sense of separate self-identity. |
| pingala (Tib.) | In tantric physiology, one of the two energy channels that run around the *shushuma*, or central channel; the red, right, or sun channel. |
| pratimoksha (Skt.) | Vows taken by the practitioner; ethical precepts; literally, "liberation." |
| prima materia | In alchemy, the original substance to be transformed. |
| psyche | The totality of an individual's psychological process, including both consciousness and the unconscious. |
| psychopomp | A psychological/mythical guide; one who shows the way. |
| rigpa (Tib.) | Insight. |
| rupakaya (Skt.) | The form body; manifestation of the Buddha's pure consciousness in a form beneficial to others. |
| sadhana (Skt.) | Literally, "method of accomplishment"; essential practices relating to the generation stage of tantric practice. |

Sakya (Tib.)            One of the four principal schools of Tibetan Bud-
                        dhism.

samadhi (Skt.)          Tranquil abiding (Tib. *shi né*).

samaya (Skt.)           Commitment or pledge made prior to entering one
                        of the stages of deity practice.

sambhogakaya (Skt.)     The purified subtle body of a Buddha.

samlado (Tib.)          "To sit within boundaries"; retreat.

Self                    The center of the totality of an individual, the
                        archetypal root of meaning; often carries images of
                        the divine and of wholeness.

Shadow                  Aspects of human nature that are repressed and
                        held in the unconscious.

shakti (Skt.)           Power; consort of Shiva.

Shakyamuni (Skt.)       "Sage of the Shakyas"; the historical Buddha.

shi né (Tib.)           Tranquil abiding (Skt. *samadhi*).

shunyata (Skt.)         Emptiness; the ultimate nature of reality.

shushuma (Tib.)         In tantric physiology, the body's central energy
                        channel.

soma                    The physical body.

siddhi (Skt.)           Spiritual accomplishment.

Spirit Mercurius        Symbolic figure representing the substance and
                        process of alchemical transformation.

thangka (Tib.)          A Tibetan icon painting.

Tara (Skt.)             Female Buddha of active compassion.

Theravada (Skt.)        "The way expounded by the elders"; Buddhist
                        school predominant in Sri Lanka, Thailand, Cam-
                        bodia, and Burma.

tigle (Tib.)            Elemental fluid drops.

transference            The act of unconsciously endowing another indi-
                        vidual with an attribute actually projected from
                        within oneself.

tsogrim (Tib.)          The completion stage of Tantra.

Tsongkhapa (Tib.)       The founder of the Gelugpa school (1357–1419).

tummo (Tib.)            "Inner heat"; perfection stage practice in which the
                        sensation of heat is generated.

vajra (Skt.)            Literally, "indestructible"; one of the symbolic
                        implements of tantric adepts.

Vajrapani (Skt.)        A wrathful deity; the power of all the Buddhas
                        made manifest as a deity.

Vajrasattva (Skt.)      An aspect of Akshobhya, associated with the Vajra
                        family; used for purification.

Vipashyana (Skt.)       Insight meditation.

Yama (Skt.)             The lord of death.

Yamantaka (Skt.)        Wrathful aspect of the deity Manjushri.

yidam (Tib.)            "Mind bound" deity; deity chosen as the focus of
                        worship in tantric practices.

Yoga Tantra (Skt.)      The third level of Tantra.

# Notes

1 C. G. Jung, *Psychology and Religion: West and East,* Vol. 11, Collected Works of C. G. Jung (Princeton: Princeton University Press/Bollingen Foundation, 1970).

2 C. G. Jung, "Commentary on *The Secret of the Golden Flower,*" in *Alchemical Studies,* Vol. 13, Collected Works of C. G. Jung, (Princeton: Princeton University Press/Bollingen Foundation, 1967), p. 37.

3 C. G. Jung, "The Concept of the Collective Unconscious," *The Archetypes of the Collective Unconscious,* Vol. 9 Part 1, Collected Works of C. G. Jung (London: Routledge, 1991), pp. 42-53.

4 Jung, *Psychology and Religion: West and East,* pp. 484, 774.

5 Unpublished translation.

6 For a more detailed discussion of this period, see Stephen Batchelor's *The Awakening of the West: The Encounter of Buddhism and Western Culture* (Berkeley: Parallax Press, 1994).

7 C. G. Jung, *The Archetypes and the Collective Unconscious,* vol. 9, Collected Works of C.G. Jung (London: Routledge, 1991), p. 212.

8 C. G. Jung, *The Archetypes and the Collective Unconscious,* p. 209.

9 Ibid., p. 208.

10 Shantideva, *A Guide to the Bodhisattva's Way of Life,* trans. Stephen Batchelor (Dharamsala, India: Library of Tibetan Works and Archives, 1979), Chapter IV, verses 35-36; Chapter VII, verses 60, 68-69.

11 C.G. Jung, *Psychology and Religion: West and East,* p. 484.

12 Ibid.

13 *The Six Yogas of Naropa,* trans. Garma C. C. Chang (Ithaca, NY: Snow Lion Publications, 1986), p. 26.

14 Ibid., p. 30.

15 C. G. Jung, *Psychology and Religion: West and East,* p. 485.

16 Ibid.

17 C. G. Jung, *Symbols of Transformation,* Vol. 5, Collected Works of C. G. Jung (Princeton: Princeton University Press/Bollingen Foundation, 1977), p. 232.

18 Ibid.

19 James Hillman defines *daimons* as " . . . figures of the middle realm, neither quite transcendent Gods nor quiet physical humans . . . . [T]here were many sorts of them, beneficial, terrifying, message-bringers, mediators, voices of guidance and caution." James Hillman, *Healing Fiction* (Barrytown, NY: Station Hill Press, 1983), p. 55.

20  Dharmarakshita, *The Wheel of Sharp Weapons*, trans. Geshe Ngawang Dhargyey (Dharmsala: Library of Tibetan Works and Archives, 1976), pp. 13-14, verse 52; p. 15, verse 57.
21  "A Song to Move the Dakinis' Hearts," from the *Guru Puja* (Tib. Lama Chopa). Translator unknown.
22  Glenn H. Mullin, ed. and trans. *Songs of Spiritual Change: Selected Works of the Dalai Lama VII* (Ithaca, NY: Snow Lion, 1985), p. 82.
23  Keith Dowman, trans. *Buddhist Masters of Enchantment: The Lives and Legends of the Mahasiddhas* (Rochester, VT: Inner Traditions, 1998), p. 104.

A.Kya Yong.Dzin. *Compendium of Ways of Knowing.* Trans. Sherpa Tulku and Alex Berzin. Dharamsala, India: Library of Tibetan Works and Archives, 1976.

Arya Maitreya and Asanga. *The Changeless Nature, The Mahayana Uttara Tantra Shastra.* Trans. Ken and Katia Holmes. Eskdalemuir, Dumfriesshire, Scotland: Kagyu Samye Ling, 1985.

Batchelor, Stephen. *The Awakening of the West: The Encounter of Buddhism and Western Culture.* Berkeley, CA: Parallax Press, 1994.

Bernbaum, Edwin. *The Way to Shambhala.* Garden City, NY: Anchor Press, 1980.

Beyer, Stephan. *The Cult of Tara: Magic and Ritual in Tibet.* Berkeley: University of California Press, 1973.

Bly, Robert. *Iron John: A Book About Men.* Reading, MA: Addison-Wesley, 1990.

Campbell, Joseph. *The Hero with a Thousand Faces.* Princeton, NJ: Princeton University Press, 1972.

Chang, Garma C. C. *The Hundred Thousand Songs of Milarepa.* New York: Harper Colophon, 1970.

———. *Six Yogas of Naropa.* Ithaca: Snow Lion Publications, 1986.

Cooper, J. C. *Fairy Tales: Allegories of the Inner Life.* Wellingborough, UK: The Aquarian Press, 1983.

Dallet, Janet O. *Saturday's Child: Encounters with the Dark Gods.* Toronto: Inner City Books, 1991.

Dhargyey, Geshe Ngawang. *The Tibetan Tradition of Mental Development.* Dharamsala, India: Library of Tibetan Works and Archives, 1974.

Dharmarakshita. *The Wheel of Sharp Weapons: A Mahayana Training of the Mind.* Trans. Geshe Ngawang Dhargyey et al. Dharamsala, India: Library of Tibetan Works and Archives, 1981.

Dowman, Keith. *Buddhist Masters of Enchantment: The Lives and Legends of the Mahasiddhas.* Trans. Keith Dowman. Rochester, VT: Inner Traditions, 1998.

———. *Sky Dancer: The Secret Life and Songs of Lady Yeshe Tsogyel.* Ithaca, NY: Snow Lion Publications, 1997.

Edinger, Edward F. *Ego and Archetype.* Boston: Shambhala Publications, 1992.

Evans-Wentz, W. Y. *Tibetan Yoga and Secret Doctrines.* 3rd. edition. New York City: Oxford University Press USA, 2000.

Fromm, Erich, D. T. Suzuki and Richard De Martino. *Zen Buddhism and Psychoanalysis.* New York: Harper and Brothers, 1960.

Govinda, Lama Anagarika. *Foundations of Tibetan Mysticism.* San Francisco: Red Wheel/Weiser, 1969.

Guenther, Herbert V. *The Life and Teaching of Naropa.* Oxford: Clarendon Press, 1963.

———. *The Royal Song of Saraha: A Study in the History of Buddhist Thought.* Boston: Shambhala Publications, 1973.

———. *Treasures on the Tibetan Middle Way: A Newly Revised Edition of Tibetan Buddhism Without Mystification.* Boston: Shambhala Publications, 1976.

Guenther, Herbert V., trans. *Kindly Bent to Ease Us.* Emeryville, CA: Dharma Publishing, 1976.

Gyatso, Kelsang. *Clear Light of Bliss: The Practice of Mahamudra in Vajrayana Buddhism.* Glen Spey, NY: Tharpa Publications, 1992.

———. *Selected Works of the Dalai Lama VII: Songs of Spiritual Change (Teachings of the Dalai Lamas).* Trans. Glenn Mullin. Ithaca: Snow Lion Publications, 1982.

Gyatso, Khedrup Norsang. *Ornament of Stainless Light: An Exposition of the Kalachakra Tantra.* Ed. and trans. Gavin Kilty. Boston: Wisdom Publications, 2004.

Herrigel, Eugen, and Daisetz T. Suzuki. *Zen in the Art of Archery.* New York: Vintage, 1999.

Hillman, James. *Anima: The Anatomy of a Personified Notion.* Woodstock, CT: Spring Publications, 1985.

———. *The Dream and the Underworld.* New York: Harper & Row, 1979.

———. *Healing Fiction.* Barrytown, NY: Station Hill Press, 1983.

Jacobi, Jolande. *Complex/Archetype/Symbol in the Psychology of C. G. Jung.* Trans. Ralph Mannheim. Princeton: Princeton University Press/Bollingen Foundation, 1971.

Johnson, Robert. *We: Understanding the Psychology of Romantic Love.* San Francisco: HarperSanFrancisco, reprint edition, 1985.

Jung, C. G. *Alchemical Studies.* Ed. and trans. Gerhard Adler and R. F. C. Hull. The Collected Works of C. G. Jung. Vol. 13. Princeton: Princeton University Press/Bollingen Foundation, 1983.

———. *Archetypes and the Collective Unconscious.* Ed. and trans. Gerhard Adler and R. F. C. Hull. The Collected Works of C. G. Jung. Vol. 9, Part 1. Princeton: Princeton University Press/Bollingen Foundation, 1981.

———. *Psychology and Alchemy.* Ed. and trans. Gerhard Adler and R. F. C. Hull. The Collected Works of C. G. Jung. Vol. 12. Princeton: Princeton University Press/Bollingen Foundation, 1980.

———. *Psychology and Religion: West and East.* Ed. and trans. Gerhard Adler and R. F. C. Hull. The Collected Works of C. G. Jung. Vol. 11. Princeton: Princeton University Press/Bollingen Foundation, 1970.

———. *Symbols of Transformation.* Ed. and trans. Gerhard Adler and R. F. C. Hull. The Collected Works of C. G. Jung. Vol. 5. Princeton: Princeton University Press/Bollingen Foundation, 1977.

Jung, Emma. *Anima and Animus.* Woodstock, CT: Spring Publications, 1981.

Kornfield, Jack, trans. *Teachings of the Buddha.* Boston: Shambhala, 1996.

Monick, Eugene. *Phallos: Sacred Image of the Masculine.* Toronto: Inner City Books, 1987.

Neumann, Erich. *Amor and Psyche: The Psychic Development of the Feminine: A Commentary on the Tale by Apuleius.* Princeton: Princeton University Press/Bollingen Foundation, 1973.

Norberg-Hodge, Helena. *Ancient Futures: Learning from Ladakh.* London: Rider, 1991.

Otto, Walter Friedrich. *Dionysus, Myth and Cult.* Bloomington, Indiana: Indiana University Press, 1965.

Phabongka Rinpoche. *Commentary on the Heruka Body Mandala* (in Tibetan). Unpublished translation.

———. *The Sadhana of Chakrasamvara* (in Tibetan). Unpublished translation.

Pearson, Carol. S. *The Hero Within: Six Archetypes We Live By.* San Francisco: HarperSanFrancisco, 1986.

Perera, Sylvia Brinton. *Descent to the Goddess: A Way of Initiation for Women.* Toronto: Inner City Books, 1981.

Preece, Rob. *The Alchemical Buddha.* Devon, UK: Mudra, 2000.

Rabten, Geshe. *The Essential Nectar: Meditations on the Buddhist Path.* Boston: Wisdom Publications, 1984.

———. *The Preliminary Practices of Tibetan Buddhism.* Dharamsala, India: Library of Tibetan Works and Archives, 1974.

Shantideva. *A Guide to the Bodhisattva's Way of Life.* Trans. Stephen Batchelor. Dharamsala, India: Library of Tibetan Works and Archives, 1979.

Sopa, Geshe Lhundup, and Jeffrey Hopkins. *Cutting Through Appearances: Practice and Theory of Tibetan Buddhism.* Ithaca: Snow Lion Publications, 1990.

Tsongkhapa. *Three Principal Aspects of the Path.* Trans. Alexander Berzin. Dharamsala: Library of Tibetan Works and Archives, 1982.

Stein, Murray. *In MidLife: A Jungian Perspective.* Woodstock, CT: Spring Publications, 1983.

von Franz, Marie. *Individuation in Fairy Tales.* Woodstock, CT: Spring Publications, 1977.

von Franz, Marie, and Emma Jung. *The Grail Legend.* Boston: Sigo Press, 1986.

von Franz, Marie, and James Hillman. *Lectures on Jung's Typology.* Woodstock, CT: Spring Publications, 1971.

Yeshe, Lama Thubten. *The Bliss of Inner Fire: Heart Practice of the Six Yogas of Naropa.* Boston: Wisdom Publications, 1998.

———. *Introduction to Tantra: The Transformation of Desire.* Boston: Wisdom Publications, 1987.

———. *Mahamudra.* Boston: Wisdom Publications, 1981.

———. *The Tantric Path of Purification: The Yoga Method of Heruka Vajrasattva Including Complete Retreat Instructions.* Boston: Wisdom Publications, 1995.

Zweig, Connie, and Jeremiah Abrams. *Meeting the Shadow.* New York: Putnam Books, 1991.

p. 224
chakras Buddhist system

5 primary types of energy winds ∴
5 " chakras

crown → "the pervasive wind" - it pervades the entire body & affects motility.

five element | throat → "the upward moving" or "voiding wind". associated w. expression thru the throat & mouth.

water element | heart → "the life supporting wind" ~~carries~~ carries the extremely suble quali of mind, the mind of clear ligh

air element | navel → "the equal place wind" wind associated w. the hea generated in process of digestion. Also tummo

earth element | secret place (5 finger widths below navel) → energy wind associated w. the release of feces, sperm, urine & gas. Known as the "downward voiding wind"!